LIBRARY, ST.PATRICK'S COLLEGE, DUBLIN 9
LEABHARLANN, COLÁISTE PHÁDRAIG, B.Á.C. 9

000162442

Urban Sociology, Capitalism and Modernity

This book is due for return on or before the last date shown below.

25/11a 14.14

30/11e 16.12

10/11e 12.09.

18/11a 13.55

26/11/09
12.06

23/11/9 @
16:42.

SOCIOLOGY FOR A CHANGING WORLD
Series Editors: Graham Allan and Mary Maynard
Consultant Editor: Janet Finch

This series, published in conjunction with the British Sociological Association, evaluates and reflects major developments in contemporary sociology. The books will focus on key changes in social and economic life in recent years and on the ways in which the discipline of sociology has analysed those changes. The books will reflect the state of the art in contemporary British sociology, while at the same time drawing upon comparative material to set debates in an international perspective.

Published
Graham Allan and Graham Crow, *Families, Households and Society*
Rosamund Billington, Annette Fitzsimmons, Lenore Greensides
   and Sheelagh Strawbridge, *Culture and Society*
Lois Bryson, *Welfare and the State: Who Benefits?*
Frances Heidensohn, *Crime and Society*
Stephen J. Hunt, *Religion in Western Society*
Mike Savage and Alan Warde, *Urban Sociology, Capitalism and Modernity*
John Solomos and Les Back, *Racism and Society*
Philip Sutton, *Nature, Environment and Society*
Andrew Webster, *Science, Technology and Society*

Forthcoming
Kevin Brehony and Rosemary Deem, *Rethinking Sociologies of Education*
Gordon Causer and Ray Norman, *Work and Employment in Contemporary Society*
Jörg Dürrschmidt and Graham Taylor, *Globalisation, Modernity and Social Change*
David Morgan, *Men, Masculinites and Society*
Julie Seymour, *Social Research Methodology*

Series Standing Order

If you would like to receive future titles in this series as they are published, you can make use of our standing order facility. To place a standing order please contact your bookseller or, in case of difficulty, write to us at the address below with your name and address and the name of the series. Please state with which title you wish to begin your standing order. (If you live outside the United Kingdom we may not have the rights for your area, in which case we will forward your order to the publisher concerned.)

Customer Services Department, Macmillan Distribution Ltd
Houndmills, Basingstoke, Hampshire RG21 6XS, England

URBAN SOCIOLOGY, CAPITALISM AND MODERNITY

Second Edition

Mike Savage
Alan Warde
and
Kevin Ward

ST PATRICK'S COLLEGE LIBRARY

palgrave
macmillan

© Mike Savage, Alan Warde 1993, 2003 and Kevin Ward 2003

All rights reserved. No reproduction, copy or transmission of this publication may be made without written permission.

No paragraph of this publication may be reproduced, copied or transmitted save with written permission or in accordance with the provisions of the Copyright, Designs and Patents Act 1988, or under the terms of any licence permitting limited copying issued by the Copyright Licensing Agency, 90 Tottenham Court Road, London W1T 4LP.

Any person who does any unauthorised act in relation to this publication may be liable to criminal prosecution and civil claims for damages.

The authors have asserted their rights to be identified as the authors of this work in accordance with the Copyright, Designs and Patents Act 1988.

First edition 1993
Second edition 2003

Published by
PALGRAVE MACMILLAN
Houndmills, Basingstoke, Hampshire RG21 6XS and
175 Fifth Avenue, New York, N. Y. 10010
Companies and representatives throughout the world

PALGRAVE MACMILLAN is the global academic imprint of the Palgrave Macmillan division of St. Martin's Press, LLC and of Palgrave Macmillan Ltd. Macmillan® is a registered trademark in the United States, United Kingdom and other countries. Palgrave is a registered trademark in the European Union and other countries.

ISBN-13: 978-0-333-97159-8 hardback
ISBN-10: 0-333-97159-0 hardback
ISBN-13: 978-0-333-97160-4 paperback
ISBN-10: 0-333-97160-4 paperback

This book is printed on paper suitable for recycling and made from fully managed and sustained forest sources.

A catalogue record for this book is available from the British Library.

Libary of Congress Cataloging-in-Publication Data

, capitalism and modernity / Mike Savage, Alan in Ward—2nd ed.
p.cm—(Sociology for a changing world)
Includes bibliographical references and index.
ISBN 0–333–97159–0 (cloth)—ISBN 0–333–97160–4 (paper)
1. Sociology, Urban. 2. Sociology, Urban—History. 3. Capitalism. I. Ward, Kevin, 1969–II. Warde, Alan. III. Title. IV. Series.
HT151.S265 2002
307.76—dc21

2002026751

Leabharlann

S.L.   000162442

CLASS. 307.76 SAV

DATE. 21 | 11 | 05

PRICE...................

DROM CONNACHT

10   9   8   7   6   5   4   3   2
12   11   10   09   08   07   06   05

Printed in China

Contents

ST. PATRICKS COLLEGE LIBRARY

Preface to the Second Edition

When we wrote the first edition of *Urban Sociology, Capitalism and Modernity* in the early 1990s, the subject was at a turning point. During the 1970s urban sociology underwent something of a re-naissance, particularly as a result of the Marxist-inspired work of Castells and his associates. In retrospect this school of thought can be seen as the last stand of classical urban sociology due to its concern to delineate precisely what the 'urban' was (or was not). The later 1970s and early 1980s saw a series of critiques of urban sociology (Mellor, 1977; Smith, 1979; Saunders, 1981), with the widespread and growing recognition that there were no distinctly 'urban' processes that could usefully be delineated from other kinds of spatial ones. The 1980s saw a remarkable new interest in the 'spatiality' of social life (e.g., Giddens, 1984; Gregory and Urry, 1985) but this tended to by-pass urban sociology, precisely because of its claims that spatial processes were omnipresent and not solely relevant to urban life.

Our book turned the tables on urban sociology by arguing that it was not of great interest to worry excessively about what pre-cisely the 'urban' was. Rather, we argued that what had been seen as the weakness of urban sociology – its inability to provide a clear definition of the urban – could actually be seen as a strength. It was precisely the fragmentation, opaqueness and vari-ability of modern social life that should inspire urban sociology. Cities, we claimed, were a contradictory interface between capi-talism and modernity, and since this relationship was one of tension, it was inevitable that there could be no easy theoretical definition of the urban. We championed an urban sociology that understood cities as prime (though not the only) sites of moder-nity, and re-read the work of Simmel and Benjamin, and the early Chicago School urban sociologists, to recover their interest in cities as laboratories of modern social life. We also insisted, against purely cultural intepretations of urban life, that it remained important to contextualise cities in terms of their involvement in capitalist economic and social relations. Cities, then, were caught up in multiple tensions. Following Simmel, modernity could be seen as fragmentary and unstable: capitalism as a mode of production itself was prone to recurrent crises; and cities, at the interface between capitalism and modernity, signalled the inherently incomplete and unfinished nature of urban life.

In the decade that has passed since the writing of the first edition, subsequent events have largely confirmed our diagnosis. Indeed, the notorious attack on the World Trade Centre in New York City on 11 September 2001 exemplified the themes of our book. The attack destroyed a leading capitalist site, based in perhaps the leading 'world city'. Ordinary, routine, urban life of millions of New Yorkers was fundamentally ruptured by one dramatic event, indicating how our everyday lives are predicated on fragile underpinnings, especially in the complex urban centres of twenty-first-century capitalism. The attack itself seems to be an outcome of different cultural frames for interpreting and understanding the meaning of 'modernity' in a world dominated by American corporate capitalism.

This event crystallises a sense in much writing that the urban is a crucial site of contemporary social life. Instead of worrying about defining the urban, there is a wave of urban studies that crosses disciplines and subject-matter with breathtaking ease (see, e.g., Westwood and Taylor, 1997; Bridge and Watson, 2000c). Many academic disciplines have rediscovered their urban interests, for instance urban anthropology (Low, 2000), or literary studies (Tanner, 1996). There is a striking revival of popular, but serious, urban writing, in which location in specific kinds of cities matters. Consider the remarkable range of writing on and about London, from Ian Sinclair (1998) through Peter Ackroyd (1999) and Michael Moorcock (2001). Urban biographies of many cities have been written, all of them exploring the particularities of specific cities in a way that also highlights the distinctive role of urban imaginations in contemporary societies.

In short, the 1990s witnessed a flowering of interdisciplinary urban studies. Yet, whilst we celebrate this current, we think it important to relate the diversity of urban studies to some overarching themes – in our case the city as interface between capitalism and modernity. Indeed, recent scholarship has developed accounts of capitalism and modernity that are highly pertinent to our account. In place of the rather generic and almost celebratory approaches to modernity and late modernity that characterised debates in the late 1980s and early 1990s, in the work of Berman, Giddens, and Beck, recent analysis has become more concerned with the particularity and problems of modern cultures. In this respect, a key figure has been Walter Benjamin, whose account of modernity is remarkably prescient for its attention to the embedding of the past in the modern, for its recognition of the role of the visual and consumption in modern life, and for his concern with the urban. For instance, Joel Kahn's book *Modernity and Exclusion* (2000) focuses on the different ways that modernity emerges in various national cultures according to the precise traditional cultures that it departs from.

Debates about capitalism have become somewhat less central than they were at the time of writing the first edition, when David Harvey's work, and that of the Regulation School in general, had a commanding influence (see Merrifield, 2000). The collapse of the Soviet bloc and the lack of viable alternatives to capitalism have in some respects muted debates. However, in other ways, analysis of capitalism has become ever more attuned to historical and spatial specificity of different modes of capital accumulation, for instance as manifested by Arrighi (1994). Contemporary analyses of capitalism are increasingly concerned with the role of consumption and the service sector in the accumulation process, and the urban context is often seen as a key zone (e.g. Scott, 1999). Perhaps the clearest indication of the close link between debates about capitalism and urbanism comes from the example of Manuel Castells in his *The Network Society* (1996). It is striking that it was a leading urban sociologist, drawing upon his urban expertise, who developed such an influential account of current globalisation. His analysis of the rise of corporate networks, the potential of new technologies, and the rise of new global elites, are all premised on his awareness of the distinctive role of world cities as key nodes in contemporary capitalism.

Whereas for much of the twentieth century, urban sociology tended to emphasise the mobile, fluctuating and fleeting aspects of social life, this situation has changed recently. The critique of structuralist sociology, and the popularity of post-structuralist approaches to social theory, as well as the rising interest in accounts of globalisation, have led to new currents of sociology emphasising the significance of flows and networks, rather than fixed structural locations (especially Urry, 2000). In our view, the relationship between fixity and mobility is a dialectical one that can never be fully resolved in favour of one of these poles. In view of the increasing interest in mobilities of one kind or another, urban sociology is increasingly likely to be important for insisting on the obduracy of place and role of fixed urban form in structuring social life.

In writing this second edition the authorship has changed to include Kevin Ward, an expert in urban, economic and political geography. Kevin's knowledge equips him to update material in these areas that neither of the original authors, Mike Savage and Alan Warde, are able. This change of authorship has not entailed a large-scale rewriting of the first edition. Since we think our general argument has been sustained by more recent work we have not made radical changes to this second edition. There is a minor change in that we have given greater prominence to debates regarding globalisation, and we have reduced our coverage of debates regarding post-modernism. Each chapter has been reworked, and arguments have been clarified where necessary. More usually we have cut material which is dated, and drawn on more recent urban research to illustrate and refine our position and to render our arguments more topical. The book now better reflects the remarkable flourishing of interdisciplinary studies of urban life and the appreciation of the social processes associated with globalisation which have required more attention being paid to spatial scale. We do not see our book as any kind of substitute for the exciting range of urban studies available today, but we hope it will be read in order to systematise and integrate topics that are often held apart.

MIKE SAVAGE
ALAN WARDE
KEVIN WARD

Acknowledgements

The first thanks for the appearance of this new edition are due to Catherine Gray, editor at Palgrave Macmillan, who refused to accept our arguments that we were too busy to write another edition, and refused to let the possibility of updating our first edition slide off our agenda. The final decision to undertake the new edition was made when Mike Savage and Alan Warde got to know Kevin Ward, a Manchester University colleague from a neighbouring Department. Kevin's insistence that the book was worth updating, and that he was prepared to use his expertise in economic and political geography to help us in this project, finally proved decisive. This book is the final result!

We would like to thank all those who have discussed urban issues with us over the past decade and more. These include Fiona Devine, Helen Hills, Kevin Hetherington, Adam Holden, Martin Jones, Patrick LeGales, Brian Longhurst, Gordon MacLeod, Eugene McCann, Jamie Peck, Steve Quilley, Bev Skeggs, Dale Southerton and Adam Tickell. Mike Savage would like to pay particular tribute to Rosemary Mellor, with whom he co-taught a graduate course in urban sociology in 1996–7 and from whom he learnt much about the development of urban studies since the 1970s. Rosemary's death in 2001 was indeed a sad blow to urban sociology.

MIKE SAVAGE
ALAN WARDE
KEVIN WARD

1 Introduction

Consider one view of why the experience of the modern city is so fascinating and compelling:

> the great buildings of civilisation; the meeting places, the libraries and theatres, the towers and domes; and often more moving than these, the houses, the streets, the press and excitement of so many people, with so many purposes. I have stood in many cities and felt this pulse: in the physical differences of Stockholm and Florence, Paris and Milan: this identifiable and moving quality: the centre, the activity, the light. Like everyone else I have also felt the chaos of the metro and the traffic jam: the monotony of the ranks of houses, the aching press of strange crowds ... this sense of possibility, of meeting and of movement, is a permanent element of my sense of cities. (Williams, 1973, pp. 14–15)

Many people will recognise elements of Raymond Williams's feelings in their own encounters with cities – for he repeats a cultural stereotype that pervades modern societies. This book, a critical reflection on the nature of urban life and experience in the context of social change, evaluates the extent to which this view of the city can be sustained sociologically.

The problem of urban sociology can be discerned initially in the short extract above: its scope is potentially enormous – from the architecture of cities to traffic congestion, the experience of urban life, the behaviour of crowds, housing, planning and so forth. The experience of urban life seems so all-encompassing that it is difficult to distinguish what might not be the domain of urban sociology. The definition of the subject has been a source of despair to its practitioners and advocates. The recurrent worry was how to define 'the urban', to specify distinctive and unique properties of the city that provided the focus for specialised scholarly attention. Thus, as far back as 1955, Ruth Glass pointed out that 'there is no such subject [as urban sociology] with a distinct identity of its own' (Glass, 1989, p. 51). She continued, 'in a highly urbanised country such as Great Britain, the label "urban" can be applied to almost any branch of current sociological study. In the circumstances, it is rather pointless to apply it at all' (Glass, 1989, p. 56).

Nevertheless, urban sociologists continued to research and write about life in cities, undaunted by the prospect of contributing to a subject whose boundaries could not be delimited. Indeed, increasingly the inability to bound the subject has been mirrored by a melting away of disciplinary boundaries, as those studying the city include those working in anthropology, cultural studies, economics, gender studies and geography, in addition to sociology. We have written this book in the belief that there is no solid definition of the urban; approaching matters from the point of view of a definition of the 'urban' produces very oblique appreciations of the role and achievements of urban sociology. The label 'urban' sociology is mostly a flag of convenience. However, the fact that the urban cannot be defined in a general way does not mean that important things cannot be said about specific processes in particular cities! This text therefore isolates the actual contribution of the subdiscipline, in order to identify the common elements explaining its persistence.

Looking at the textbooks published over the past forty years, it would be hard to isolate a core to the subject, for their principal organising themes are extraordinarily various. Some are about planning improvement of life in cities, others describe urban forms and structures; some offer histories of urban growth while others seek the biological or ecological bases of urban behaviour; some are theoretical treatises on the quality and disparate nature of the urban experience, others epistemological reflections on the concept of the urban (e.g., respectively, Greer, 1962; Pahl, 1970; Reissman, 1964; Dickens, 1990; Smith, 1980; Jacobs and Fincher, 1998; Saunders, 1981). This prompts our view that the history of urban sociology is discontinuous, unamenable to an account of its linear evolution around a single theme (cf.

Saunders, 1981). Yet, although there is no cumulative tradition, there is a number of recurrent threads and themes around which urban sociology revolves.

Themes examined within urban sociology and the types of topics that we discuss include:

1. what it feels like to live in a modern city and whether there is a unitary or universal 'urban' experience. Defining characteristics have been sought: e.g. anonymity – being just another face in a vast crowd; the uncertainty and unpredictability of events in complex urban environments; the senses of possibility and danger induced by cities;
2. whether, by contrast, places are distinctive, what makes for attachment to particular neighbourhoods or cities, given that people certainly perceive places to have their own identity and characteristics;
3. how urban life is affected by the features of local social structure, e.g., class position, gender, ethnic group, housing situation, and so forth;
4. how informal social bonds develop and to what extent the nature of affective relationships – with kin, neighbours, friends and associates – are determined by the external social context and environment, much discussion having been devoted to whether different kinds of settlement engender concomitant types of social ties;
5. how to explain the history of urbanisation and the concentration of population in towns, cities and conurbations;
6. what are the basic features of the spatial structure of cities and whether different spatial arrangements generate distinctive modes of interaction;
7. the nature of, and solutions to, 'urban' problems like congestion, pollution, poverty, vagrancy, delinquency and street violence;
8. how urban political affairs are conducted, what influences political participation and what impact the different agencies of the local state have on daily life.

Urban sociologies oscillate in their focus as they select among themes and try to reconcile divergent concerns. In this book we argue that a coherent programme for urban sociology would be concerned with the mutual impact of two analytically separate entities, *capitalism* and *modernity*. Moreover, past achievements too are best appreciated as an extended enquiry into the relationship between modernity and capitalism. Definitions of modernity are highly contested. In the last decade and a half a vast literature has emerged focused on a putative transition to post-modernity and causing an intensive re-examination of what is meant by the term 'modernity' (for a summary, see Smart, 1992; Kumar, 1998). We prefer to reserve the concept 'modern' to describe a particular mode of experience. One insightful formulation is that of Berman (1983) who makes 'the experience of modernity' a central organising principle of his study of Western aesthetic reflections on life in cities:

> There is a mode of vital experience – experience of space and time, of self and others, of life's possibilities and perils – that is shared by men and women all over the world today. I will call this body of experience 'modernity'. To be modern is to find ourselves in an environment that promises us adventure, power, joy, growth, transformation of ourselves and the world – and, at the same time, that threatens to destroy everything we have, everything we know, everything we are. Modern environments and experiences cut across all boundaries of geography and ethnicity, of class and nationality, of religion and ideology: in this sense, modernity can be said to unite all mankind. But it is a paradoxical unity, a unity of disunity; it pours us all into a maelstrom of perpetual disintegration and renewal, of struggle and contradiction, of ambiguity and anguish. To be modern is to be part of a universe in which, as Marx said, 'all that is solid melts into air'. (Berman, 1983, p. 1)

The ambivalent experience of modernity contrasts with traditional ways of life, which were socially more secure and predictable because less open and manipulable. Most urban sociologists, and particularly the early ones, were fascinated by this experience of modernity. Yet this dominant preoccupation has always existed in tension with another, the way in which capitalist economic structures affect urban life.

Capitalism refers to the economic order of Western societies in which production is organised around the search for profit. The private ownership of the means of production – land, tools, machines, factories and suchlike – entails that their owners ultimately retain profits, and those who do not share ownership are forced to work as employees. These economic relations of exploitation generate social class inequality, an inherent feature of capitalist societies. The search for profit leads also to a dynamic, competitive, conflictual, economic system prone to crisis. These powerful economic forces cannot but affect the nature of cities, and in the 1960s and 1970s urban sociologists, influenced by the revival of Marxist political economy, concentrated attention on the capitalist roots of urban conditions.

Today the tide is turning again. After a period when urban sociology focused on issues of modernity in the context of debates about post-modernity, the most recent work has tended to move beyond this binary contrast, to argue for a fine-grain and less totalising approach to the analysis of cities. In light of this, we continue to believe that urban sociology needs to synthesise the best elements of the political economy of capitalism with more cultural analyses of modernity, realigning the subject near the heart of the sociological discipline as well as illuminating the multiplicity of urban experiences.

The book contains six substantial chapters. Each deals with a different set of issues and body of literature; each chapter, for purposes of study, may be read separately. However, there is also a sustained argument running throughout the book about the nature and functions of urban sociology and how the analysis of the interacting mechanisms of capitalism and modernity constitute differential urban experiences.

Chapter 2 provides a brief history of urban sociology, primarily as practised in Britain and the USA. In the 1970s and 1980s older work was heavily criticised and radical new approaches were promulgated. Much of value in the older tradition was prematurely condemned as inquiry into the social conditions of modernity and was discarded. At the end of the 1990s some of the work by authors like Simmel and Lefebvre was embraced once again, as political economy and cultural approaches to the production of urban sociology existed alongside one another, with some even attempting to integrate the two. Chapter 3 explores economic theories of urban development and decline. Here we show how recent analyses of capitalism have used the concept of uneven development to explore the differentiation of cities within the global economy. Instead of a uniform process of urbanisation, where all cities grow according to the same logic, attention to uneven development identifies variation in accordance with location within the capitalist world system. In outlining the ways in which cities experience uneven development, we argue that such theories are insufficient alone to express the cultural dimensions of modernity.

Chapter 4 examines urban manifestations of the inherent inequalities of capitalism that powerfully affect the spatial and social organisation of cities. We discuss processes that produce inequalities within cities, such as gentrification, suburbanisation, and household divisions, and how each is closely interlinked with the others. Hence we argue that the experience of modernity is not a universal one: its costs and benefits are differentially felt according to class, ethnicity, gender and sexuality.

Chapter 5 shifts the focus directly onto the city and modernity. We consider the classic works of Georg Simmel and Louis Wirth, in search of a 'generic' urban culture. Is there an urban way of life, which can be defined in terms that apply, in some way, to all cities? We examine Wirth's attempt to show that urban ways of life could be contrasted with rural ways of life and Simmel's endeavours to specify the city as the locus of modernity. Protracted investigation, we contend, has failed to provide a convincing demonstration of the existence of an urban way of life.

Chapter 6 therefore considers how places gain different meanings. We argue that no account of urban culture is adequate unless it takes seriously personal, unique, experiences of urban life, but that this occurs in the context of broader cultural forces. In particular, we focus on debates about the relationship between globalisation and urban meaning. It is suggested that the work of Walter Benjamin offers a series of valuable beginnings for this project. His ideas implicitly criticise the fashionable claim that an era of post-modernity has emerged.

Chapter 7 surveys analyses of urban politics, showing their responsiveness to changing political agendas and the impact of the forces of capitalism and modernity. We examine, in particular, the shifting geographies of the state, the growing role of the local state in economic development, the political manipulation of place identities and the growing use of surveillance methods in public spaces.

2 The Roots of Urban Sociology

In this chapter we present a brief and selective survey of the history of urban sociology. Section 2.1 deals with the concerns of urban sociology in its 'golden age' between 1910 and the 1930s, when it was central to the development of the discipline. We focus on the Chicago School and identify elements in its legacy, which are relevant for analysis today. We contrast the development of urban sociology in the UK to indicate some of the specific strengths of the British tradition of urban research. After the Second World War urban sociology became more marginal to the discipline, and in section 2.2 we indicate some of the reasons for this. The pressing sense of social turmoil and political unrest which had earlier generated an interest in cities was replaced by more complacent political attitudes in which it was assumed that economic growth and social harmony were destined to be permanent features of capitalist welfare states. The rise of functionalist and structuralist social theory altered the terrain of sociological inquiry. By the middle of the 1970s most commentators were contemptuous of the contribution of the Chicago School and of urban sociology more generally. We consider in particular the influential Marxist critique of urban sociology of Castells and elements of its subsequent development as 'the new urban sociology'. In section 2.3 we turn to the most recent work in urban sociology, where disciplinary boundaries have melted away, as efforts to theorise and explain urban change have embraced an eclectic range of approaches (Allen et al., 1999; Low, 2000; Bridge and Watson, 2000a, 2000b, 2000c; Borden et al., 2001). In addition to discipline-specific works on urbanisation we find at the beginning of a new millennium, a rash of interdisciplinary edited collections, which embrace and celebrate both the diversity of urban life and the approaches to make sense of it. In conclusion we suggest that aspects of the research agenda of contemporary sociology signify a return to some broad objectives of urban sociology implicit in the work of Henri Lefebvre, Georg Simmel and the Chicago School. Here the study of urban life is seen as integrally linked to an investigation of 'modernity', and wider society more generally.

2.1 The development of urban sociology 1900–30

At first glance our claim that the early twentieth century was a 'golden age' for urban sociology may seem strange. Modern sociology frequently traces its roots back to three leading theorists – Karl Marx, Max Weber, and Emile Durkheim – all of whom (Weber partly excepted) were relatively uninterested in urban phenomena (Giddens, 1971; Alexander, 1982). These three were preoccupied with analysing other principal characteristics of new industrial societies of the nineteenth century (Kumar, 1978; Lee and Newby, 1982).

Saunders (1986) claimed that they all advanced rather different arguments in support of the view that in modern societies cities had lost any distinctive properties they might once have possessed. Whilst in ancient societies the distinction between town and countryside was socially significant, and in feudal Europe cities had distinctive social and political autonomy from the rule of rural landlords, by the nineteenth century this was no longer true. In modern societies there are no social activities that happen only in cities or only in the countryside. In an age of high geographical mobility it does not make sense to treat the city and the countryside as self-contained social orders, detached from each other.

If the 'founders' of sociology were uninterested in urban phenomena, how could urban sociology be of prime importance to the discipline in its early days? The paradox is more apparent than real, since the influence of Marx, Weber and Durkheim on early sociology was not as marked as is sometimes suggested in later accounts. Of the three only Durkheim had a strong influence on the development of sociology as an academic discipline, helping to found one of the earliest sociological journals, *L'Année Sociologique,* in 1896. Even so he was important in only one of the two French sociological schools which emerged at the end of the nineteenth century, and the other, strongly based on the work of Frédéric Le Play and the journal, *La Science Sociale,* arguably had a more important short-term impact.

Thus, irrespective of the theoretical writings of Marx, Weber and Durkheim, sociology emerged in the early twentieth century as a discipline primarily concerned with the nature of urban life and the analysis of what might loosely be termed 'urban problems' – unemployment, poverty, social unrest, rootlessness, congestion and so forth. The sociology of cities dominated early sociological work, both in Britain and America, and it proved of particular value in examining social relationships in an increasingly individualised and fragmented society.

2.1.1   The Chicago School

The Chicago School played a particularly important role in the establishment of urban sociology. The University of Chicago was founded in 1892 and the Department of Sociology soon came to have a commanding influence in the USA, partly because the leading journal, *American Journal of Sociology,* was based there. By the First World War the concern with the urban life had been made apparent by Robert Park's publication of his article on 'The City', which laid down an exhaustive research agenda for urban sociology. The School subsequently produced two distinctive bodies of work: one is associated with the ecological mapping of the so-called 'natural areas' of Chicago, the other with a series of ethnographies of diverse social groups in the city.

The Chicago School is often best known for Burgess's model of urban form, based on patterns of land-use in 1920s Chicago, which attempted to delineate the basic patterns of social segregation in modern cities. This, the concentric zone model (see Figure 2.1), was an ideal-type representation of city growth, assuming the absence of natural features like waterfronts and hills. It postulated the existence of a Central Business District (CBD), in the middle of the city, and then, further out, a zone of transition characterised by urban decay, which was 'invaded' by business and industry. This made it unattractive to residents who, when they had the resources, moved outwards either to the zone of working-men's homes or, if they could afford it, to the suburbs, where the middle classes tended to predominate. Burgess saw this model as testifying to the importance of ecological processes: as cities expanded so successive waves of 'invasion' took place as people spilled out of their areas into others, leading to competition between differing communities, and a changing urban form. Corroboration and qualification of this model eventually resulted in considerable, statistically based, research, involving mapping land-use, the distribution of particular populations and the incidence of social pathologies like suicide and crime.

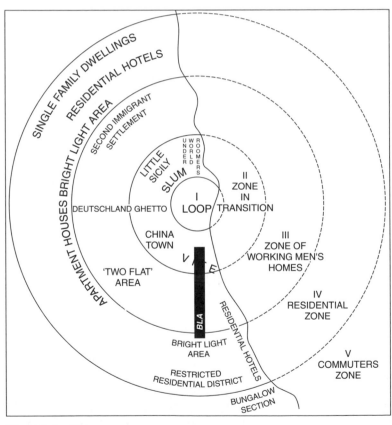

Figure 2.1   *Urban areas*

Source: R. E. Park, E. W. Burgess and R. D. McKenzie (eds), *The City* (University of Chicago Press, 1967), p. 55.

The ethnographic strand of Chicago School research has been less developed within urban sociology, although its influence on urban anthropology has been great (see Hannerz, 1980; Low, 2000). From the 1920s a series of famous ethnographies on different aspects of Chicago life began to emerge in response to some of the questions raised by Park (see the summary of these in Hannerz, 1980). These ethnographies were all detailed studies of particular facets of urban life in Chicago, and tended to focus on the disadvantaged, insecure, and transient. The most famous of these included: *The Gang* (Thrasher, 1927) – a detailed study of 1,313 gangs in different parts of Chicago; *The Hobo* (Andersen, 1923) – a study of migrants and tramps; *The Taxi-Hall Dancers* (Cressey, 1932) – a study of women who danced with men in return for payment, and of the men who bought female company in this way; and *The Gold Coast and the Slum* (Zorbaugh, 1929) – a study of social relationships in two adjacent areas of central Chicago.

These ethnographies were all written from field research based on participant observation. They were written by researchers who sought to gain access to the people they were researching, examining the motivations and attitudes guiding the actions of gang-members, tramps, slum-dwellers and so forth. They began to contribute to a project suggested by Park: 'anthropology, the science of man, has been mainly concerned up to the present with the study of primitive peoples. But civilised man is quite as interesting an object of investigation' (Park, 1967, p. 3). Hannerz (1980) sees them as the first attempts to carry out micro-research using anthropological techniques in modern societies.

The key themes still relevant today that can be extracted from the Chicago School do not concern formalised ecological theory nor early versions of urban ethnographic method, but are three interconnected substantive elements: sociation, its changing modes within modernity, and social reform.

Sociation

The first and the most general of these elements is an interest in the nature and patterns of social interaction and processes of social bonding. Questions included why people associated with particular others, how social groups, bonds and loyalties developed, and how they changed. This concern drew upon the insights of

Simmel, who was highly influential for the Chicago School, and for whom the main focus of sociology was to account for patterns of 'sociation' (Frisby, 1984). Simmel argued that:

> just as the differentiation of the specifically psychological from objective matter produces psychology as a science, so a genuine sociology can only deal with what is specifically societal, the form and forms of sociation. (quoted in Frisby, 1984, p. 52)

The concept of sociation is not an easy one, and Simmel develops it by contrast with 'society'. Society consists of 'permanent interactions ... crystallised as definable, consistent structures such as the state and family'(Simmel, 1950, p. 9). Sociation, however, comprises the 'less conspicuous' ties that bind people together:

> that people look at one another and are jealous of one another: that they exchange letters or dine together; that irrespective of all tangible interests they strike one another as pleasant or unpleasant ... the whole gamut of relations that play from one person to another and that may be momentary or permanent, conscious or unconscious, ephemeral or of grave consequence, all these tie men (*sic*) incessantly together. (Simmel, 1950, p. 10)

Sociation is concerned with the informal ordering of social life, the moral codes and conventions underlying apparently haphazard and incoherent forms of human action. Forms of social action, which may appear meaningless, volatile or anarchic, nonetheless have a meaning when situated in spatial and social context.

Sociation's changing modes within modernity
The interest in patterns of sociation was related to a second main issue, a more empirical question of how processes of sociation were changing in contemporary America in the early twentieth century. Park, in his research agenda written in 1915, laid out the issues clearly enough. Economic growth, he wrote, breaks down or modifies

> the older social and economic organisation of society, which was based upon family ties, local associations, on culture, caste

and status, and to substitute for it an organisation based on occupational and vocational interests, division of labour, the concentration of industries and groups or special tasks have
continually changed the material conditions of life, and in
doing this have made readjustment to novel conditions increasingly necessary. (Park, 1967, pp. 13, 19)

Here is the empirical concern of the Chicago School: understanding the importance of the rise of modern industrialism and
its impact on processes of sociation. Modernity, for Park, involved the breaking down of formal, structural bases of human
action, and the growth of informal social life. Park's view was
that the division of labour meant that work and occupation
tended to fragment social bonds (e.g. Park, 1967). The only way
in which social ties could be built up lay in the rise of neighbourhood solidarities. He argued that families, and what he termed
'primary attachments', had been eroded in modern cities. His
concern was with the nature of other social bonds, to see how
they might, or might not, build up collective organisation. Many
Chicago studies focused upon the unattached – those without
primary bonds – to see whether they were forming other sorts of
social ties. Hence the interest in people who inhabited the lonely
world of the taxi-hall dancer, the hobo, and the tramp.

The work of the Chicago School is best seen as an extended
empirical inquiry into the nature of social bonding in the
modern, fragmented, city. The city interested them for empirical
rather than conceptual reasons. It was where the division of
labour was most elaborate and developed, and hence where the
fragmentary nature of modern life could most profitably be
studied. Moreover, in Chicago as in other American cities, the
extent of immigration also posed a challenge to the establishment
of orderly and comprehensible social relationships.

Social reform

A third important characteristic of the Chicago School's work
was its directly political concern. As Smith (1988) argues, what
bound the Chicagoans together was less a common theoretical
position than shared liberal political ideals and the desire to translate them into political practice. He maintained that 'they believed American democracy, properly functioning, should enable

men and women to achieve the satisfactions embodied in what has become known as the American dream' (Smith, 1988, p. 5). The School accepted the basic parameters of a capitalist economy and a liberal democratic electoral system – which partly explains their relative lack of interest in employment or the state – but were concerned with how cooperative sorts of interaction could be developed to replace the fragmenting forms evident in contemporary Chicago. The Chicagoans believed in a reformist politics, involving experimenting with social institutions to examine how they might affect the character of sociation in specific environments. The contemporary problem was how individuals could deal with the disorienting, exciting, unstable, insecure, disembedded, polyvalent and anomic conditions that an industrial city like Chicago posed. These scholars confronted the intellectual and practical problems associated with what we would now describe as the experience of modernity.

Despite the novelty of their approach, and the diversity of their empirical research, the Chicago School lacked any currently viable theoretical orientation. This is not to say that various Chicago writers did not write theoretical papers or speculate on social theory – they did, for they are usually seen as endorsing 'human ecology' and its attempt to adapt biological ideas to the study of cities (Bridge and Watson, 2000b). Saunders, for instance, argues that the Chicago School developed a form of 'human ecology', in which patterns of urban life were seen as driven by principles similar to those evident in plant ecology, where different species of plant competed to gain dominance in a particular habitat. As this form of biological reductionism is generally considered completely unsustainable, most urban sociologists have used such interpretations as grounds for dismissing Chicago's contemporary relevance.

Park used human ecology to indicate the importance of processes of conflict and competition within cities for scarce resources. The social structure of cities showed that different communities – of ethnic groups, or social classes – tended to concentrate in differing areas. This was not a static or unchanging pattern however, and just as types of plants moved from area to area, so did different urban communities. Park referred to this process as one of 'succession', which went through a cycle of competition (between groups, for instance), dominance (as one ethnic group gains the upper hand and the other begins to move out), succession (as the new group establishes itself as the sole group in that area), and invasion (as it then expands into another area, so beginning the cycle all over again). By using this ecological perspective it seemed that the Chicago School were taking the emphasis away from processes of racism and class conflict, instead seeing patterns of settlement in urban areas as the product of evolutionary processes of 'the survival of the fittest'.

Although there is no doubt that these 'ecological' themes were evident in the work of Park, and other Chicago School writers, this was not the sole theoretical preoccupation of the Chicago School, and nor should evaluation of the whole school rest upon this one idea. Park himself had other ideas, too, tending to emphasise cultural factors in social life, being quite explicit that cultural factors could modify ecological processes (Lal, 1990, pp. 28–9). Smith (1988, ch. 7) argues that Park only attempted to systematise his ecological arguments after he retired, his strongest statements of ecological principles being written in the 1930s (e.g. Park, 1938). This was well after most of the Chicago ethnographies had been written and when he was no longer especially influential within Chicago. In his first and most important paper, 'The City: Suggestions for the Investigation of Human Behaviour in the Urban Environment', written in 1915 (see Park, 1967), which set the research agenda for the ethnographers, Park mentions the ecological approach only briefly, at the beginning. Here he sees it as only one of four approaches to the city: the others being 'the geographic', the economic, and the cultural. Most of his article concentrates on the economic aspect of urban change, especially – echoing Durkheim – on the sociological significance of the division of labour.

Nor should one assume that human ecology is necessarily a form of biological determinism. Many commentators have asserted the weaknesses of drawing parallels between natural and human ecology, among the first and most elaborate being Alihan's (1938) demonstration of the inconsistencies and absurdities involved in the Chicago School's use of concepts like environment, sustenance, competition and succession. Yet Park's writing deserves to be treated carefully. He frequently refers to the way in which sociologists study 'human nature'. Today the term 'human nature' is taken to mean a fixed biological essence and is treated with suspicion by social scientists. For Park, though, the term does not have these connotations: 'human nature, as we have begun to conceive it in recent years, is largely a product of social intercourse; it is therefore, quite as much as society itself, a subject for sociological investigation' (Park, 1921, p. 172). As Donna Harraway (1989) has shown, ecological ideas, rather than being biologically derived, were largely forms of evolutionary social theory imported into the study of animals. In later years the ecological research was simply taken to refer to a particular method of gathering data about certain areas, rather than to any explicit link with biological arguments.

As Harvey (1987) argued, the 'Chicago School' was actually rather diverse. Other Chicago writers drew hardly at all upon ecological arguments. W. I. Thomas, for instance, saw social life as driven by 'four wishes' – the need for new experience, security, response and recognition – an observation which emphasised the specifically human dynamics of social life and tended to undermine any simple association of human and plant life. Indeed Thomas was seen by contemporaries (Ellwood, 1927) as being concerned to develop a rounded account of the role of 'culture' in social life which proved difficult to square with biological reductionist views. Instead the ethnographies of Chicago life carried out in the 1920s were explicitly critical of reductionist arguments. In one of the most famous of these, Thrasher's *The Gang*, the writer spends some considerable time criticising the idea that there is a 'gang instinct' and emphasises how gangs emerge for social reasons, paying particular attention to the way they might emerge out of youthful playgroups. This idea shows signs of being influenced by Cooley's (1909) stress on the importance of socialisation processes in affecting social life – again an idea that is not linked to biological arguments.

It is sometimes argued that ecological arguments were developed through Burgess's formulation of ecological principles in the concentric zone model of the city. However, whatever its value, it was of only marginal importance to the Chicago ethnographies. Virtually all writers mention this model as a point of reference, but nearly always to show that the subject of interest to them could not be fitted easily into its dimensions. Thrasher argued that Chicago gangs were located in 'interstitial' sites between the main zones discussed by Burgess, whilst Cressey's taxi-hall dancers were not located in any particular site within a city. The ethnographies were primarily interested in the unattached, lonely worlds of the migrant, transient population, which almost by definition evaded being mapped fixedly to a particular place within the city.

Instead of arguing that patterns of urban life were the same as those of plant life (which a moment's thought tells us is a ridiculous argument) the biological arguments are used as analogies, in order to show how comparison with biology might throw light on urban life (Bridge and Watson, 2000a, pp. 14–15). Human ecology, as Smith (1988, pp. 136–7) writes, was 'at best a loose framework of ideas oriented to both measurement and meaning which drew upon the borrowed prestige of the natural sciences'. The development of a more explicit ecological approach in the 1930s was caused by the need to attempt to systematise what had previously been loose notions into an apparently scientific statement which could satisfy the increasingly positivist climate of the times.

The Chicago School's most valuable legacy was its conception of sociology as concerned with forms of interaction in the contemporary city and its vision of the sociologist as a promoter of cooperative relationships. They were analysts of what recent sociologists have termed 'modernity', the specific experience of living in a modern world where any overriding social customs and values have been swept away. Furthermore, it was the combination of these three elements, sociation, modernity and reform, within a distinctive research programme based on the empirical, ethnographic study of inter-war Chicago that marked out the School. The School were not interested in analysing the general or formal properties of social action in the manner of Garfinkel (1967) or Goffman (1959). The School's interest was always in studying patterns of social bonding in a given historical situation and in particular spatial settings – the American city in the early twentieth century. What marked out the Chicago contribution was the interconnection of these three elements: the concern with studying the contemporary nature of social interaction in the context of a broad set of reformist political concerns. The city was thus of interest because it allowed their three focal concerns to be reconciled and elaborated. The city was interesting not for anything intrinsic to cities *per se,* but because it was where economic development and hence the modern division of labour was best established, because it was where diverse types of social interaction took place, and because it was the scene of major local political interventions in inter-war America. This explains Park's frequent evocation of the idea that cities were a 'social laboratory' (e.g. Park, 1967, p. 46).

Before turning to consider how this ambitious research programme in urban sociology declined after the 1930s, we consider the case of early British work in the area, which also had some distinctive strengths.

2.1.2   *British urban sociology before the Second World War*

In Britain, academic sociology was much slower to develop than in the USA, and it was not until the 1960s that it became a widely taught subject in higher education. Nonetheless, there was a long tradition of social research in Britain, as in the USA, preoccupied with the nature, causes and consequences of 'urban problems and issues'.

This was especially true in what Halsey, Heath and Ridge (1980) have called the 'political arithmetic' tradition of Victorian social research of Henry Mayhew, Charles Booth, and Seebohm Rowntree. They were primarily concerned to measure the extent of poverty in urban areas. Mayhew, in the 1850s, spent considerable time interviewing the poor in London, publishing his findings as newspaper articles. The style was not ethnographic in the Chicago sense. What marked out Mayhew from other contemporary reporters was his attempt to understand theoretically the causes of poverty. He saw these as stemming from low pay resulting from the cyclical nature of production in many urban handicraft trades, rather than from individual defects of the poor themselves (Thompson and Yeo, 1971; Kent, 1981).

His successors, Charles Booth and Seebohm Rowntree, had similar concerns, but abandoned Mayhew's style of interviewing in favour of more rigorous statistical surveys. In an extensive study of London, carried out in the 1880s, Booth tried to enumerate the causes of poverty by distinguishing the effects of individual habits from those of specific types of employment, a concern also taken up by Rowntree in his studies of poverty in York.

There were major differences between British and American traditions of urban research. In Britain there was less concern with the transient and rootless, more with issues of poverty and social class. Booth developed an elaborate classification of social classes, which he used to construct the social geography of London. When his work was drawn upon by Chicago writers, it was to bring out the significance of class as a social force (see Pfautz, 1967). Pfautz argued that Booth was one of the first sociologists to show systematically how social class affected urban social segregation and involvement in institutional life, for example religious activity. This concern with class was to give a distinctively British flavour to some urban sociology, in contrast to the Americans' greater interest in race and ethnicity. Moreover, work, unemployment, poverty and associational activities were the central tradition of urban surveys. The principal research instrument was a steadily more sophisticated version of the sample survey, cultivated by sociologists seeking professional accreditation and by social reformers of the liberal and Fabian types.

Institutionally, another tradition of early British sociology was based on the Sociological Society, founded in 1903 (Abrams, 1968). This Society developed a direct interest in the study of towns and cities. Branford (1926), discussing the intellectual lineage of the Sociological Society, saw it as drawing upon the two French sociological schools of Durkheim and Le Play. Nonetheless, Le Play, rather than Durkheim, was the more important figure for the Sociological Society.

This stress on Le Play is instructive. Le Play was no theorist, but focused upon the role of sociology as a survey-based discipline that investigated the relationships between what he termed 'Place, Work and Folk'. He argued that sociologists needed to examine households in their regional context in order to investigate the reciprocal relationship between environment and society. For Branford this formula, which we maintain remains useful, allowed sociology to unite otherwise disparate disciplines. 'Through the master concept', wrote Branford, 'that place determines work and work in turn conditions family life and folk organisation, his [Le Play's] observations become alive with the breath of unity' (Branford, 1928, p. 335). Branford saw the attempt to unite the Durkheimian and Le Play traditions as occurring more especially by applying the characteristic methods of each towards studying the evolution of cities and their regions. For this school (i.e. the Sociological Society) it is living cities and their regions which most fully offer to the plain, scientific student, as well as to the plain man, the directly observable aspects of civilisation. (Branford, 1926, p. 315)

The research instrument chosen by Branford and Geddes was the 'regional survey', not to be confused with the sample surveys of later social researchers. Geddes, an idiosyncratic scholar, originally biologist, sometime geographer, sociologist, propagandist and educationalist before becoming influential in the town-planning movement, advocated this method. His was a much more totalising sense of the term 'survey', for it included considering the natural environment and the history of a place as well as the activities of its current inhabitants. He genuinely sought to incorporate the insights of natural science, geography, economics and anthropology, all of which, being influenced by Comte, he thought might be subsumed as sociology. In the three decades after his 1903 study of Dunfermline he persuaded many groups of people in different places to undertake such surveys, for reasons of self-education and civic awareness as well as for scientific purposes. Most later commentators (e.g. Abrams, 1968, p. 118; Mellor, 1989, p. 136) think Geddes contributed little, agreeing with Glass that:

> His failure to devise an adequate method for urban sociology and his premature diversion into planning propaganda and educational projects were critical. They discredited urban sociology among sociologists and they established an essentially non-sociological use of the social survey among planners. (Glass, 1989, p. 120)

Branford maintained that sociology could only proceed by the inductive generalisation of facts from a regional survey. In 1928 he wrote that 'Regional Surveys ... are now in progress throughout Britain ... thus arises the need and practicability of a social observatory for each city, with departments of study on all the ... levels with their various outlooks' (Branford, 1928, p. 337).

We have seen that the Chicago School saw urban sociology as involving three general concerns: sociation in the modern city;

the nature of modernity; and a liberal political project. Britain was somewhat different. The interest in 'sociation' was almost entirely absent. Whilst the Chicagoans focused upon the social life of the neighbourhood, gang or informal social group, the British mainstream focused upon the household survey, probing issues based on household income and expenditure, and were not especially concerned with the extent of wider social bonds. The British tended to assume that social class identities provided social bonds, even in otherwise diverse urban settings.

The British were, nevertheless, interested in the nature of 'contemporary' life and were also politically involved. Geddes's ideas were central to the Town Planning and Garden City movements, also associated with Ebenezer Howard, which argued that most urban problems could be resolved by planning cities more rationally. It is interesting to speculate whether it was the Utopian and visionary aspects of Geddes's thought that led to his lack of acceptability within British social science. But he and Branford also added a dimension missing in the Chicago school. From Le Play they adopted the idea that sociology was vitally concerned with the context and environment of social life. For Branford the main viewpoint was 'that of the essential interconnexion of all main aspects of any given community and its civilisation' (Branford, 1926, p. 317). The regional focus allowed them to show how it was impossible to abstract individuals from their wider social environment, and that sociology was a contextual discipline, concerned not to partition social action into a series of subdisciplines but to integrate different aspects of social activity. They showed the way to examine the total configuration of forces that provided the basis of everyday activities in different places.

Through the 1930s more local surveys were accomplished, foremost of which were the Merseyside Survey, published in 1934, the *New London Survey of London Life and Labour* (1930) and the York survey (Rowntree, 1941). The two last-mentioned were follow-up surveys of earlier research, and concentrated on assessing the extent to which poverty levels had changed. Their success began to suggest that cumulative sociological knowledge could be developed. The emerging hegemony of the sample survey, influenced by statistical ideas such as random sampling, was perhaps indicated by the largely adverse reaction to the appearance of Mass Observation (Kent, 1981). This social movement of 'observers', instead of conducting interviews using a pre-designed schedule, employed simple ethnographic techniques, including the use of direct observation of social activities in certain towns. Although the techniques were rather closer to those of the ethnographers of Chicago, its project of 'a science of ourselves' received little attention in British academia.

2.2   The decline of urban sociology: towards the 1990s

In both Britain and the USA, until the 1930s, urban sociology was scarcely a specialised sub-branch of the discipline. Rather, empirical sociological issues revolved around urban conditions: mass immigration, poverty, social pathologies, conflict groups and social bonding. Sociologists were thus directly concerned with the environments and contexts that generated social action. Developments after the 1930s displaced the urban focus of sociology and, hence, its contextual logic.

Most generally, sociology began to be organised around a different set of intellectual problems. The main theoretical concern of the reconstructed sociology was the nature of social order. Talcott Parsons, in his book *The Structure of Social Action,* published in 1937, introduced Pareto, Weber and Durkheim as the key figures in sociological thought, the first two having been largely ignored earlier. His subsequent *The Social System* (1951) fixed the problem of order at the centre of American sociology. In European sociology the study of inequality and social control remained prominent but, particularly because of the increasing legitimacy of statistically based research methods, the contextual focus characteristic of urban research was diminished.

The Parsonian conception of social order had no place in the older sociology in America or Europe. One of the few points of agreement within the Chicago School was a belief that there was no social order in the modern city, but only an uncoordinated struggle for resources and survival. The question of social order was seen as a political rather than a sociological issue, as something that might be achieved through political engagement, but which did not presently exist. Whilst not uninterested in inequality, the prime focus was on the bonds within, rather than between, social groups and classes. This apocalyptic view of social disorganisation seemed increasingly out of place in the post-war, planned, Keynesian era of steady economic growth, declining mass migration and muted social conflict. In the new age, the vitality of urban sociology was lost; its theoretical relevance diminished and its political concerns grew more parochial.

Of course, urban sociology never ceased to exist in the USA and specialist scholars continued to work in the field. However, technically, inquiry became increasingly positivistic and issues of urban planning seemed to predominate. Louis Wirth's article 'Urbanism as a Way of Life' (1938), discussed in detail in Chapter 5, proved an influential starting-point for comparing urban and rural social relations by observing measurable differences. His distinction between urban and rural ways of life fuelled nostalgic debates about 'the decline of community' (e.g. Stein, 1964) and investigation of the personality types of urban dwellers (e.g. Riesman, 1950). Both concerns were infused by the mass-society thesis which, despite some affinity to depictions of the experience of modernity and its prominence in American social science in the 1950s and 1960s, added little to sociological insight. In addition the techniques of urban analysis that in part emerged from the statistical wing of the Chicago School – the ecological analysis of Hawley (1950) for example – while providing useful descriptive material about segregation in American cities, subdued many of the appealing aspects of the pre-war research agenda. Post-war urban sociology in many ways resolved the methodological debate in Chicago between case studies and survey methods in favour of the latter (Bulmer, 1984). Though there continued to be some fascinating ethnographic studies of areas of cities, working-class communities and suburbs (e.g. Suttles, 1968; Gans, 1962 and 1968a), qualitative research became less prestigious and less widely practised than statistical methods.

The substance of urban research became more the investigation of ways of dealing with urban problems, though as an issue of management rather than political reform. While attention centred on enhancing community and neighbourliness, this academic status quo was disturbed by the US riots of the 1960s. This brought issues of social justice and order to the fore, and led to increasing dissatisfaction with Parsonian theory.

In Britain, too, changes in preferred methods of investigation coincided with new concerns. In place of contextual study of the interaction between people and their environment came an overriding interest in occupational stratification. In post-war empirical sociology, social class, rather than region or neighbourhood, became the central concept integrating sociological subdisciplines. By the 1970s it was joined by a growing concern with gender and racial inequality. Rather than examining how social actions were rooted in specific places, social practices were related to the operations of common, national, class (and later, gender and race) systems. Thus key concerns of pre-war urban sociology receded.

The immediate post-war period saw the proliferation of community studies, increasingly influenced by the concerns of anthropology, a discipline stronger than sociology in the UK. The community-study approach owed relatively little to the 'regional survey' tradition and became concerned predominantly with the internal mechanics of social relationships within small geographical areas. Though deeply and rightly concerned with sociation, research was framed, as in the USA, largely by the contrast between rural order and urban anomie and the project of re-establishing a lost sense of community (see Frankenberg, 1966). The call by Mass Observation for 'a science of ourselves' (evocative because the British anthropological tradition had previously been largely devoted to exotic peoples of the Empire) was thus to some degree answered. Much good work was done, but it was relatively little appreciated, typically being criticised from a positivist viewpoint for being non-cumulative, unverifiable, and parochial (see Chapter 5).

These inquiries did contribute to a more theoretically informed interest in social class, though the local focus was used simply as a frame. This was true of Stacey's (1960) work on Banbury and also particularly true of the famous study *Coal is Our Life* (Dennis *et al.*, 1956). This report of a Yorkshire colliery village showed how the culture of the miners was rooted in their work and community. In many ways it was a classic example of Le Play's axiom that cultures emerged out of people's relationship to nature in specific geographical milieux. Nonetheless, class, rather than place, was the organising focus of the book.

Stacey and Dennis *et al.*, like other British sociologists, concentrated on the abstract nature of social groups, organisations and institutions, rather than their contextual, spatial and environmental aspects. Before the 1950s social classes had been studied only in specific social settings. Research was on the working class in London, or poverty in York. The new approaches to social class abstracted from the particular places in which people lived. Social mobility research was an early example. David Glass and his associates (Glass, 1954) reoriented sociological interest towards analyses of the mobility between classes at the national level, using sample surveys. This trend was not instantaneous. Still in the mid-1960s social mobility was frequently related to spatial mobility. Likewise, David Lockwood's influential explanation of variations in 'working-class images of society' emphasised the importance of community as a vital determinant of people's values (Lockwood, 1966). Workers living in one-industry towns tended to be more class-conscious and oppositional than those living in new housing estates alongside the middle classes. It was symbolic, however, that the famous 'affluent worker' study of the 1960s (Goldthorpe *et al.*, 1968, 1969), which examined the social and political attitudes of car workers in Luton, was interpreted as applying to affluent workers anywhere, the evidence rarely being put in its particular local context.

By the 1970s social environment played little or no part in analyses of social class. Moreover, in social theory, a structuralist analysis inspired by the French Marxist, Althusser, emerged, maintaining that class analysis should be focused not upon people but upon the forces affecting class positions – the 'empty slots' into which people were fitted. Social class became more closely related to purely economic processes, affecting the nature of work and employment relations, rather than to wider social milieux of everyday life, social networks and residence. Structuralism left a legacy in many branches of empirical sociology. In social mobility research John Goldthorpe's (1980) influential analysis depended entirely upon a national random sample, collected in the early 1970s, without concern for regional variation or spatial mobility (see also Payne, 1987).

The same tendency is apparent in the British sociology of the family, originally an offshoot of community studies (Young and Willmott, 1962). In related work by Elizabeth Bott (1957) the social networks of marriage partners in the neighbourhood were the primary influences on relationships within the household. Where couples were strongly integrated into networks outside the household, gender roles inside the household were more segregated. This research suggested that families and households could best be understood in relationship to their encompassing, external, social environment. In the 1960s this view began to be undermined. Young and Willmott (1962) argued that the social environment was not, in fact, especially significant in shaping family structures. Apparent differences in family type in old working-class areas and on newer estates could be explained simply because traditional social arrangements had not had time to re-emerge. For them, whilst social environment seemed relatively unimportant, class became vital, hence their contrast between extended working-class and nuclear middle-class families. Willmott and Young later became even less interested in the neighbourhood context of family life, adopting random-sample-surveys designs for their Symmetrical Family inquiry (Young and Willmott, 1975). As with social mobility research, the survey replaced the local case study. Specific urban contexts became incidental (see locality research in Chapter 3).

One of the crucial concerns of both the Chicago School and the early British urban sociologists was their sense of political engagement. On both sides of the Atlantic social research continued to be wedded to a politics of social democratic reform, by and large supporting state intervention to ameliorate the position of those to whom the market offered least. However, increasingly, sociologists found themselves agitating less at the local level and becoming more concerned to lobby central government. Moving away from the concerns of the Chicago School and inter-war British urban sociology, national survey research was viewed as carrying more weight, especially since government departments tended to hold statistical knowledge in highest esteem.

By the late 1960s the sociological wheel had turned full circle. Georg Simmel, in his account of 'The Field of Sociology', had argued that sociology should not simply concern itself with 'definable, consistent structures such as the state and the family, the guild and the church, social classes and organisations based on common interests' (Simmel, 1950, p. 9). Rather, it should make the study of 'sociation' central. By the 1960s, however, mainstream sociology was focused almost exclusively on these institutions. Urban context and the moral order implicit in everyday actions were consequently neglected. National studies of class structures based on sample surveys replaced local studies of inequality and social interaction. With prospects for urban sociology bleak, the 1970s and 1980s saw an attempt at its reconstitution to fit the revised state of the social sciences. Thus emerged 'the new urban sociology'.

2.2. 1   The 'new urban sociology'

Urban sociology survived, in the USA especially, despite being out of step with post-war theoretical developments in sociology. Much of its output consisted of statistical description of urban conditions, offering some informative basis for addressing urban problems. It also continued to explore questions of city growth and, particularly, to explore a contrast between urban and rural life. Despite some exceptional studies, urban sociology became something of an intellectual backwater. This tranquil existence was fractured by a series of devastating critiques of its theoretical failings. The most famous and original was the Marxist critique by Manuel Castells in *The Urban Question* (1977), which condemned the older traditions of urban sociology and sought to reconstitute it on an alternative basis. Castells's critique coincided with the resurgence and widespread adoption of Marxist analysis in Europe. Once again, general trends in social theory propelled urban studies onto new terrain. The concerns of neo-Marxism included isolating the specifically capitalist aspects of economic life, stressing the role of classes as historical agents and a critical rejection of the way in which welfare arrangements were socially incorporating the working class without significant redistribution of wealth or power. The particular version of neo-Marxism associated with the French philosopher, Louis Althusser, proved most influential in the attempt to develop a more rigorous and theoretical 'new urban sociology'. This provided a starting-point not only for Marxists but also for some Weberians, including Peter Saunders in his book *Social Theory and the Urban Question* (1981). He, too, sought to pull down the final curtain on the older traditions of urban sociology.

The starting-point of the critique was the argument that a scientific discipline needed to have a proper 'theoretical object'.

In this claim both Castells and Saunders were heavily indebted to Althusser, who argued that what distinguished scientific from 'ideological' works was the way that the latter began with taken-for-granted notions whilst the former constituted their concerns theoretically. The creation of a scientific discipline required a distinct 'theoretical object' specific to it. Within this framework it was argued that all existing urban sociology was ideological since it began with commonsense concepts such as community, the city, or urban problems, which it was unable to ground theoretically.

Urban sociology proved an easy target for criticism from this epistemological viewpoint. What was the specific 'theoretical object' of urban sociology? Was it the city? If so, there were distinctive problems in specifying social activities which only took place in cities. Forms of industry, patterns of interaction, leisure activities, class conflict, and so forth could be seen in the city and the countryside. What, possible reason was there, then, for distinguishing the city from the countryside?

Perhaps, instead, the theoretical object of urban sociology might be a concern with 'space', and the way in which spatial arrangements affected social life? But it proved very difficult to show how space itself – taken as physical distance between natural and social objects – could really help sociological explanation. To give a simple example, close physical proximity to others may make you very fond of them, or heartily tired of them. The mere fact of physical proximity seems far less important in explaining people's actions than the type of social and personal relationships between them.

The critique developed by Castells and Saunders was extremely powerful. Urban sociology has no theoretical object, and it is difficult to know how one might be constructed. Castells attempted to reconstruct urban sociology by integrating it with his analysis of the contradictions of capitalist societies. He argued that in late capitalism cities had a distinctive role not in the process of production, the usual Marxist emphasis, but rather as centres of 'collective consumption'. Collective consumption referred to forms of services collectively provided, usually by the state – mass housing, transport, health facilities, and so forth. Because collective consumption is geared to people living within a certain spatial radius, it has a spatial referent. Moreover, the provision of such services was identified as a source of political mobilisation, as it spawned urban social movements, protest groups aiming to improve urban conditions through contesting the existing pattern of collective consumption. Castells maintained that because these protests were linked to the reproduction of labour power, they might have revolutionary potential if linked into working-class movements.

Castells's account initially appeared to solve some problems both for urban sociology and for Marxist political practice. Urban sociology acquired a theoretical object, collective consumption, while Marxism was nourished by the notion that disparate urban protests of the 1970s, squatters' movements, tenants' movements, and the like, were connected to class struggle. Academically, the analysis of cities specifically as sites for the reproduction of labour power became the distinctive feature of 'the new urban sociology'. Symptomatic was a new journal, the *International Journal of Urban and Regional Research,* launched in 1977 and heavily influenced by Castells and French Marxism, though open also to other materialist theoretical perspectives. Various trend reports around 1980 (e.g. Zukin, 1980; Lebas, 1982) perceived enormous potential in the Marxist approach of Castells as a way to reinvigorate urban sociology. Castells was a vehement critic of culturalist approaches to the city like that of Wirth, of evolutionary accounts of urban development and of spatially determinist theories. He emphasised the changing nature of economic production and the contemporary role of the state in organising consumption. His concern with urban social movements, as vehicles for social opposition, had practical political ramifications. Above all it promised a theoretically coherent framework for urban studies.

Ultimately Castells's arguments raised as many problems as they solved. Politically, urban social movements proved difficult to fuse with Marxist politics, at least outside the developing countries. Throughout Europe, communist parties failed to mobilise on the basis of urban social movements and, in his later work, Castells (1983) repudiated the vision of an association between class struggle and urban protest. Although Castells did help to introduce Marxist concepts to urban sociology, in the course of the 1980s production processes, rather than collective consumption, became the focus of Marxist scholarship and the new urban sociology subsided. Geographers, David Harvey, Doreen Massey, Dick Walker, Allen Scott and others developed a Marxist–informed political economy in which the concept of collective consumption played little part.

Castells's formulation of the concept of collective consumption proved more popular in Britain amongst non–Marxist writers like Patrick Dunleavy and Peter Saunders, though they appropriated it critically. As Saunders pointed out, collective consumption is not a purely 'urban' process. The collective consumption of education and health services occurs in both city and countryside. Furthermore, Saunders observed, not all the consumption practices within cities are collective: many are private, purchased by individuals. Saunders, following Dunleavy, used this distinction as a way of identifying social groups possessing distinctive material and political interests by virtue of the extent to which they depended upon either collective or private consumption. Hence Saunders proposed that the correct focus of urban sociology should be consumption in all its forms, and that it should lose any residual spatial reference. This raised another question, however. Why not abandon urban sociology entirely and develop a new subdiscipline, the 'sociology of consumption', for such a project seemed not to require the ideas, empirical findings or theories of earlier urban sociology?

The 'new urban sociology' was very challenging and it did manage to inspire empirical study and theoretical analysis of some of the most pressing political issues of the 1970s and 1980s. The concept of collective consumption implicitly addressed the role of, and changes within, the welfare state, the declining quality and recommodification of services being probably the major social issue of the period. It directed attention to urban movements and the mobilisation of political actors around issues of urban planning. Because of its Marxist derivation it also encouraged a much deeper analysis of the relationship between city life and capital accumulation. Nevertheless, it consciously renounced the intellectual traditions of urban sociology, which contain more of value than was appreciated. In particular, while accepting that it is not possible to constitute 'the urban' as a theoretical object, excessive concern with defining 'the urban' distorted the history of urban sociology. For, in fact, few urban sociologists ever claimed that the city was a theoretical entity. Park, for instance, was quite clear about this when stating that the city 'was a laboratory, or clinic, in which human nature and social processes may be profitably studied' (Park, 1967, p. 46). He and his colleagues were concerned with social bonds in a fragmented world, and cities were arenas in which such a topic might be examined. What motivated the Chicago School and the early British sociologists was, rather, a broad set of social and political concerns about the nature of contemporary social life. And it was to dismantling boundaries, both disciplinary and as a way of conceptualising the city, that sociologists and others have most recently turned.

2.3 Urban sociology and beyond: the new millennium

In a hidden-away footnote in *Postmetropolis: Critical Studies of Cities and Regions*, Edward Soja (2000, p. 271) reflects on the decline in the US of urban sociology. He cites two reasons for its apparent demise. First, conservative sociologists reacted badly to the radicalism of the Marxist approach that came to dominate in the 1970s, moving away from producing urban sociology *per se* to work on issues such as ethnicity, race and gender. Second, new urban sociology was weak in 'dealing with the urbanization processes and their specifically spatial manifestations' (2000, p. 271). He claims that those US sociologists who have continued to produce what might reasonably be referred to as 'urban sociology' now find themselves in urban planning faculties in the US. Yet, the last decade has seen a renewed intellectual vigour in the analysis of the city. On both sides of the Atlantic, and beyond the Western world, cities have been conceptualised as 'sites of complex global/local interconnections producing a multiplicity of social, cultural, political, economic spaces and forms' (Bridge and Watson, 2000a, p. 1). In adopting this view, urban sociology, like all sub-disciplines in the social sciences, has been informed by post-structuralism and an attention to issues of discourse and representation, by the emphasis on fluidity and on difference. Ironically one of those cited as leading lights in what Soja (2000, pp. 271–2) terms 'the reconfiguration of cityscape', Saskia Sassen (2000, p. 144) has recently speculated on the 'new frontiers facing urban sociology at the millennium'. Taking a line similar to ours, she argues that:

> It is perhaps one of the ironies at this century's end that some of the old questions of the early Chicago School of Urban

Sociology should re-emerge as promising and strategic to understand certain critical issues today, notably the importance of recovering place and undertaking ethnographies at a time when dominant forces such as globalization and telecommunications seem to signal that place and the details of the local no longer matter.

Yet, the conducting of contemporary urban research in a very different academic environment from that in which earlier urban sociology was produced raises a host of intellectual challenges. Theoretical developments have led to a diverse set of disciplines being represented alongside one another in a range of recent works. These include, for example, 'the unknown city' (Borden *et al.*, 2001), 'theorizing the city' (Low, 2000) and 'unsettling cities' (Allen *et al.*, 1999). What is emphasised in this work by anthropologists, architects, ethnographers, geographers and sociologists is the need to think in terms of flows of ideas, images, money, people, etc. and in terms of the relations that exist across time and space but between places.

In light of this, recent work on the urban can be organised around two themes. First, is the heightened sensitivity to how cities and the urban processes are represented. Often drawing upon the work of Simmel (1964) and Lefebvre (1991) this work centres on the ways through which cities are represented in film, literature, in urban scholarship and in urban planning and politics (Bridge and Watson, 2000b). This emphasis, as perhaps part of the wider 'cultural turn' in urban studies, is summed up by Borden *et al.* (2001, p. 14):

> Cities are complex systems of representations, in which space and times are understood and experienced in the form of a representation. All systems of representation are composed of signs: written words, speech, painting, photographic images, maps and signals, filmic narratives, choreographic movements, installations and events, buildings and places.

This acknowledgement of the importance of representation and the other non-material elements of everyday life has accompanied a wider turn in social sciences towards taking meanings as socially constructed rather than pre-given. In this spirit, sociologists have begun to analyse cities as sites of multiple representations and meanings, which are open to being contested by actors and those with interests in the city.

A second theme is the analysis of cities in terms of networks or connections, of relations across space (Castells, 1996/97; Massey, 1999). On the one hand this marks a return to earlier work in urban sociology, conceptualising the city as un-bounded. Yet it also stands in contrast to the urban sociology of the 1980s:

> This is ... not the city as a bounded unit, but the city as a node in a grid of cross-boundary processes ... This type of city cannot be located simply in a scalar hierarchy that places it beneath the national, regional and global. It is one of the spaces of the global, and it engages the global directly, often by-passing the national. (Sassen, 2000, p. 146)

This emphasis on flows and networks is neatly summed up in Smith's (2001) *Transnational Urbanism* and in work on 'a new transnational political geography' and defined as:

> a marker of the criss-crossing transnational circuits of communication and cross-cutting local, translocal, and transnational social practices that 'come together' in particular places at particular times and enter into the contested politics of place-making, the social construction of power differentials, and the making of individual, group, national, and transnational identi ties, and their corresponding fields of difference. (Sassen, 2000, pp. 151–3)

Sassen (2000, p.151), mirroring this relational emphasis, talks in terms of an approach that 'connects sites that are not geographically proximate yet are intensely connected to each other'. In essence, sociologists and others interested in the urban experience have turned toward an analysis of the city that celebrates difference, which examines the connections between places, which acknowledges the importance of non-economic as well as economic networks, and which conceptualises cities within wider societies.

2.4 Conclusion

If anything, the end of the 1990s marked a return in urban sociology to pre-Marxist approaches to the city. After a period when structural readings dominated, the last few years of urban research have seen a partial return to an emphasis on context and on place. Hence our assertion that the critique on which the new urban sociology was based is both true and misleading. Urban sociology does not have a clear theoretical object, and it is not simply the study of cities, understood as physical units with large populations. Instead it should be conceived as a broader inquiry into the nature of contemporary social relations in their contextual settings. It has been part of a sociological venture that concentrates on the ways in which institutions and practices combine in particular places. The attempt has been to explore the interrelationship between institutional domains: 'place, work and folk' for the admirers of Le Play; 'production, consumption and exchange' for the Marxists; perhaps race, class and family for many American urbanists. It was not the particular characteristics of urban spaces that justified such inquiries; rather, it was the appropriateness of urban areas as sites of research where sociologists could examine in considerable detail the interdependence of the social institutions that form everyday experience. In many ways synthetic theories were being formulated and tested empirically in confined areas where context could be appreciated.

Informed by external changes in social theory and contemporary political issues, which combine with an internal technical dynamic, urban sociology has grappled with the concerns of social theory, particularly the attempt to understand the nature of modern, individual and collective, experience. In this sense the city may be considered as a sociological laboratory, for it is regularly used to address, to some degree empirically, particularly those matters concerned with the experience of modernity.

Urban sociology has also responded regularly to changing political agendas and priorities. This is partly because abstract social theory itself is also guided by the vagaries of contemporary political predicaments. In the time of the Chicago School emphasis was on the political problems emanating from explosive industrial-city growth, mass migration, and the concentration of apparently rootless, and dangerous, people. Simultaneously in the UK, urbanists depicted urban poverty and inequality during the years of the Depression, advocating state intervention, planning and the preservation of community as political remedies. In the post-war era the priority seemed to become more one of effective planning, management and control of urban living. Urban managerialist approaches, for instance, explored issues regarding the routines of state administration and what an interventionist commitment can do to mitigate inequality and inadequate standards of living. This was disrupted in the USA initially by the civil rights movement and violent urban protest that brought 'the urban question' to the fore as politicians sought some response. At this stage urban sociology took a much closer interest in urban conflict, the actors and the social movements involved in promoting urban change. Subsequently, the issue of welfare provision and debates about the merits of privatisation versus state intervention became a key contemporary issue. The new urban sociology of the 1970s offered a diagnosis of the pacifying influence of welfare, the stifling of dissent and the faltering progress of class struggle. Most recently, work in urban sociology has revealed the diversity of forms and experiences that constitute contemporary cities, and all this might mean for efforts to decode social exclusion.

We have argued that changes in the prestige of different kinds of method are an important factor explaining the history of urban sociology. Before the Chicago School urban investigations were either based on histories of cities or on simple observation. The Chicago School pioneered both systematic urban ethnography and statistical methods of ecological analysis. There has been some oscillation ever since between case-study approaches, including community studies, and statistical approaches, increasingly of the sample-survey type. Most recently, greater confidence has been expressed in the use of imaginative description, hermeneutic interpretation of meanings, the readings of urban landscapes, etc. Despite the variety of methods deployed, aspects of what Thomas Kuhn would describe as 'normal science' have developed, where specialised techniques for inquiring into social segregation and patterns of sociability have steadily improved providing the basis for reliable analysis. These are pursued constantly and are regularly redeployed to deal with pressing political issues of urban inequality and social or cultural disorganisation. Chapters 4 and 7 deal with the former and 5 and 6 with the latter.

It remains our contention, then, that the contribution of older forms of urban sociology has been somewhat misunderstood and that there is a number of themes within it, particularly in the Chicago School and Simmel, that deserve further development, especially those of modernity, sociation and political engagement. The recent rediscovery of issues of public space and of the practices of everyday life underscores this point. From a rather fragmentary and minor British tradition we can also draw on concerns with social inequality and a structural-contextual approach to place. Of course, early urban sociology had grave defects. Among these was an almost total ignorance of political economy, of both the wider logic of the system of capitalist production and the role of the state. The next chapter considers how recent scholarship, much of it developed by human geographers, has attended to that lacuna.

3 Cities and Uneven Economic Development

Though best seen as an extended inquiry into the relationship between capitalism and modernity, urban sociology has characteristically concentrated on cities as sites of modernity, rather than on how capitalist economic systems structure cities. It has also underplayed the on-going relationship between capitalism and cities. In this chapter we draw on the work of urban geographers to show how cities need to be placed in the broader context of the world capitalist system. Such contextualisation, we argue, is important in specifying the relationship between different cities, and between cities and rural areas, so allowing urban sociologists to avoid the mistake of seeing cities as self-contained objects with clear boundaries – as exemplars of a universal modernity. Instead, we argue in this chapter that cities need to be understood as part of a wider economic system, and as precise conjunctures capable of mediating and shaping economic restructuring processes. The significance of examining the economic bases of urban form is that it allows urban specificity to be comprehended, in terms of the particular role which different cities play within the worldwide economic system.

However, it is not easy to register the importance of the economic context of cities. There is no consensus as to how capitalism operates as an economic system and in particular how it operates over space, between places, and hence how it affects urban development. This chapter clarifies differing views of the relationship between economic systems and urban development, in order to assess their value in placing cities in their context. It is structured around the way different writers emphasise the temporal or spatial dimensions of urban differentiation and uneven spatial development.

In section 3.1 we consider approaches, largely non-Marxist, which adopt a temporal focus, where cities are related to particular stages of historical development, but are rarely analysed in terms of their spatial relation to each other. The principal axiom is that cities evolve in line with broader economic development. This evolutionary perspective is typical of the early urban economists, such as Alfred Weber, Jane Jacobs, Peter Hall and others. The problem with such accounts is that they tend to assume that there is only one type of urban development, which all cities from whatever culture follow, and hence they ignore the diversity and specificity of cities. This leads us to the work of urban geographers who have concentrated their research on the analysis of urban differentiation. Section 3.2 examines Marxist theories of uneven development whose focus is a spatial one, where cities are seen as occupying specific places within a worldwide capitalist economic system. Within this broad perspective we evaluate three competing and rather different ways in which such differentiation is explained. The first version is that associated with the early work of David Harvey, which is explicitly concerned with the historical specificity of differing processes (or 'circuits') of capital accumulation, and with the significance of social struggle. In section 3.2.2 we contrast Harvey's account with that offered by Doreen Massey, which places greater importance on industrial restructuring and has produced a well-documented account of contemporary urban change in Britain and other advanced industrial countries. Both Harvey and Massey incline towards a certain economic reductionism. In section 3.2.3 we examine the accounts derived from the 'Regulation School' which has become increasingly influential in urban studies, and pay particular attention to the most recent work on the geographies of regulation. Finally, we set out the self-styled 'LA School' and assess their contribution to the explanation of contemporary spatial patterns of uneven development.

3.1   Limits to evolutionary theories of cities

In the work of Simmel and the Chicago School cities represented the new and the modern, epitomes of the emergent economic and social order produced by industrial capitalism. Implicitly they drew upon an evolutionary model of economic change. The city of Chicago, in particular, was taken as representative of the modern industrial city, and attempts to apply the concentric-ring model (developed by Burgess and modified by others) to other industrial cities were legion. Within this frame of thought the city was seen as the product of the elaborate division of labour characteristic of modern industrial society. Cities owed their economic role to their pivotal place in this new industrial order as centres of commerce, sites of production, and bases for the most specialised economic activities. In this line of reasoning the city was the most advanced manifestation of an evolutionary process of economic change, 'the workshops of civilisation' in Park's words (see Harvey, 1973, p. 195).

Evolutionary approaches to urban development argued that the industrial city was the culmination of a long evolutionary process, stretching back to the earliest historical periods. Lampard (1965) distinguished two urban epochs in human history. These were, first, 'primordial urbanisation' where settlements first emerged in the years between 15000 BC and 4000 BC, as a collective form of organisation additional to the usual migratory agricultural activities. The importance of the second period of 'definitive urbanisation', which began in Mesopotamia after 4000 BC, was that cities developed as fixed sites. Hence, 'by means of its capacity to generate, store, and utilise social saving, the definitive city artefact is capable of transplanting itself out of its native uterine environments' (Lampard, 1965, p. 523). This period of 'definitive urbanisation' is itself split into two epochs, before and after AD 1700. In the first of these, cities were centres for a hinterland and existed in a stable hierarchy, in which hamlets formed a hinterland for villages, villages for towns, towns for cities, and cities for capital cities. Urban expansion was limited since cities were essentially parasitic on a limited agricultural economy. After 1700, the industrial city emerged as a dynamic force, able to increase in size because of the ability of economic production based in cities to sever their dependency on agriculture.

The industrial city was hence seen as the locus of the new industrial society and as ushering in a new period in history when urban growth could continue at a vastly expanded level. Yet since the 1930s the industrial societies which cities were seen to embody have themselves been transformed by deindustrialisation

(Bell, 1973; Gershuny, 1978). Manufacturing industries in many urban heartlands have collapsed and service industries have arisen while industrial production has developed in new, rural, areas, appearing to cut the apparently close connection between cities and industry on which the evolutionary ideas were based.

Attempts to apply evolutionary thinking have persisted into the present day and have taken a new turn as industrial economies have changed. A good example is the work of Peter Hall, who has developed the evolutionary model of the city to encompass deindustrialisation as well as industrialisation (see Hall and Hay, 1980; Hall, 1988). Hall begins by arguing that the urban system has been massively transformed in recent decades. Drawing upon American evidence he argues that four linked processes have undermined the centrality of the large, industrial urban conurbation which characterised earlier periods of industrial capitalism. These are:

1. suburbanisation, where urban growth takes place in suburban rather than central urban areas;
2. de-urbanisation, where the urban population reduces relative to the population of rural and non-urban areas;
3. the contraction of the largest cities;
4. the rise of new regions and the decline of old.

Hall explains this transformation by distinguishing six evolutionary stages through which cities go as industrial economies change and decline. His emphasis is upon the way in which, as regions industrialise, cities develop in size and concentration. After a period of time, however, any industrial area begins to stagnate as innovation occurs elsewhere. Hence cities begin to decline. Because this process of industrial growth and fall is inevitable, all cities pass through the same six-stage cycle.

The six stages Hall specifies are divided into two groups. The first three stages occur during industrialisation, the last three when deindustrialisation begins to take effect in any given region:

1. The stage of 'centralisation during loss' happens during early industrialisation. People migrate from the country to the city, leading to a growing urban population, but the overall population in any region is in net decline as more people leave the region overall.

2. As industrialisation continues, the overall proportion of people living in cities within regions increases.
3. 'Relative centralisation' occurs when the city stretches over its boundaries and begins to develop suburbs. Nevertheless the proportion of urban dwellers continues to grow. This is the type of city which was the focus of the Chicago School studies, where there were large and dense urban populations and suburbs had begun to emerge.

Hall's argument, however, is that urban evolution has now continued beyond this, and a process of urban decline marks a new stage from that studied by the Chicago writers:

4. Suburbs begin to grow faster than the urban core, so that 'relative decentralisation' occurs as people move to the outer reaches of cities.
5. Starting about 1900 in the largest European cities (but generally much more recently) 'absolute decentralisation' occurs as people begin to move out of the inner city as it becomes increasingly specialised around office and commercial functions.
6. The entire city begins to decline as people begin to move out to the rural areas as deindustrialisation proceeds.

This process of 'counter-urbanisation' has been much debated since the 1960s (Fielding, 1982). The period of industrial urban expansion, which earlier writers had expected to continue unabated, gives way, in Hall's view, to a situation of urban decline.

Hall is wary about applying his evolutionary model. It is derived from research in the USA chronicling the decline of large cities from the 1960s. In Western Europe there are different patterns, and 'the different countries' urban systems ... display marked differences from one another' (Hall, 1988, p. 116). In Britain and Germany the largest cities were declining in population by the 1970s, as Hall would have expected. However in France, Italy and the Benelux countries they were not.

Although many cities are seeing significant population loss, there are a number of difficulties with an evolutionary model such as Hall's. First, there is a problem with the way that Hall, in common with other writers referring to the phenomenon of 'counterurbanisation', characterises the decline of cities in the current period. There is no doubt that in many parts of the developed world population and employment is moving from central urban locations, but whether this should be seen as testifying to the decline of cities rather than their further expansion into new areas is a moot point. If fixed boundaries are drawn round a city at any one point in time, it is always possible that when the population within these boundaries decreases this may be interpreted as urban decline. In reality, however, the city may be expanding outside these boundaries and increasing in significance. Scott, for instance, emphasises the continuing urbanisation process in capitalist societies (Scott, 1988a, p. 63). Second, there is a problem about generalising from Hall's study of urban trends in twentieth-century Western Europe. Even if we were to accept that cities have historically shared a common set of characteristics, contemporary cities are becoming increasingly differentiated according to their role in the world economy, which makes it unhelpful to generalise about a single evolutionary path for all. Indeed, over the last two decades there has been a mushrooming of city types, the defining of each depending on whether it is economic, political, or religious criteria that are used. There is now a rich literature on cities that uses a range of metaphors and images as lenses on to different processes. Low (2000, pp. 5–21) identifies twelve 'images' organised in terms of 'social relational processes', 'economic processes', 'urban planning and architecture approaches' and 'religious and cultural aspects of urban life'. Building upon the economic category, we outline four urban types – developing cities, global cities, older industrial cities and informational cities – all of which have a different set of characteristics.

Developing cities are themselves heterogeneous but tend to possess a number of distinctive features. They are 'over-urbanised' (Timberlake, 1987). This means that they tend to be extremely large relative to the population of the country–a result of the fact that inward capitalist investment often focuses upon these capital city sites, a phenonmenon described as 'urban bias'. They also tend to be deeply divided, along a number of lines. Strong demarcations exist between the formal and informal economy, between city and country and between social (and sometimes ethnic) groups. This dualistic format is related, in many cases, to the colonial legacy of 'urban apartheid' (Abu-Lughod, 1980; King, 1990), where colonial rulers lived in separate parts of the city and were subject to a different jurisdiction from that applying to native dwellers.

Global cities (or world cities) are ones that increasingly depend on international financial services and are linked to the circulation and realisation of wealth. They are frequently where the corporate headquarters of multinational enterprises are located and are the sites of what Massey (1988) and Sassen (1991, 2000) refer to as 'control functions', where the control and management of corporate enterprise is directed. London, New York and Tokyo are examples of this type of city. They tend to be large, centralised (with a distinct urban core specialising in international financial services), and contain alongside one another an élite group of workers and lower-paid servicing workers (Kasarda, 1988; Fainstein and Harloe, 2000). In the last two decades the world city thesis has evolved, as an adjunct to the global city literature.

Older industrial cities, now in precipitate decline following the collapse of urban manufacturing, and with a few making the successful transition to post-industrial-city status, constitute the third type – Glasgow, Liverpool (a trading rather than industrial city), Bradford and Manchester being especially prominent. Other noted examples have been found in the north-east and mid-west of America (Detroit, Buffalo, Cleveland), and in Germany (Essen, Duisburg). These cities are characterised by decay and dereliction, high levels of unemployment, poor housing conditions and so forth.

Informational cities are distinctively new urban developments (global cities and older industrial cities being adaptations of older urban forms), which are not necessarily organised around an urban core with suburban hinterland. Instead, they tend to be more decentralised and cover a large area. In this city the 'space of flows' – how information technology and the service economy is organised geographically – dominates over the 'space of places' – or the everyday spaces in which people organise their lives. In essence, Castells (1989, 1996, 1997) argues that in this type of city, which reflects a wider societal move towards the information society, the ability of groups to resist some of the changes is undermined because the economy is organised through placeless flows.

The foregoing typology is not exhaustive. Instead, as Low (2000, p. 5) argues, these images 'provide a guide to the diverse ideas, concepts, and frameworks that authors use to analyze and write about the city and should be considered different lenses that offer the reader as well as the writer other ways to communicate about an often elusive and discursively complex subject'.

Many urban centres fall into several of the categories. The point is that it is impossible to see one form of city as archetypal of the current economic and social order in they way in which Chicago was taken as an exemplar of industrial capitalism in the early twentieth century. Although Los Angeles has often been portrayed as *the city of the future* (Scott and Soja, 1996) no one city reflects the diversity of all possible urban futures. It is not true that all cities experience the same logic of development, nor do they feed into and shape that logic in the same way. Rather, some cities obtain distinct roles in the global economy, and once established they become differentiated from other cities occupying different roles within the same environment. At the heart of the analysis is the fact that cities exist within a wider world system. The dynamics of this world system affect the way that cities develop and decline. A recognition of this belies a linear historical view of urban differentiation – where different urban forms are reflections of the specific period which any given city has reached in an evolutionary urban cycle – implying instead that spatial dynamics of the world system profoundly shape urban form. It is to a greater consideration of these processes that we now turn.

3.2   Competing explanations of uneven development

We have shown that evolutionary approaches fail to recognise the specificity of cities and the distinct roles they perform in a wider world economy. Let us consider in greater detail how these differences are sustained, and even deepened, by spatial processes of uneven development. Various theories address this issue. Many are of Marxist provenance, emerging from the revived intellectual reputation of Marxist analysis in the social sciences in the 1970s. The effect was to focus attention on the specifically capitalist mechanisms operating to create the geography of economic life. Thus, rather than beginning from the nature of industrialism, as did much orthodox economic sociology and geography in the post-war period, the central concerns were ones of capitalist accumulation, competition, exploitation and restructuring. When applied to the area of urban studies this constituted a more rigorous and detailed approach to the economic bases of urban systems.

Theories of uneven development, however, are bedevilled by a number of problems. Since these problems recur many times in the following pages it is worth listing them briefly:

1. Spatial analyses of uneven development may be ahistorical, failing fully to deal with its historically specific forms.
2. These theories may present static approaches, where the explanatory weight of the theory is geared to explaining how uneven development between places is sustained. It then becomes difficult to explain why some places are able to change their economic standing, possibly against the odds, the theory being insufficiently attuned to specificity (although see Chapter 7).
3. Theories may be unable to register the significance of human agency in affecting processes of uneven development, particularly in the form of social conflict.
4. Such theories may be overly determinist, trying to explain more about the character of places or cities than can usefully be derived from the process of uneven development itself.

In order to put our later discussion of the three different approaches in context it is worth just very briefly setting out the thesis presented by Frobel, Heinrichs and Kreye in their *New International Division of Labour* (NIDL) first published in German in 1977. They sought to explain the growing internationalisation of production since 1945 and its effects on the world economic system. Their main point was that manufacturing production processes which had once been undertaken in core countries in Western Europe were increasingly located in the Third World, which as peripheral countries within the world economy had previously concentrated on agricultural produce and raw materials for export to the advanced countries. Whereas in the 1950s Western Europe imported scarcely any manufactured goods, by 1975 much of the production in certain industrial sectors, like textiles and electrical goods, was carried out overseas, financed and controlled by metropolitan companies.

This process seemed to mark a new phase in the relationship between the global core and the periphery (Wallerstein, 1974). The prime reason for the emergence of the NIDL, according to Frobel *et al.*, was the change in the labour process as levels of skill involved in manufacturing production were reduced sharply. In such circumstances, a vast pool of unemployed or under-employed unskilled labour could be exploited on a world scale. The terms of employment of unskilled labour in developing countries were especially favourable to capital: wages are much lower, working conditions poorer, trade unions weaker, labour forces easier to discipline, etc., than in the West. The improvement in methods of communication and transport made it possible to exploit these new reserves of labour. Other factors such as tax concessions to multinationals, absence of pollution control, and the absence of health-and-safety legislation enhance the attractiveness of these locations. Also, certain other conditions have to be fulfilled to make overseas sites acceptable: transport costs which depend on the size and weight of the product; the political stability of overseas political regimes; property law; the corruptibility of officials, etc. (see Frobel *et al.*, 1980, pp. 145–7, for a list). But where such conditions are met it becomes profitable to transfer machinery to sites outside Europe to take advantage of favourable labour conditions.

The NIDL thesis was intellectually of enormous importance. It brought to scholarly attention a new form of internationalisation of the capitalist economy, explained recent changes in patterns of employment and indicated how multinational and transnational corporations could exploit spatial differences in labour markets, in conjunction with a new technical division of labour within particular industrial sectors. It offered a relatively simple explanation of the phenomenon of deindustrialisation. Derived in part from the neo-Marxist world-systems theory of Wallerstein it did not depend on any particularly sophisticated economic theory.

What is of particular concern to us is the implication of the NIDL for urban systems. The NIDL thesis can be used, in some ways, to explain the differentiation of cities in different parts of the world. Rather than see cities inevitably decline as an evolutionary concomitant of deindustrialisation, as Hall suggests, the NIDL thesis is able to explain the differential fate of cities in various parts of the globe. At one level, the prime position of

Western capital cities could be explained by their coordinating role in the new international division of labour. At another level the growth of large cities in the periphery, such as Mexico City, could also be explained by the role they played as sites for the new decentralised production.

Despite these insights, Frobel *et al.* were heavily criticised, partly by people unsympathetic to world-system theory (see Cohen, 1987; Hill, 1987; Gottdiener and Komninos, 1989, passim). Cohen advanced a comprehensive critique of the general proposition of the NIDL thesis, seeing it as conceptually weak, historically inadequate and empirically exaggerated. Conceptually, Cohen argued that the thesis was excessively economistic, derived from the logic of capital accumulation at the expense of social struggles and that there was too much emphasis on labour costs as against technological innovation. Historically, he claimed, there was nothing very new about the international division of labour, for there had been many phases in the past – mercantilism and imperialism among them. Finally, Cohen argued that the numbers concerned were not so enormous – that only a small proportion of total global employees worked in multinational companies.

There are three main problems with the NIDL thesis as a tool to analyse urban change. First, it is economistic, since it is incapable of systematically analysing anything other than economic change. As a result it gives few insights into changes internal to any particular city, and can only indicate the broad views of a city's general prosperity. It thus says little about processes such as suburbanisation, social segregation or housing provision.

Second, it ignores human agency; in particular there was an assumption that jobs, not people, were mobile, and hence that deskilled work would be moved to peripheral locations. This simplistic assumption precludes the possibility that unskilled labour may migrate to existing urban centres, or to growing urban areas in developed countries. The migration of Hispanic workers to south-west USA, for instance, has been of major significance in the development of the Californian economy, pointing to the variety of possible strategies which firms can use to find suitable labour for jobs. The decisions of particular firms are not structural necessities, but are partly choices in the light of a number of alternatives.

Finally, it has problems explaining why some cities were able to carve out particular places for themselves in the NIDL and others were not. In other words it is insufficiently attuned to the way in which urban actors can create a role for a particular place in the NIDL. Why are some manufacturing cities better able than others to readjust to the NIDL and change the basis of their local economies? The role of corporate actors and local political forces in affecting any city's economic position, even given the broad economic changes sketched out by the NIDL thesis, is largely ignored (see Chapter 7). While persuasive descriptions of local economic change could be offered, the roles of the state and politics were always included as historically contingent responses. The theoretical link between the activities of the capitalist corporation and the political apparatuses of national or local state was absent. Links were explicitly considered usually only if the local state had fiscal problems because major employers were closing down their operations. This would encourage them to offer incentives to private firms either to persuade them to stay or to attract new inward investment. Similarly, at the level of local popular resistance, although urban social movements, community groups, etc. were perceived as organising opposition (e.g. Fainstein, 1987), there was no *theoretical* basis for appreciating their significance. These limits were indeed partly recognised by Smith and Tardanico (1987) in their attempts to improve the understanding of the reproduction of labour power within this school of thought. Failings in this respect are partly the result of exaggerating the mobility of capital. The NIDL thesis would lead one to expect much higher levels of geographical mobility among firms than actually occurs, partly, as the 'LA School' considered below would contend, because they underestimate the importance of economic networks and the benefits of agglomeration. We next turn to the three contrasting explanations of uneven development, beginning with the seminal work of David Harvey.

3.2.1   *David Harvey, the second circuit of capital and urbanisation*

In the 1970s David Harvey attempted an ambitious theoretical approach to the analysis of uneven development, derived from a new appreciation of Marx's economic theory and its implications for urban growth. In many ways it offered a powerful contrast to the NIDL thesis, since it tried to build a theory which is historically sensitive, aware of urban specificity, and deliberately emphasising the importance of social conflict for urban development.

Harvey's starting-point was to develop Marx's own analysis of capital accumulation and draw out the implications for urban structure. This primarily involved an examination of landed property and its role in capital accumulation, a subject about which Marx said relatively little. In Harvey's early work (1973) he specified the distinctive nature of land as a commodity in capitalist society. While land is something which can be bought and sold — like any other commodity — it has a number of peculiarities. It is spatially fixed, since land cannot be transported. It is necessary to human life, since we all need to live somewhere. It allows assets and improvements to be stored. And finally, it is relatively permanent, since improvements to land (e.g. buildings) tend to survive considerable periods of time, longer than the time it takes for clothes to wear out or food to be eaten, for instance.

Much of Harvey's work can be seen as an exploration of the implications of the specific character of capital investment in land rather than in other spheres. He emphasised that such investment is both highly significant for the functioning of the capitalist economy — since a great deal of capital is usually tied up in the built environment — and also that such investment leaves a relatively enduring physical legacy. The resulting built form can help to aid capital accumulation, if it is a profitable avenue for investment, but can also be a barrier to it, when its enduring qualities render it outdated and anachronistic in a relatively short period of time. Much of Harvey's work can be seen as an elaboration of this idea of the double-edged nature of property for capital accumulation.

Harvey, in later work (1977, 1982) developed his analysis of the precise role of land for capital accumulation by examining the three 'circuits' of capital. The primary circuit — the production of commodities within manufacturing — is the one to which Marx gives greatest attention. Harvey emphasised how the accumulation of profit by the exploitation of labour within capitalist enterprises runs into severe contradictions, most notably when goods are overproduced without adequate money in the economy to purchase them. As a result of this, profits may fall and capital will lie idle. It is this crisis of 'over-accumulation' that causes capital to be switched into the 'second circuit' – where capital is fixed in the built environment. Money is moved from the primary circuit to the secondary – so long as a supportive framework for this transition exists, as when a state encourages such investment. The tertiary circuit of capital involves scientific knowledge and expenditures to reproduce labour power. Expenditure in this circuit is often the result of social struggle rather than being a direct opportunity for capital to find new avenues for accumulation.

Harvey's analysis illuminated urban processes in two ways. First, it conceptualised the significance of investment in the built environment in relation to other economic processes, suggesting links between urban restructuring and economic restructuring. Harvey's principal example attributed the growth of suburbs in America after the Second World War to the switching of capital out of the primary circuit, where crises of over-accumulation were emerging. The changing structure of the capitalist city was thus related to broader trends in the capitalist economy. The property boom of the early 1970s in USA and Britain, which saw the development of office blocks in many urban centres, owed much to similar pressures.

The built environment, however, is not simply a means of resolving crises in capital accumulation: it can, in turn, cause further crises. As capital is invested in the built environment and hence the economy is more generally 'cooled down', new opportunities for capital accumulation in the primary circuit open up again. Capital moves back into this circuit, capital of the secondary circuit is devalued and it becomes a less attractive avenue for investment. Once constructed, the existing built environment is no longer as 'efficient' as new building and may prove a barrier to effective capital accumulation, so causing capital investment to move to newer and more advanced sites. One result is that the older built environment is abandoned or downgraded such that capital moves elsewhere to restore profitability.

Harvey's model of the urban process under capitalism is hence the very opposite of the evolutionary view we discussed above. For Harvey, investment in the urban form offers a temporary solution to crises in capitalism, but then in turn it becomes a problem, which needs to be addressed by switching capital investment elsewhere. Cities – and other spatial units – hence grow and decline in an almost cyclical way. Yet Harvey is also attuned to the social and political struggles that can attempt to 'fix' the role of a particular city, against particular economic forces. Struggles by social groups threatened by the removal of capital can prevent capital flight and ensure the survival of an urban infrastructure. The miners' strike in Britain in 1984/85 is an example of a failed attempt to fix investment to particular traditional coal-mining areas, as is the trend of local community and labour groups working together to retain investment in a locality. In other cases 'growth coalitions' may succeed in attracting investment. Ultimately the way that tendencies within capitalism make *and* break places is linked to political struggles. This point is taken up in Chapter 7, where we examine urban politics.

Harvey also helped to draw attention to the social and political role of one group within the bourgeoisie – landlords – who had a particular stake within any one place. Capitalists owning land are committed to their investment in a specific place. They often play a crucial role in defending local economies and engage in civic 'boosterism' to encourage the economic prosperity of their place, which will enhance property prices and the value of their land. This theme has been developed extensively by American writers such as Gottdiener (1985) and Logan and Molotch (1987) who identify the central role of landed interests in affecting urban fortunes (see Chapter 7).

The strengths of Harvey's account are several. First, it is possible to use his ideas to explore the *variety* of urban processes in the contemporary world. Whilst his discussion of the tendencies of capital to move between circuits very usefully explores the bases of switches of investment in the built environment, he is also cognisant of the role of political struggle. Thus, he is able to show how social and political forces in a particular city may act to modify, or even thwart, attempts by capitalists to disinvest. His stress on the way in which the built environment is at different times a help and a hindrance for capital accumulation, and thus how dramatic changes can occur to the same city within relatively short time-spans, makes sense of dramatic episodes of contemporary urban change. His theory of uneven development allows historical specificity and recognises the role of human agency.

Harvey's analysis is not unproblematic, however. The major difficulty is that his work is empirically largely unsubstantiated, for little research has actually used Harvey's insights to shed light on processes of urban change. The main exception to this concerns studies of suburbanisation and gentrification, which we examine in the next chapter. Harvey's own case studies, such as that of Paris in the nineteenth century, seem to lapse all too quickly into detailed historical descriptions.

One reason why Harvey's work remains weakly developed empirically emanates from some underlying theoretical weaknesses in his approach. His arguments can be seen as circular. Decisions to invest in the built environment can be seen as resulting from a crisis in the primary circuit, which causes a shift of capital to the secondary circuit. How do we know that there is a crisis in the primary circuit? Because capital is being switched into the secondary circuit. In other words, it can be difficult to distinguish the evidence for the causes of urban change from evidence about urban changes themselves. Harvey's theory can be used to explain anything that happens. His more recent work, possibly aware of such a problem, has therefore become more concerned with analysing the dynamics of capitalist economies, and in the 1980s he turned to 'Regulation School' Marxism, discussed below in section 3.2.3.

More specifically, it is possible to question Harvey's rather static conception of the built environment. In his view once the built environment has been produced it is relatively unchangeable, and hence can be a drag on capital accumulation in the future. There are clear examples of this: elaborate motorway systems, for instance, may appear to offer solutions both to over-accumulation problems and to the general economic problems associated with traffic congestion in one year, but shortly afterwards they pose more problems as they attract more traffic than they are designed for. Yet other forms of built environment are arguably more flexible and are less of a constraint once built. Residential and office buildings, for instance, can be used by different people in varying ways, and the extent to which a given built environment is a constraint to future users would appear to be an empirical matter (see also Saunders, 1986, pp. 253ff).

Third, one of the attractions of Harvey's view is his insistence on the role of social and political struggle in shaping urban processes. This has been developed, in different ways, by other writers, such as Manuel Castells (1983) and American writers on 'growth coalitions', 'the entrepreneurial city', and the like (Logan and Molotch, 1987; see Chapter 7). The problem with Harvey's account, however, is a certain reductionism to social class relations, which diverts attention from the significance of other social groups and actors. This is in sharp contrast to Castells who emphasises that urban struggles are rarely based purely on class lines, but are organised around such issues as gender, ethnicity or neighbourhood. This is not to say that Harvey (1985a and b) fails to recognise the complexity of class relations. He does refer to intra-class conflicts, divisions within the capitalist class and the way in which 'regional class alliances' can form as members of the working class and the bourgeoisie ally together to defend their stake in a particular area. However, he still says nothing about the social significance of groups other than classes.

Finally, there is also a certain tension in Harvey's work between his emphasis upon the dynamics of capital accumulation and his stress on social conflict as forces behind urban development. Ultimately, he sees struggle as caused by the contradictory nature of the relation between classes. Hence, his references to the significance of social conflict for urban development do not, in the end, make serious concession to the argument that social groups, by their own efforts, have important historical effects. Although he tries to resist implications of his position (see e.g. Harvey, 1982, p. 450), in the final instance his position is economically determinist.

3.2.2   Industrial restructuring and class struggle

The relationship between social conflict and capitalist restructuring lies at the heart of a third account of uneven development, pioneered by Doreen Massey. Sometimes called the 'restructuring' approach (see Bagguley *et al.*, 1990), it led to a large amount of empirical research, particularly in the UK, concerning the relationship between economic restructuring, urban and regional change, and political conflict.

Massey's approach differs from those discussed above in being concerned less with the abstract logic of capital accumulation, and more with how the strategies adopted by enterprises to survive and prosper in the world capitalist economy affect patterns of spatial inequality. She examines the ways in which organisations restructure in response to changes in their economic environment and the spatial consequences. Whilst the other theories operate at a macro-level, Massey's work occupies a middle ground, providing conceptual guidance as to how specific places are affected by differing types of restructuring.

In her earlier work with Richard Meegan (Massey and Meegan, 1979; 1982), it was argued that firms in different sectors of the economy responded to international economic pressures by adopting different strategies. The most important of these were rationalisation (the closure of specific units of production and centralisation of production in other sites), intensification (making employees work harder), and investment and technical change (involving capital investment and better productivity). These strategies make for uneven development, for some areas lose employment as production is rationalised away from them, whilst others gain employment because they are subject to fresh investment. Spatial differentiation is also linked to the way in which firms deal with resistance to their restructuring strategies. One repeatedly used strategy is to shed skilled workers in one location and replace them, when necessary, with unskilled people somewhere else. Thus, workplaces in the inner cities, often employing union-organised skilled workers, might be closed down and the production process, with perhaps new technology, shifted to, or expanded in, other areas where new, unskilled, often inexperienced, and often female, labour will be engaged. There are plenty of examples of this. In Britain, rural regions like East Anglia and North Wales have been fastest growing in terms of manufacturing employment in the years after 1970. Again, car production in the USA has been moved out of Detroit and Chicago to sites further south where labour is more docile. For Massey, labour becomes locally (or perhaps more correctly, regionally) specialised as workers with specific skills congregate together.

In her best-known work, *Spatial Divisions of Labour* (1984), Massey developed and systematised this argument by showing how, as firms restructured, they tended to specialise activities in those areas where the cheapest and most pliable labour force could be found. Research and development work, along with the administrative functions of Head Office, was located in those areas where professional and managerial workers were plentiful and which were near the corridors of power. As a result, she argued, Britain could increasingly be seen as a country divided between a prosperous south-east, where the 'control functions' of large organisations were concentrated, and the depressed peripheral regions, where employment tended to be concentrated in branch plants and largely involved unskilled workers. This polarisation marked a new spatial division of labour. It was a major change from the older patterns, where parts of Britain had semi-autonomous regional economies, typically based on a specific product (textiles in north-west England, shipbuilding in north-east England, and so on), and in which skilled, unskilled, and managerial workers were employed in smaller, less spatially disaggregated firms.

The logic of Massey's account is that capital has come to use spatial differentiation in the competitive search for profit, as it invests in those areas where it can draw upon a suitable labour force. Spatial advantage is most readily obtained by discriminating among available labour forces. This acknowledges that capital is nowadays highly mobile, and certainly more mobile than labour, thus implying that many constraints on industrial location, which characterised earlier epochs, have been overcome.

Unlike the NIDL theorists and David Harvey, Massey avoids a purely economistic account, and finds a way of exploring how the social character of specific places impacts on processes of restructuring. The social qualities of labour are significant in repelling or attracting capital, and hence, Massey argues, it is important to consider how local work cultures are formed and how they facilitate types of militancy or passivity. In the UK, for instance, industrial employment in the Home Counties expanded in the 1980s partly because firms chose to locate to areas without trade-union traditions where workers might be more compliant (Wills, 1996). Trade-union membership has become much more dispersed recently, indicating the demise of densely unionised towns and regions. As their population has declined, some of the larger industrial cities have lost some bases for labour militancy.

Massey's work avoids many of the problems we have identified in other research. Her account is historically sensitive, and she is not committed to a static view of uneven development where the fortunes of places are fixed into core or peripheral status from the beginning of world capitalism. Most important of all, she is explicitly concerned to elaborate on the way that social conflict and local forms of agency impact on forms of economic restructuring and uneven development. It was in developing this insight that research focused in the 1980s, as attention turned to detailed consideration of the way that economic restructuring was both affected by, and in turn impacted upon, local social relations and local cultures. The promise was to find tighter connections between economic restructuring and social and cultural changes within particular places (see Cooke, 1989a; Bagguley *et al.*, 1990). The principal way in which Massey was taken up in UK studies has been through a series of 'locality studies', including a programme of research into the Changing Urban and Regional System (CURS) (e.g. Cooke, 1986; Cooke, 1989b). This research programme attempted to explore in greater detail both how the social complexion of various places affected forms of economic restructuring, and how restructuring impacted on these 'localities'. This research strategy entailed detailed localised inquiry, taking the distinctive features of different places seriously and trying to describe and explain differentiation. The promise of such an approach is a better understanding of social and economic activity in its material context, connecting together general forces and specific outcomes.

Massey's framework offered a sophisticated attempt to theorise urban differentiation as the interplay between the restructuring strategies of firms and the social and cultural characteristics of particular local areas. It appeared to resolve many of the weaknesses of other research, and in particular it laid a path from theoretical formalism to a detailed research programme. This programme expanded on Massey's ideas in a number of ways. Important among these was the successful application of her analysis, which was based primarily on restructuring in manufacturing, to the restructuring of 'service' employment, for instance in the health services. Bagguley *et al.* (1990) and Pinch (1989) were able to show that even in the British health service, not organised on a profit-making basis, many of the restructuring strategies discussed by Massey, and others, were in operation, causing serious job losses. Even though it had been traditionally supposed that service industries were much less spatially mobile than manufacturing firms, since they had to be situated closer to their market, they were shown to be subject to a process of the spatial separation of functions similar to those analysed by Massey (see e.g. Marshall *et al.*, 1988; Gentle, 1993; Marshall and Richardson, 1996).

Despite this success, Massey's impressive research agenda came increasingly under attack. One theoretical problem was how the 'local' was to be conceptualised. When firms invested in a place were they investing in a neighbourhood, a locality, or a region? One response was to develop the idea of locality, seen as a local labour market area (e.g. Cooke, 1989b; see the discussion in Duncan and Savage, 1989). If the principal relevant characteristic for location decisions is the nature of available labour, then that might seem a sensible demarcation. However, labour markets are very heterogeneous and are not usually salient for people themselves, even though the life chances of substantial proportions of the population are affected by employment opportunities available (Hanson and Pratt, 1995). Furthermore, local labour markets are segmented and divided, with professional workers, for instance, usually being able to travel much further to work than a labourer. Local labour markets are also of limited cultural importance to people, who might be more likely to identify with specific neighbourhoods or towns (Peck, 1989; 1996).

The issue of whether localities were meaningful entities, whether their boundaries could be drawn, was one basis of dispute about locality studies. Several critics thought that the implication of the studies was to return to bad habits of empiricist and descriptive geography that looked at places as if they were unique entities whose characteristics were not explained in proper national and international context (Smith, 1986). Others thought that there was a tendency to reify space, to suggest that particular spaces – localities – had causal powers of their own (Duncan and Savage, 1989). Accounts that conceptualised such localities as actors in their own right, by referring to their 'proactive' properties (e.g. Cooke, 1989a), gave grounds for such criticism.

During the 1990s further research cast doubt on the significance of local differences. The publication of research from the ESRC-funded Social Change and Economic Life initiative (Gallie *et al.*, 1994; Penn *et al.*, 1994), which drew on sample surveys of employees in seven different towns in the UK, argued that local differences in areas, such as the experience of unemployment, were not that significant. During the 1990s, it became increasingly clear that localities cannot be usefully seen as self-contained entities, but that it was the stretching of social relations over spatial distances that was important (see Castells, 1996, 1997a, 1997b).

It also proved difficult to relate local political mobilisation to processes of economic restructuring in any simple way. Massey (1991) insisted that the way in which 'locality research' was designed was to throw light on the way that political organisation might best be developed locally. Yet many of the local studies concerned ended up by asserting the autonomy of local political processes from economic determinants. In the case of Lancaster, for instance, battles over town planning fought in the mid-1980s were not dominated by conflicts between capital and labour, but instead involved a great number of social groups. Amongst the most active were different elements of 'service class' (managers and professionals), which had not been studied by those examining restructuring in any detail. Elsewhere, Urry (1990b) emphasised the role of professional interests within local councils in creating local policy: the connections with economic restructuring were now highly tenuous. Increasingly the most interesting research arising from the CURS programme pointed to the social indeterminacy of economic restructuring.

So far, restructuring theory has offered a series of major insights into processes of economic restructuring, but it was limited in its attempts to explain social and cultural processes.

3.2.3   *Regulation theory and neo-Marxism*

The third approach to uneven development and urban differentiation that we consider is associated with the Regulation School. Important in its own right in terms of its ability through 'third generation' work to explain the spatially uneven way the state regulates economy and society, regulation theory was also influential on the 'LA School', as we will see in the next section. As with work inspired by Massey, one of the main attractions of this theoretical current is its ability to support a wide-ranging research programme. Also in common with Massey this approach is historically sensitive and attuned to urban specificity.

Regulation School theory is descended from French structural Marxism of the 1970s (see Jessop, 1990; MacLeod, 1997 for overviews). Its principal figures, Aglietta, Lipietz, Boyer and Jessop, have employed a distinctive set of theoretically generated concepts – regime of accumulation, mode of regulation, Fordism – to explore relationships between capital, labour and the state. The main starting-point for these writers is the argument that nation-states play a crucial role in regulating capital accumulation, and they see the differing ways in which capitalism is regulated as historically specific 'regimes of accumulation'. Much of their work is thus an historically grounded attempt to consider the implications of the contemporary shift from one 'regime of accumulation', Fordism, to another 'regime of accumulation', neo-Fordism, post-Fordism, or after-Fordism. In its most recent configuration, regulation theory has introduced an overtly spatial element to theorising the regulatory capacity of the state. Through the work of geographers and sociologists, such as Goodwin, Jessop, Jones, MacLeod, Painter, Peck and Tickell, regulation theory has been used to explain the emergence of urban and sub-national modes of social regulation, as one part of what has been referred to as the 'hollowing out' of the nation-state.

The Italian Marxist, Gramsci, apparently coined the phrase 'Fordism' to characterise the mass-production methods pioneered by Henry Ford in the inter-war years of the twentieth century, and some of their effects on social and family life in Italy. The concept re-entered contemporary social and economic thought through the writings of the Regulation School who referred to a complete era in capitalist development as Fordist. Their argument is that Fordism was the dominant mode of industrial organisation in the mid twentieth century and that it constituted a distinctive 'regime of accumulation'. The regime of accumulation is based on a specific 'mode of regulation' (whence the name of the School), where regulation refers to things like the forms of the state, the nature of intervention, welfare arrangements, legal forms, and so forth. In addition, for the Regulation School, phases of capitalist development are defined by the mode of both production and consumption. The Fordist era was characterised by mass production and mass consumption. However, they argued that in the 1970s this regime was gradually giving way to a neo- or post-Fordist one, with less demand for mass-produced goods and in which competitive pressures required much more flexible methods of production.

The concept of post-Fordism, like many other concepts prefixed by the delimiter 'post', is primarily constructed as a negative ideal-type, identifying characteristics that were not present in a preceding, and better understood, institutional setting. The model of Fordism is relatively well established, and many commentators would think of Fordist arrangements as characterising the leading manufacturing firms from the 1930s through to the 1970s. The Fordist firm is one characterised by scientific management, economies of scale, mass production, and technical control. Post-Fordist production arrangements are associated with the declining size of production units, small batch production, customised products, flexible working practices, greater worker discretion and more responsible autonomy.

Critics of regulation theory see it as bearing many of the alleged defects of its structuralist predecessors: functionalist, econ-omistic, reductionist, excessively abstract, ignoring individual action and under-emphasising social struggles. Nevertheless, the technical vocabulary of the Regulation School is frequently slipped into discussions of new flexible forms of production, though often in a highly eclectic way (e.g. *Society & Space,* 1988). Quite often the concepts are invoked without regard to the theoretical scheme from which they were derived. In the late 1980s and early 1990s regulation work was nearly synonymous with the notions of Fordism, post-Fordism and flexibility. These were widely deployed in analyses of new patterns of economic and spatial inequality, an important example of which is David Harvey's book, *The Condition of Postmodernity* (1989). In this Harvey dissects the demise of the post-war settlement. His account is based on the proposition that

> the contrasts between present political-economic practices and those of the post-war boom period are sufficiently strong to make the hypothesis of a shift from Fordism to what might be called a 'flexible' regime of accumulation a telling way to characterise recent history. (Harvey, 1989, p. 124)

Fordism was the regime of accumulation that supported the 'long boom' after 1945 and was epitomised by the operations of the Ford motor company which produced cheap automobiles using assembly-line techniques while paying their (generally very bored) workers comparatively high wages. Harvey, consistently with other exponents of regulation theory, observes: 'Post-war Fordism has to be seen, therefore, less as a mere system of mass production and more as a total way of life' (ibid., p. 135). The post-war settlement generally worked well, productivity rose, wealth increased, and the gains were in part redistributed through the mechanism of the welfare state and social democratic political policies – a particular mode of regulation. Not everyone was satisfied or contented: there were many workers on poor wages; poverty was not eliminated even in the core countries; immigrants into Europe, of whom there were many, were particularly disprivileged; and the effects on the Third World were far from positive. Nor was it a permanent solution. It began to show signs of difficulty in the mid-1960s, and the early 1970s, which saw not only the end of a stable international financial system, but also oil-price rises and inflation; and the beginning of a fresh recession effectively ended an era. For Harvey, 1973 was the turning-point, a change that he sees associated with the emergence of post-modernism as an aesthetic (see Chapter 5).

Harvey interprets this in terms of a transition to a regime of flexible accumulation. He observes changes in the labour market, with a growing disparity between core and peripheral workers; changes in industrial organisation, especially the emergence of subcontracting, but also of homeworking, sweat-shops, and the use of women's domestic labour. Small-batch production entails a move away from the economies of scale that Fordism offered. New products – particularly responding to quickly changing fashions – require constant innovation from capital. This also has cultural consequences:

> The relatively stable aesthetic of Fordist modernism has given way to all the ferment, instability and fleeting qualities of a post-modernist aesthetic that celebrates difference, ephemerality, spectacle, fashion, and the commodification of cultural forms. (Harvey, 1989, p. 156)

Employment in service industries increased. The dialectic between monopolisation and competition in capitalist economy works out in a new way, with tighter organisation achieved through access to, and control over, information and a complete rejigging of the financial system since the mid-1970s. This is a result partly of new information technology and its rapid transmission, partly of new opportunities for capital gains and partly of powers beyond the control of nation-states. Moreover, Harvey discerns changes in attitudes and norms, seeing the emergence of a 'rampant individualism' associated with entrepreneurialism.

Harvey explains the shift in terms of his older stress on the logic of over-accumulation, but sees the 1970s as a particular configuration of conditions. He develops a distinctive analysis in terms of 'time-space compression'. In the world of new information technology the circulation-time of capital is reduced. Effectively the size of the globe shrinks as it becomes possible to trade stocks and shares throughout 24 hours – when the London Exchange is closed either New York or Tokyo will be open, and vice versa. The capacity of firms to use different spaces for different purposes is another aspect of time-space compression. Economically we live in a smaller world.

Whilst Harvey might have strengthened his analysis of the contemporary transformation of capitalism, he has not applied his framework to uneven development and urban and regional change in any detail (see Goodwin *et al.*, 1993). One of the so-called 'missing links' in regulationist research, which is of interest to us in looking at urban processes, is the decoupling of regulation theory from analyses of the nation-state. This most recent work emphasised the role of the state, political factors, and most importantly *space* (Jones, 1997). As Peck and Tickell (1995, p. 26) argue:

> If regulation theory is to be spatialised, it must loosen its exclusive grip on the nation-state: although the nation-state will no doubt continue to be one of the key arenas of struggle, this may not be the scale at which institution-building is rooted. The question of functionality in accumulation-regulation relationships consequently needs to be opened up at other spatial scales.

What third generation regulation theorists sought to do was to draw out of the theory an *approach* that would enable them to make sense of contemporary changes in the relationship between local, regional, national and global scales of accumulation. In light of increasing regulatory efforts at the global and EU level, and the heightened role prescribed through state restructuring to the 'local' in economic development (see Chapter 7), Peck and Tickell (1992) devised the 'local mode of social regulation' concept. Concerned to link conceptually localities and regions within wider regulatory systems, this work attempted to move beyond the initial insights of regulation theory. Working alongside the Local Governance Research Programme of the UK Economic and Social Research Council (Stoker, 2000), Peck and Tickell (1992, 1995) integrate their regulationist research on uneven development and the evolution of the British state with Massey's (1984) work on industrial restructuring (see MacLeod and Goodwin, 1999). In arguing for a more scale-sensitive deployment of the regulation approach, this group of authors was also pushing for a system-based and more fluid reading of regulation. As Peck and Tickell (1995: 27, original emphasis) make clear:

> Local [modes of social regulation] should not … be seen as the domain of exclusively local regulatory practices … *but as regulatory systems distinctive more for their unique position within wider (national and international) structures of accumulation and regulation.*

Hence, the most recent work on regulation theory has sought to address explicitly the inherent *spatiality* of accumulation and regulation. Localities and regions are connected into wider structures, reflecting the spatially selective nature of state regulation (Jones, 1997). At the same time as sociologists and geographers in the UK were wrestling with issues of economic and social regulation, the so-called 'LA school' was working on the restructuring of urban and regional economies.

3.2.4 The LA school: towards 'geopolitical economy'

Since the early 1980s the geographers of the 'California School' have made great strides in explaining the restructuring of the urban and regional economies of the western world. Triggered by an attempt to provide a theoretical account of the dramatic development of the Californian urban conglomerations of Los Angeles, this work quickly became 'exported', cast as explaining more than the 'peculiarities of the industrial geography of Southern

California and the Bay Area' (Scott, 2000, p. 492). In the last two decades Los Angeles became perhaps the most discussed city in the world (Jameson, 1984; Soja, 1989; Scott and Soja, 1989; Davis, 1990; Keil, 2000, etc.). Los Angeles was to the 1980s and 1990s what Chicago was to the early twentieth century, a particularly stark example of the urbanising processes that are to be found throughout much of the world economy. The focus of the work is the changes in the organisation of the economy, the restructuring of the urban metropolis, and the relationship between the two (Scott, 2000; Soja, 2000).

The LA School sees the rise of the Californian economy as tied to the decline of the old industrial regions of the north-east of the USA (the 'Rust Belt'). The new industries, such as electronics and defence, are located in California, while contracting ones, like shipbuilding, are in the Rust Belt. They concentrate on the experience of recently growing industrial sectors and argue that establishments in these sectors are tending to cluster in 'new industrial districts' – leading to what Scott (1988b) call 'new industrial spaces'. They provide evidence for a variety of sectors – for example, motion pictures (Christopherson and Storper, 1986) animated pictures (Scott, 1988b) printed-circuit fabrication (Scott, 1988b) – where factories tend to cluster together in the same district of a large metropolitan area. The reason for this is to obtain economies of scope rather than the economies of scale that were the objective of Fordist mass production.

Although the Californians deploy Marxist concepts (particularly of regulation theory), the core of their current position is a theory of the firm associated with the economist Oliver Williamson, (for a summary, see Williamson, 1990) who has developed the theory of 'transaction cost analysis'. Very simply their theory distinguishes those situations under which firms find it best to internalise contributory activities (such as marketing, or research, or various production functions), and those where it is best to externalise them, by using subcontractors or buying services on the market. Scott (1988b) pursues the spatial implications of this contrast, observing that when firms externalise their activities they tend to congregate close to the other firms involved in their production network, leading to agglomeration economies and the emergence of New Industrial Districts. Alternatively, if activities are internalised, firms may be able to separate functions spatially onto different sites.

Massey's account of the spatial separation of production functions will apply only to such cases.

These writers largely accept the empirical trends identified as flexible accumulation in Piore and Sabel's (1984) analysis of the Third Italy, and argue that they testify to the rise of new industries, based on external linkages. Firms tend to be smaller and to subcontract activities, leading to vertical disintegration. The development of new products encourages the concentration of small firms that can share expert knowledge, for which purposes social networks, often based on face-to-face interaction, are ideal. New industrial districts tend to contain firms in advanced innovative sectors, attracting and retaining workers with appropriate knowledge and expertise. In some versions strong priority is accorded to technological developments (e.g. Storper and Walker, 1989) where the development of new products is deemed conducive to external links between firms as, for instance, new companies cluster round the innovating enterprise.

Although much of the initial work of the California School was directed purely towards explaining industrial location, starting with Scott's (1988a) *Metropolis: From the Division of Labour to Urban Form*, the focus of research widened to include analyses of urban development. Having outlined the process through which firms reorganise, compelled by the benefits of vertical disintegration, Scott makes a series of claims about the way in which the concentration of workers' residences near to the new 'neo-Marshallian' industrial districts in which they work has effects on social segregation, ethnic differentiation and community formation.

Beginning from the premise of the spatial separation of home and workplace in capitalist economies, Scott (1988a, pp. 217–30) argues that the employment relation is a key determinant of residential location. He uses data to show that although there are other cross-cutting bases of residential segregation, occupation is primary, universal and constant in large cities of the advanced capitalist societies. Blue-collar and white-collar workers live in different zones of the city. The reasons for this are several: blue-collar workers who travel shorter distances to work will concentrate around workplaces; state practices of zoning segregate social groups; and there are group preferences as regards housing that are mediated by cost. However, Scott goes beyond these factors to try to make out a case that

> neighbourhoods are the privileged locales within which social reproduction of the determinate forms of life engendered in the capitalist city goes on ... Here, I use the term reproduction in its double sense to mean both generational replacement and the maintenance of stable subjective/ideological accommodations with workaday life. (Scott, 1988a, p. 223)

The significance of this is threefold. First, neighbourhoods are sites of educating and socialising children, and families tend to choose them on the basis of their educational facilities with a view to ensuring that children get an education appropriate to their anticipated class position. Parents try to prevent their children becoming downwardly mobile and choose schools accordingly. Second, neighbourhoods signify social prestige and status, and social groups differentiate themselves by adopting particular behavioural and cultural traits that are reinforced and sanctioned in local communities. Third, neighbourhoods are places where inter-family social networks develop. Sometimes in poor neighbourhoods a network is protection against the insecurities of employment, in others it constitutes the source of information by which new jobs are found. On this third basis the concentration of ethnic groups can also be explained, Scott claims, because they tend to have access only to limited niches in the labour market: 'ethnicity in the American metropolis is thus pre-eminently a contingent outcome of local labor market pressures and needs' (Scott, 1988a, p. 226). Ultimately industrial location gives rise to neighbourhoods composed of people who work in the industries, and the social homogeneity of these neighbourhoods becomes self-reinforcing over time.

Scott's account is not entirely convincing simply because firm reorganisation and labour market are insufficient as basic mechanisms to generate the complex range of social effects. The Californians, unlike Harvey and certainly Massey, say very little about social conflict and its impact on economic restructuring and social change. Their analysis is conducted at the level of economic theory, and even at that level it is probably too narrow. The Californians take little notice of trends in the service industries and their role in employment, since they see services as largely dependent on manufacturing production (see Sayer and Walker, 1992). If urbanisation is connected only to industrialisation, as it is by Scott, then we have a limited grasp on the impact of most economic activity.

One final problem with the Californian account, and another sense in which it may be seen as unduly economistic, is that it almost entirely ignores the state. Here again this may be the result of focusing attention on one country, the USA, where the federal government in particular is relatively non-interventionist in regional planning. Alternatively, this silence may be taken to be more representative of an approach, also witnessed in the work on 'third Italy' and other 'new industrial spaces' (Scott, 1988b), which tends to underplay the role of the state in economic restructuring (Feagin and Smith, 1987; Gottdiener, 1989). It also fails to draw attention to the unbounded nature of contemporary economies, which has accompanied the growth in the number of scales at which the state regulates economic and social activity. In this sense, and as Peck and Tickell (1995: 26) argue about the coupling of economic and social regulation of uneven development,

> Whereas we now know a great deal about how Emilian firms relate to one another, for example, less is known about how they articulate with the wider Italian, Europe and global economies.

3.3 Conclusion

In the past two decades, theories of uneven development have become increasingly sophisticated and attuned to the demands posed on them by contemporary economic restructuring. Accounts have grown more sensitive historically and have identified explicitly how different places may be affected in diverse ways by uneven development. It has been demonstrated that urban development is not some evolutionary process through which all cities pass. Rather these new theories have demonstrated the instability of urban fortunes and the reasons why cities rise and fall, fall and rise. Causes include the dynamics of the world capitalist economy which allow the relocation of industry across the globe; the cycles of investment and disinvestment in the built environment; forms of corporate restructuring; and the dynamics of product innovation. As a result, particular cities cannot be deemed emblematic of a form of social organisation, in the way that the city of Chicago stood for industrial capitalism. Instead we should recognise the inherent impermanence of the economic foundations of cities and the multiple roles of cities in a world capitalist economy.

Jointly, these theories succeeded in analysing the economic foundations of urban change and identifying a series of forces that derive specifically from mechanisms of the capitalist organisation of production. As such they have proved an important corrective to the previous neglect by urban sociology of such matters. Individually, each seems to have identified some characteristic recent strategies and processes of the global economy. Their disagreements stem partly from concentrating on different nations and different industrial sectors, though there are more fundamental theoretical sources of dispute too.

Theories of uneven development have been far less successful at explaining the sources of intra-urban change and social change within cities. Once they move away from delineating the economic position of particular places, and begin to refer to the impact of uneven development on their urban structure, social order and cultural patterns, they begin to falter. Although Harvey sought to capture the importance of social conflict for urban development, Massey sought to show how economic restructuring is related to local social and political change and Scott sought to try to demonstrate how neighbourhoods are produced by industrial location, their solutions are at best partial. Even the more scale-sensitive, third generation regulation work struggles to overcome the economic determinism attributed to its earlier manifestations.

Theories of uneven development need to be supplemented by a much fuller analysis of the social, cultural and political processes that shape, and are themselves shaped by, cities. Much might be gained by uniting some aspects of classical urban sociology with the enhanced understanding of capitalist spatial development. Subsequent chapters examine material inequality, sociation, the cultural specificity of place and the nature of political conflict in the contemporary city, all themes that have featured prominently in urban sociology. Typically, though, they were explored through analysis of the nature of modernity, rather than of capitalism. What is required is better specification of the relation ship between capitalist dynamics and the social conditions of modernity. A principal connection is through the analysis of the inequalities constantly generated by the mechanisms of accumulation which are reproduced, modulated or transformed in the course of the mundane practices of daily life captured by analyses of the experience of modernity.

4 Inequality and Social Organisation in the City

Social inequality is inherent within capitalist societies. In this chapter we will examine how capitalist inequalities based on social class relate to other inequalities – notably those of gender and ethnicity – and how these inequalities affect urban form, and how they are themselves shaped by urban processes. Traditional approaches to urban inequality were primarily interested in segregation, the spatial expression of inequality. This chapter begins, in section 4.1, by briefly considering this research, documenting entrenched patterns of segregation as exemplified by studies of Britain and North America.

General analyses of segregation have increasingly given way to analyses of specific urban developments in terms of the cultural ramifications of social concentration. The ghetto, suburb and the gentrified enclave are all expressions, through segregation, of inequality. In such areas, groups visibly display some distinctive cultural characteristics in their daily activities which constitute the reproduction of social identity and, to a variable degree, social solidarity. In section 4.2 we consider ways in which material inequality arises through unequal access to housing. We show that processes of economic production and restructuring, whilst not determining patterns of segregation, exercise a powerful mediating role.

The interplay of inequality, group identity and organisation is the subject-matter of the later sections of the chapter (and is further developed in parts of Chapter 5). In section 4.3 we show how the social character of particular urban spaces – suburbs and gentrified inner-city areas – emerges out of structured inequality and appears as a type of (sub)cultural expressiveness. Drawing upon both Marxist and Weberian views, we show that suburbanisation and gentrification cannot be explained purely in terms of economic production, but nevertheless both are closely related to social divisions of class, gender and ethnicity. Indeed, we argue that in the last two decades we have witnessed the sub-urbanisation of British and North American city centres (Crawford, 1992). We show how the creation of these new social zones in cities brings about new cultures, and are themselves partly the product of cultural change.

In section 4.4 we move on to consider whether some of the trends we have discussed indicate that cities are becoming more polarised. In order to address this question we examine the role that the analysis of households is coming to have in urban studies – in some respects a return to the British tradition of urban research based on Le Play's trilogy of 'Place, Work and Folk'. We look in detail at one study of a specific local environment in the context of arguments about increasing social polarisation occurring between households.

4.1 Urban space and segregation

Segregation of urban space occurs because land is limited. In cap-italist cities land is mostly privately owned, each parcel of land having a different value depending upon its size, its location and its current and potential uses. Property in land has many uses: some of it will be devoted to industrial purposes (increasingly those of service industries); some will be residential; and some will be devoted to urban infrastructure like roads and parks, most of which are publicly owned and accessible to anyone. Much land is already built on, and built-form contains historic residues and new opportunities, which affect its value.

In these propertied spaces different kinds of human activity are sited. What happens on any given site is partly a result of a history of struggle, competition, planning and regulation. It is also partly the result of the ways in which people currently use the space. As we pointed out in Chapter 3, usage of the urban fabric is partially constrained by the original purposes for which it was designed, but it may also be adapted to new purposes, as is instanced by the innovative uses in most large cities of old factories and warehouses (for housing, museums, offices, and so forth). The resulting patterns on the ground are complex; there is much flux; hence the difficulties of explaining the spatial distribution of activities.

More important for urban sociology than segregation of land use is the segregation of social groups. Social inequality is expressed spatially. It is rare indeed to find millionaires living alongside unskilled labourers. One can also detect a spatial separation of family types: nuclear families tend to live in suburban areas, whilst single people tend to live in more central urban areas. As a result, the analysis of the segregation of cities tells us much about the nature of social differentiation, about how different forms of inequality are related, and trends in urban segregation can be read as evidence of social changes.

Early interest in examining segregation took the form of detailed studies of individual cities: Booth's study of London in the 1880s classified every street according to its social grading. One of the most publicised achievements of the Chicago School was their attempt to systematise a general model of segregation in the modern city. In this concentric-ring model (see Chapter 2) Burgess identified a number of typical zones that tended to radiate from the centre of the city. These included the Central Business District in the middle, surrounded by a 'zone of transition' – an area which was being 'invaded' by light industry and commerce, but into which the most marginal groups of city dwellers were also forced. This area contained ghettos, and what Burgess described as a 'black band'. Outside this was a working-class ring and, on the urban periphery, middle-class suburbs.

This model was largely based on impressionistic research, and hence since the 1920s there have been attempts to gain precision by quantifying the incidence of households with different social characteristics in defined small areas within cities. Beginning with that of Burgess, a variety of techniques for measurement and mapping were developed: land-use modelling, social-area analysis, factorial analysis – all with some affinity to human ecology approaches. This provided a basic, positivist, description of social differentiation within cities (a useful summary of these techniques can be found in Ley, 1983, pp. 60–84).

As a result of these exercises, a variety of models of segregation were advanced, each of which hypothesises a typical pattern for the distribution of major urban activities. The Chicago School

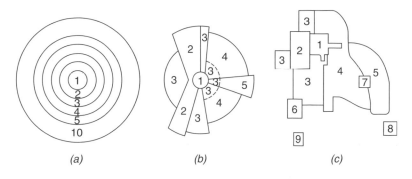

(a)   *(b)*   *(c)*

District
1 Central Business District
2 Wholesale Light Manufacturing
3 Low-class Residential
4 Medium-class Residential
5 High-class Residential

6 Heavy Manufacturing
7 Outlying Business District
8 Residential Suburb
9 Industrial Suburb
10 Commuters' Zone

Figure 4.1 Models of urban land use: (a) Burgess's concentric zone model; (b) Hoyt's sectoral model; (c) Harris and Ullman's multiple nuclei model.

Source: C. D. Harris and E. Ullman, 'The Nature of Cities', *Annals, American Academy of Political and Social Science*, 242(1945): 7–17, fig.5.

model (a (see Figure 4.1) identified zones, radiating out from the centre of cities, each with its own specialised activities. Another model (b) suggests a sectoral pattern, with concentrations of activities in wedge-shaped corridors emanating from the middle. The third model (c) accepts that there are concentrations of activities in particular spatial areas, but that there is no regular pattern, with clusters of specialised activity spread around the city. According to Herbert and Johnston (1978, p. 20), testing the two main competing models – Burgess's concentric rings and Hoyt's (1939) sectors – indicated that

> the geography of socio-economic status (i.e. social class) was largely sectoral; that of family status was largely zonal (with young families in the outer suburbs and the apartment renters close to the city centre), whereas that for ethnic status indicated significant clusters in both zones and sectors.

The original Chicago interest in spatial analysis of urban life continued to flourish in the USA until the 1970s, and in many ways it remains a starting-point for geographical studies of the city. Subsequently, though, British and American geographers and sociologists lost interest in segregation. One reason for this among geographers was the reaction of the discipline to positivist and statistical techniques which came out of the growing influence of Marxism in the late 1970s, which had little use for that kind of empirical data, and an increasing recognition that statistical description was often wanting in providing explanations of social process or giving the feel for the texture of everyday life (see Ley, 1983, for an attempt at the latter). In particular, analyses of changes in urban segregation became more preoccupied with cultural processes that could not be examined simply by statistical methods (see section 4.3). Nevertheless, mapping social segregation in cities remains an important descriptive exercise and older methods of estimating levels of social segregation do play an indispensable role in the explanation of the processes involved in the production of social space.

4.2   Ghettoisation

Nowhere is the importance of segregation more apparent than in studies of the processes of ghettoisation. The term was initially coined to describe the areas of cities wherein Jews were contained in early modern Europe, densely packed residential tracts of land to which they were restricted by law. The ghettos of the contemporary western world most remarked upon by urban sociologists are in the cities of the USA, where black African Americans are disproportionately concentrated.

In America the process of segregation is severe and has been addressed in terms of ghettoisation and the emergence of an 'underclass'. Thus Massey and Denton (1993) talk about an American 'apartheid', so significant is the spatial concentration of, particularly, African Americans, but also Puerto Ricans, while Davis (1990) talks of a 'spatial apartheid', in referring to how the city is divided up, and the processes through which these divisions are maintained and enforced. As Massey and Denton (1993) show, ghettos emerged in the early twentieth century. In 1900 the typical black urban dweller lived in a predominantly white neighbourhood. The black ghetto emerged not as a reflection of the wishes of African Americans but 'through a series of well-defined institutional practices, private behaviors, and public policies by which whites sought to contain growing urban black populations' (p. 10). Other substantial immigrant groups to the US – Italians, Poles and Jews – had initially concentrated in particular neighbourhoods, but they had never been locally in a majority and they had gradually left those areas as they became more prosperous. African Americans, by contrast, have remained in urban locations which are very homogeneous. For example, in 1950, 80 per cent of the black population of Chicago were living in areas where 90 per cent or more of the total population was black. Levels of segregation approaching this proportion have continued to characterise especially the deindustrialised metropolitan areas of the north-east and mid-west – Buffalo, Cleveland, Newark, New York and Philadelphia.

Massey and Denton go on to show how residential segregation itself concentrates poverty and creates the social characteristics which have come to be attributed in political debate to an underclass. As they argue:

> Deleterious neighborhood conditions are built into the structure of the black community. They occur because segregation concentrates poverty to build a set of mutually reinforcing and self-feeding spirals of decline into black neighborhoods. When economic dislocations deprive a segregated group of employment and increase its rate of poverty, socioeconomic deprivation inevitably becomes more concentrated in neighborhoods where that group lives. The damaging social consequences that follow from increased poverty are spatially concentrated as well, creating uniquely disadvantaged environments that become progressively isolated – geographically, socially and economically – from the rest of society.
>
> The effect of segregation on black well-being is structural, not individual. Residential segregation lies beyond the ability of any individual to change; it contrains black life chances irrespective of personal traits, individual motivations, or private achievements. (Massey and Denton, 1993, pp. 2–3)

For Massey and Denton, it is the combination of very poor economic opportunities for employment, and political powerlessness – both of which conditions are magnified by isolation in areas of residence which are homogeneously black – that results in the concentration of social deprivation which is manifested as crime, violence and family breakdown.

How the social conditions that characterise the ghettos affect life experience is powerfully captured by Wacquant who has contributed much recently to the understanding of the life of ethnic groups situated in the inner-cities. Wacquant graphically describes aspects of a black American ghetto in offering an account, based on interviews, of the experience of a professional hustler in central Chicago. The skills of the hustler include 'the ability to manipulate others, to inveigle and deceive them, if need be by joining violence to chicanery and charm, in the pursuit of immediate pecuniary gain' (1999b, p. 142). In an account of how 'Rickey' gets by, Wacquant describes a distinctive social world which is precarious and dangerous, and from which there is little hope of escape for any of its members. Street fights, shootings, drug trafficking and prostitution are commonplace. 'Born in Chicago the seventh and last son of a family of eleven children, Rickey has lived all his life in a large South Side project notorious across the country as a high-risk area.' His high school, 'with all the charm of a barracks (reinforced steel doors, barred windows, and beat-up sports facilities), ... attended exclusively by poor African-American children in the vicinity', provided no adequate education (1999b, p. 147). 'At 29, he has never had a steady job; his subsistence has always depended on hustling and mandated participation in a broad spectrum of more or less illegal activities' (1999b, p. 148). This is a story of misery, lost opportunity, contextual constraints, habituation to degraded social environments and social relationships, and damage caused by the inadequate distribution of resources. Rickey, and others like him, are experts in their own daily lives, who at a practical level know exactly what they are doing and what they must do in order to look out for themselves and make the best of their circumstances. As Wacquant concludes, 'Rickey is neither a social anomaly nor the representative of a deviant microsociety: rather he is the *product of the exacerbation of a logic of economic and racist exclusion* that imposes itself ever more stringently on all residents of the ghetto' (1999b, p. 151).

In a polemical analytic essay, Wacquant (1997) argues that much discussion of the American ghetto is mistaken and misleading. He insists that the phenomenon is not just a concentration of poor people, but rather that those people are poor because of the structural features of 'ethnoracial closure and control' (1997, p. 343). 'The ghetto is an ethnoracial formation that combines and inscribes in the objectivity of space and group-specific institutions all four "elementary forms" of racial domination, namely, categorization, discrimination, segregation and exclusionary violence' (1997, p. 343). He reminds us that the ghetto has a social organisation of its own which can be revealed through ethnographic investigation and which shows that it 'is *organized according to different principles*, in response to a *unique set of structural and strategic constraints* that bear on the racialized enclaves of the city as on no other segment of America's territory' (p. 346). Wacquant goes on to describe the constraints as including:

(1) the unrelenting press of economic necessity and widespread material deprivation caused by the withering away of the wage-labor economy, translating into outright deproletarianization for growing segments of the urban poor; (2) pervasive physical and social insecurity, fuelled by the glaring failings of public sector institutions and the correlative debilitation of local organizations, fostering in turn irregular socio-cultural patterns; (3) virulent racial antipathy conjoined with acute class prejudice resulting in a severe and systematic truncation of life chances and conduits of opportunity; (4) symbolic taint and territorial stigmatization, contaminating every area of social endeavor, from friendship and housing to schooling and jobs, reinforced by (5) bureaucratic apathy and administrative ineptness made possible by the electoral expendability of the black poor in a political field thoroughly dominated by corporate lobbies and moneyed interests. (Wacquant, 1997, pp. 346–7)

In another essay, Wacquant (1993) compares conditions in the Black Belts of America with those of the poorest suburbs of Paris, the Red Belt. Towns in the outer ring of Paris, previously the stronghold of working-class French communism, thrown onto bad times by the collapse of manual jobs in manufacturing industry, and more recently a major source of housing accommodation for immigrant populations, show some similarities with the

American situation. Respondents feel that their neighbourhoods are stigmatised, and they often accept these negative images of their own locations, though they are more likely to attribute this to their neighbours' behaviour rather than their own. This leads to a lack of trust and collapse of local solidarity. However, French traditions, which militate against ethnic mobilisation, together with greater diversity of ethnic groups in any one location, mean that this does not lead to the same type of stigmatisation as in the USA.

Life in the ghetto is one of habituation to extreme circumstances which, as Wacquant (1999a) points out, are largely a function of neglect at the level of state policy. While the situation in the French housing projects in working-class suburbs, *les banlieus*, is substantially different from the situation in the USA, he warns that if the French government begins to copy American policies it is in danger of introducing similarly degraded and dangerous conditions.

Britain scarcely has ghettos, according to Peach (1996), who used the 1991 Census, which asked about ethnic group identification for some minorities, to examine trends in the UK. He points out that the ethnic minority population is concentrated in England, in the major metropolitan county areas (London, Birmingham, Manchester and West Yorkshire), and living in the inner-city rather than the suburbs. He shows not only concentration in a relatively small number of urban areas, but also that some groups form very high percentages of the population in small areas. At ward level, for instance, 61 per cent of the population of Spitalfields, in Tower Hamlets, London, is Bangladeshi, and 53 per cent of the population of University ward in Bradford is Pakistani. Nevertheless this is highly unusual: 'these populations, either individually or collectively, rarely achieve a majority of the population of urban wards and relatively low proportions of the ethnic populations are found at such high concentration' (1996, p. 232). Peach uses what he refers to as 'the dual definition of the ghetto – that all the inhabitants of the area are of that group and that all members of that group are in such areas', by which criteria Britain does not exhibit the hyper-segregation typical of African Americans in the USA. Against such criteria Bangladeshis are most segregated, followed by Pakistanis and Indians. Black groups, of which Afro-Caribbeans comprise the vast majority, are much less segregated than South Asians, and the level is decreasing.

The American pattern of segregation thus indicates the important intersection of class and ethnicity as it is expressed through residential location. Urban black people are deprived of economic opportunity, a situation which is explained and exploited through racialised practices, and this is stamped upon the urban environment through spatially restricted access to housing. Similar processes, with much less sharp social consequences, can be observed in many other circumstances. Generally, research has shown that ethnic segregation is more pronounced than class segregation (Badcock, 1984, p. 205). In general, European cities are less segregated than those of the USA: ethnic minorities live in very high concentrations in micro-areas of cities but because they are relatively few in numbers they make less of an impact on overall patterns. Hence one should be wary of assuming that the patterns of segregation identified in America apply to Europe.

Segregation in European cities is more likely to be along class lines, though religious affiliation is also sometimes important. But while we can see patterns, it is rare to find class-homogeneous social areas. Such homogeneity is greater in recently built housing, since any new residential development will tend to attract people in similar material circumstances (Young and Willmott, 1975, p. 193). In Britain in particular, the focus has been more on the relationship between class and housing tenure, identifying privileged access of middle-class households to owner-occupied property.

There has always been a practical, reformist interest in housing among urban researchers, as expressed in concern about housing shortages, overcrowding, sanitary facilities, level of rents, ease of access, and so forth. It was only from the 1960s, however, that it began to be a subject of theoretical attention. It was the work of Rex and Moore (1967) on the role of housing in race relations in Birmingham, England, that triggered debate. They were concerned with the way in which access to housing disadvantaged immigrant households, pushing them into inner-city 'zones of transition' where they rented or bought old and often dilapidated houses. The causes included various forms of discrimination, the city council's policies for the allocation of public housing among them. In Britain, increasing attention was paid to understanding what difference housing *tenure* made to people's life chances, a particularly interesting issue in the UK where there was a dramatic shift from private renting to owner-occupation and council-tenancy after the Second World War. Another outcome was that much more attention was paid to the buying and selling of domestic property – in other words, to housing markets.

Although there are now many working-class owner-occupiers, entry into owner-occupation is powerfully affected by one's class situation, and it remains much easier for middle-class individuals to become owner-occupiers than for working-class individuals. Table 4.1 shows that the middle classes in Britain remain more likely to be owner-occupiers, while semi-skilled and unskilled manual workers disproportionately rent from the state. Savage *et al.* (1992a) carried out a survey of the housing destinations of the children of council tenants in Surrey, England. Around 85 per cent of children in middle-class jobs had moved into owner-occupation, but only 42 per cent of those children who were unskilled workers had done so. Second, Saunders' (1990) survey of the housing histories of a sample of owner-occupiers in Burnley, Derby and Slough showed that because middle-class people have, by and large, been in owner-occupation longer than working-class people, they have accrued more money from the housing market with which to improve their housing position. This is because they were more likely to buy their houses when they were extremely cheap, and have therefore gained more as their house prices have increased. Saunders's figures suggest that the average professional or managerial household accrued £30,523 in capital gains, compared with only £6,734 for the average working-class household (Saunders, 1990, p. 171). Third, inheritance of housing is becoming more significant, but it is predominantly middle-class people who benefit because the generation currently dying, and leaving their houses to kin, tend to have been owner-occupiers a long time. Since working-class households have only moved into owner-occupation on a large scale since 1960 they are, on average, younger and usually still alive. Finally, middle-class employees are often entitled to occupation-related benefits – mortgage subsidies and so forth – and hence are often able to have their housing costs paid by their employers (see the discussion of these points in Savage *et al.*, 1992b, ch. 5).

Table 4.1 Socio-economic group* of head of household: by tenure, 1998–9 (UK, %)

United Kingdom					Percentages
	Owned outright	Owned with mortgage	Rented from social sector	Rented privately[+]	All tenures
Economically active					
Professional	16	74	..	10	100
Employers and managers	14	75	4	6	100
Intermediate non-manual	14	66	6	13	100
Junior non-manual	14	59	17	10	100
Skilled manual	15	62	16	8	100
Semi-skilled manual	14	42	32	13	100
Unskilled manual	16	36	41	7	100
All economically active	15	63	13	9	100
Economically inactive					
Retired	62	8	26	4	100
Other	20	17	51	11	100
All economically inactive	50	11	33	6	100
All socio-economic groups	29	42	21	8	100

*Excludes members of the armed forces, economically active full-time students and those who were unemployed and had never worked.
+ Includes rent-free accommodation.
Source: Social Trends, 30(2000) Table 10.6.

Perhaps the best theoretical formulation of the way housing and employment processes work together to generate urban inequalities is Badcock's (1984) book, *Unfairly Structured Cities*. Badcock conceives the city as a mechanism that redistributes real income between social groups. He argues that the demand for housing is primarily the result of the structure of employment. Position in the labour market is the principal determinant of household financial resources which is, in turn, the main factor constraining access to housing. City institutions, such as the transport system, educational provision, public amenities, etc., act as a secondary mechanism in the distribution of resources. Living in a 'good area' means easy access to a supply of high-quality facilities and services that are unevenly spread geographically. He argues that the urban land and housing markets operate to reinforce and compound the inequalities initially arising from the labour market. Local and central states intervene sometimes to moderate the tendency for privileges to concentrate through redistributive policies in favour of the initially disadvantaged. Moreover, groups of people unprepared to accept the existing al- location of benefits organise to improve their own circumstances – though then the more powerful the group the more likely it is to succeed. The ultimate outcome of these mechanisms determines important dimensions of the quality of life.

4.3   Suburbanisation and gentrification

We have maintained that processes of social segregation in the city should not be seen as operating independently from those in the sphere of employment, but that they combine together to produce distinct forms of urban inequality. This section will elaborate this argument by considering how important recent developments in urban segregation are linked to wider forms of social and spatial inequality. Particular built forms, with their associated social tone, are linked to the operation of wider social inequalities, and are not the simple product of economic processes.

Furthermore, we also want to show that the urban form is not simply the result of the housing preferences of preconstituted social groups. Although structural inequalities are not themselves affected by urban residential patterns, the wider formation of people into social groups is very strongly affected by the existence of a suitable habitat. Hence the production of specific types of urban environment is itself a vital factor in the formation of groups with shared cultural values and outlooks. The rise of suburbia went hand in hand with the hegemony of the middle-class nuclear family; and the more recent development of gentrification is a new form of cultural expression of those middle classes seeking to find alternatives to the nuclear family.

4.3.1 *Suburbanisation*

Most residential areas, especially those of the working class, lay in close proximity to places of work during the nineteenth century. In the absence of quick means of private or public transport, people's place of work was likely to be within walking distance of home. This 'employment linkage' was broken with the onset of suburbanisation, a process that occurred from the later nineteenth century in Britain and the USA. In some countries, but not all, new means of transport coincided with the building of new houses on the outer edges of cities, much as the Chicago School concentric ring model described. First trams and railways, then the automobile, made relatively longer journeys to work possible.

Suburbanisation, defined as the decentralisation of population from the cities, happened in class waves. First the bourgeoisie, then sections of the middle classes and eventually the working class, began to live away from the city centre. The rate of growth of suburbs varied from decade to decade and from country to country. The USA has the most extensive suburban development, and mass suburbanisation occurred after the Second World War. The effect has been a shift in land-use from relatively concentrated cities to sprawling metropolitan regions. Such spreading of housing has often been opposed by planners, city authorities worried about losing revenue, conservation interests, and so on, but without much overall success, and the US remains, at heart, a staunchly anti-urban society. The UK is somewhat different, partly because despite its prevalent anti-urban sentiment, it has maintained comparatively compact cities, with London still bounded by its Green Belt designed precisely to preclude urban sprawl.

The development of large tracts of land as new suburbs, the typical form of new private housing development in the USA and Australia, has the effect of creating new settlements that initially attract a fairly homogeneous population – nuclear families with children, each with similar financial means, are typical new residents. This probably was one basis of the notion that the suburban location produces particular styles of life. Such uniformity usually declines as the housing ages and is sold as requirements change. In the US and more recently in the UK, the last two decades have seen the creation of purpose-built 'gated communities', where access is restricted through high-level security, as suburbanites seek to protect their way of life from others.

Not all housing on the peripheries of cities can be seen as suburban. In Britain, Swenarton and Taylor (1985) identified the tendency for the new inter-war suburban areas to be owner-occupied. But policy changed thereafter, many council estates being built on the periphery of large cities, as in Glasgow, Liverpool, Manchester and London. Initially these had a fairly wide mix of social classes – indeed the early estates were deliberately designed for the lower middle class and respectable working class – though like all British public-sector housing, they have increasingly become the homes of the least skilled manual workers, the unemployed and the retired. Shifts in industrial location (since manufacturing industry has also decentralised from central urban locations) significantly expanded employment in suburban workplaces from the 1960s onwards in Britain. In the USA that process began earlier, from the turn of century when, as Gordon (1984) argued, it was seen as one way of dealing with heightening class struggle in industrial cities.

Descriptions of the process of suburbanisation are fairly well agreed but explanations are contested. There are disputes between neoclassical economists, Marxists and feminists, among others. The orthodox accounts tend to assume that the growth of suburbs represents the meeting of supply and demand for a particular type of housing and residential environment. More specifically it is held that land is cheaper and more plentiful on the fringes of cities and that people prefer to live in reasonably priced, spacious houses with gardens providing they can conveniently get to work. Such an explanation does not explain why the suburban solution emerges in particular times and places.

This is the starting-point of Marxist accounts (Walker, 1981). Distinctive to these is the idea of the second circuit of capital and the building of urban infrastructure as a way to solve problems of over-accumulation (see the discussion in section 3.2). The building of the suburbs allowed capital to be invested in the built environment, so resolving the problem of over-accumulation. This explains the precise period when suburbanisation developed on a mass scale, in the period immediately after the Second World War, since this was a period of economic growth, when the tendency for over-accumulation reached particular heights, and a period when the state provided specific inducements for suburban building. The Marxist account also stressed that suburbs tended to be class-exclusive and, in the USA, were influential in class formation, both increasing the solidarity of the middle classes and creating fragmentation within the working class. As Walker put it: 'The suburbs are not middle class because the middle class lives there; the middle class lives there because the suburbs could be made middle class' (Walker, 1981, p. 397).

Weberian accounts, while accepting many of the economic factors just described (though not subscribing to their theoretical premises) usually emphasise more the market for housing. Suburbs were originally built largely for owner-occupation – single-family houses, detached in Australia and USA, more likely semi-detached in the UK. They developed a particular image – as containing the nuclear households of the middle classes, often with a particular life-style (see e.g. Fox, 1985, for strong claims about the homogeneity of the American suburbs in the 1950s as middle-class and privatised). To the extent that such a portrayal is true – and there are strong arguments advanced by Gans that we can no more talk of a suburban way of life than we can of an urban one – it is more a function of the way in which houses are financed, built and initially populated. New housing estates tend to be occupied by people in similar income brackets who are at similar life-cycle stages. But it is doubtful whether the explanatory factor is the suburb itself.

Feminist accounts offer yet another explanatory perspective on the suburbs. Davidoff and Hall (1983) document the coincidence in Birmingham, England, of moves by bourgeois households to suburban locations and the intensification of domestic life for women in the Victorian era. Wives became household managers, directing servants, but lost any public or business roles they previously occupied. For the middle classes in both the UK and the USA, the disappearance of the domestic servant, which began round the time of the First World War, altered some of the constraints on suburban living. This partly reflected the unpopularity of the job, and partly the growth of average wages, which made servants comparatively more expensive to their employers. Thus, whereas many middle-class women had been effectively domestic managers, overseeing the work of sometimes quite a number of servants who tended to do the most labour-intensive, dirty and monotonous jobs, they now became housewives, working alone to complete the many tasks that comprise housework. The position of women living in the suburbs was perhaps even less envious than those in more dense urban areas since there were fewer services available. One response to this new situation was the adoption of new domestic technology; the purchase of mass-produced consumer durables increased sharply in the inter-war years, with advertisements typically showing the suburban housewife as the user of such machines. The advertising clichés, linking housewives, nuclear families and assorted industrial products, are legendary (see Glucksmann, 1990).

Cowan's book *More Work for Mother* (1983) examines the changing content and technological context of domestic labour in the USA. It shows how housework alters over time, and differs between groups (richer and poorer) at the same period, but never reduces in quantity. One might have thought that with more services available for purchase and new domestic technology it would become less onerous. However, it continues to be said that a woman's work is never done; and there is little perceptible difference in women's response to their labours. The reasons are many, but one is that some new technologies create extra tasks; this was the case with the automobile in inter-war years in America where increased suburban living meant that housewives then had to travel to shops and ferry children around – a new set of jobs. Other technologies encourage standards of living to rise: new laundering techniques, a more readily available water supply and washing machines, not to mention more clothes, also make more work for mother.

Suburbanisation, then, emerged from and reinforced social inequality. The building of the suburbs made profits for builders and landowners. It left the poorest sections of the population in the central areas of cities. Residence in a smart middle-class suburb reduced some of the negative consequences of the experience of modernity and, because the housing market effectively excluded the less affluent, helped to create solidarity among the middle classes. However, quality of life varied from one suburb to another, with the ones furthest from the urban cores housing the working classes and providing limited amenities. In addition, suburbanisation reproduced gender inequalities, for location in the suburbs restricted job opportunities for married women and further entrenched the division of labour within the household. It was in the suburbs that the nuclear family reached its mid-twentieth-century prominence. Here the husband went out to work, often in the city centre, whilst the wife stayed at home, carrying out domestic tasks, without help from servants.

In the recent past, revisionist accounts of the suburb have argued that the meaning of the suburban space has shifted from its association with nuclear middle-class families (Silverstone, 1997). It has been suggested that the increasing individual freedom possible in low-density suburban developments allows individual non-conformity to be nurtured. The suburban roots of British popular culture have been commented on by Firth (1997) and Medhurst (1997). However, whilst some aspects of cultural diversity may be nourished by suburban space, this seems to be most common amongst those bought up in the suburbs but who have subsequently moved elsewhere. Baumgartner's (1988) powerful account of privatised suburban lifestyles in the United States, in which residents morally withdraw from each other's actions, seems a more telling account of contemporary suburbia. This explains why urban living is attractive to those rejecting middle-class suburban values.

4.3.2 *Gentrification*

Since the beginning of the 1970s there has been a lot of scholarly debate about gentrification, which in its loosest definition means the movement of middle classes back into city centres. Ruth Glass apparently coined the term in the 1950s to refer to changes in the housing stock of London. Gentrification is identifiable as the coincidence of four processes:

1. resettlement and social concentration entailing the displacement of one group of residents with another of higher social status;
2. transformation in the built environment exhibiting some distinctive aesthetic features and the emergence of new local services;
3. the gathering together of persons with a putatively shared culture and lifestyle, or at least with shared, class-related, consumer preferences;
4. economic reordering of property values, a commercial opportunity for the construction industry, and often an extension of

the system of the private ownership of domestic property
(Warde, 1991).

This process has occurred in most of the larger Western cities.

A classic description of gentrification was described in Sharon
Zukin's *Loft Living* (1988). She describes change in an area of
Manhattan, New York, which shifted from being an area of
garment industry sweatshops, through deindustrialisation, to an area
where Bohemian artists took over factory-floor spaces and turned
them into domestic 'lofts'. This was an expression of a certain
aesthetic taste for restored industrial premises and was a cheap way
of obtaining an inner-city place of residence. It made the area
'interesting', and as it encouraged the opening of art galleries and
some specialist shops, the place became relatively habitable and
carried some radical chic. This, in turn, attracted the attention of
property developers who began to see opportunities for profit in
further expanding desirable residential accommodation. At that
point much wealthier middle-class people began to buy lofts and
effectively priced Bohemian artists out of the local housing market.
As a result the New York City Council pronounced the area an
artists' quarter, actually protecting the artistic community to some
extent, in order to retain what had become a tourist attraction.
With the social upgrading of the resident population went also the
opening of assorted specialist boutiques and service facilities, which
completely transformed the area over a period of less than twenty
years. It amounted to the revitalisation of an inner-city area and it
made vast fortunes for firms in the property and building trades who
bought up and converted lofts for upper-middle-class use. What this
shows, among other things, is the link between capital accumulation
and aesthetic taste or lifestyle and the process whereby social areas in
cities change their functions over time. Zukin frames her
explanation in concepts derived from Harvey, but gives
considerable weight to cultural factors shaping living spaces.

Much of the academic debate has concerned the relative
importance of economic and cultural factors, often presented as
supply-side versus demand-side explanations. It is now agreed
that explanation requires sustained consideration of both. On the
supply-side, the nature of the inherited built environment and
changes in the value of land and property are the basis for
economic opportunities for large and small capital investors.

Financial considerations of ground rent and accumulation from property determined that real-estate development in certain areas of cities becomes a profitable use of capital. An early and coherent account was formulated in terms of the logic of the 'rent gap'.

The 'rent-gap' explanation, developed by Neil Smith and drawing on Harvey's work, offered a theoretically concise account of why gentrification occurs. It explains why some areas become ripe for gentrification. It is a matter of the financial returns to landowners on their property. If in a particular district the rent obtainable from letting houses falls, because of deterioration of properties, for example, the value of the land declines with respect to current usage. Hence existing landlords often allow properties to deteriorate even further because they will never get returns on investment in maintenance. At a certain point in this cycle of decline, though, it becomes profitable to change the use of the land. Land, and the buildings on it which have effectively been abandoned, can be bought up very cheaply and houses attractive to middle-class tenants or owners can be erected at a profit. This account probably applies most forcefully to the USA where some areas of cities tended to become largely derelict before housing was renovated by big property developers. The sociology of 'real estate business' is of major importance in America. Dereliction occurs less frequently in the UK, where gentrification often initially resembles more an informal social movement as individual purchasers renovate their newly bought Victorian working-class cottages in an approved style: Williams (1986, p. 57) claimed to be able to spot gentrification by 'brass door knockers, pastel colours, paper lanterns, bamboo blinds and light, open interiors, now supplemented by iron bars, security screens and alarm systems'. However there are intra- and international variations in approved aesthetic styles of gentrification: what is considered worthy of restoration varies between Melbourne, Sydney and Adelaide, for example. There are also international differences in the proportions of restorations of old houses (prominent in Australia and the UK), as against demolition and new construction (more prevalent in USA and Canada). Further, there comes a time when some of the housing gentrified in one round gets redeveloped in a further wave of investment and restructuring. Thus Lees (2000) notes how the very rich personnel employed in financial services property have bought housing near the financial cores of New York and London, raising prices to levels which people like the first-generation of gentrifiers cannot afford. The process of the sequential reutilisation of land for different purposes creates cycles of redevelopment that vary from place to place, partly indeed as a result of public policy. Many urban authorities now see encouragement of gentrification processes as means to revitalise their city infrastructure and increase revenue from local taxation.

Hence, urban sociologists have identified commercial and production interests lying behind a process that is often thought of as a matter of individual taste. However, rent-gap theory does not, of itself, explain shared taste. Its critics concede that it might identify one precondition of gentrification, but that it offers no purchase on the cultural aspects of the preference for living in the city. In particular, as Zukin emphasises, it ignores the fact that an essential prerequisite for gentrification is also a process whereby a cultural vanguard initially move to an area to give it cultural legitimacy.

Gentrification, it is widely agreed, is primarily a class phenomenon; the upgrading of the class composition of an area is a defining feature of the process. However, compared with suburbanisation and the movement of the middle classes to rural locations, it is not a very popular choice of the middle classes. It is the trend of a middle-class minority. The role of 'the new middle class' has often been considered central (Ley, 1996; Smith, 1996). Explaining what are the key characteristics of that minority of gentrifiers has, however, proved difficult because they come from several different sections of the middle class (Bondi, 1999). The middle classes of the first wave, following the bohemian artists, were typically college-educated professional households, not necessarily with very high incomes, whose social values were influenced by the counter-cultural movement of the 1960s. However, the employment characteristics of gentrifiers do not differentiate them from the middle classes who live elsewhere.

This can be illustrated from Butler's (1995, 1997) study of Hackney, London. His account shows that the well-established middle classes are also present in inner urban locations. In a study in 1988–9 of two newly gentrifying enclaves in Hackney, one of the poorest boroughs in inner London, Butler showed that the residents typically held cosmopolitan values, with positive images of city-living based on a deep dislike of suburban environments, an attachment to the area in which they were living, and strong political aversions to the Conservative Party and reductions in public expenditure. Leisure activities tended to involve sociability, with quite extensive usage of the cultural facilities of central London. These features distinguished the interviewees, who were predominantly professional and administrative workers, from the average members of their occupational groups; indeed the gentrifiers had higher incomes, longer education and came from higher social classes than the average. If not living alone, they were overwhelmingly (88 per cent) in dual-earner households. They represented, thus, a fraction of the British middle class, distinctive in economic, cultural and political dispositions.

Subsequent research by Butler (2002) indicates that very specific fractions of the middle class can be found in different kinds of gentrified areas within London. Battersea has been transformed by the deregulation of City of London financial services and appeals to affluent city workers looking for a congenial space to raise their families. Gentrification in Brixton by contrast, draws on the alternative culture of its black residents and is presented as an alternative to mainstream white middle-class culture. This suggests that gentrification is a differentiated process whereby various social groups are being sorted according to increasingly specific and particular criteria. Rather than seeing the emergence of urban spaces that lose specificity as suggested by Eade *et al.* (1997), this indicates the growing importance of urban specificity (see also Savage *et al.*, 2002).

The class dimension of the process can perhaps be appreciated more clearly from consideration of the relationships between classes than from the socio-demographic characteristics of gentrifiers. As authors like Jacobs (1996), Marcuse (1986) and Smith (1996) have emphasised, the process is often, though certainly not always, a process of displacement which benefits the incoming middle class at the expense of working-class local inhabitants, as witnessed by overt social conflict. The development of housing for executives employed in the City in Docklands in the East End of London provides examples of conflict that involves both class and ethnic antagonism. As Foster (1997) shows, construction of walled private estates for the rich in an area that contains poor white working-class households and a substantial group of Bangladeshi households too, generated considerable social tension and political friction.

Such research disabuses us of the notion that gentrification is an unambiguously beneficial process of inner-city revitalisation. For a start, it often means displacement for indigenous, poorer groups who usually become more marginalised as they move on to other areas within the city. Improved services and renovated exteriors are only beneficial to part of the population. Concentration of wealthier, better-educated citizens in particular districts merely deepens residential segregation. According to Smith (1996), gentrification is the re-taking of the central city by the middle class from the poor and marginal people who had inhabited it in previous decades. Through what he calls *urban revanchism* – meaning in French 'revenge' – he contends that the centres of cities are being suburbanised. Christopherson (1994) in her work on the North American city points to this process and argues that we have witnessed the downtown (or the city centre) being recreated in the image of the mall – as a theme park (Crawford, 1992; Sorkin, 1992).

Careful empirical studies of gentrifying areas indicate that class processes are strongly inflected by gender, sexuality and life-course stage. One sociologically important precipitating factor in the growth of gentrification has been the rate of new household formation. Demand for houses increased sharply in the mid-1960s as the children in the baby boom of the immediate post-war years began to set up their own homes. There was not sufficient new suburban building to meet the demand and anyway suburban housing was often too expensive for young couples; hence, the search for 'improving neighbourhoods' within the city. Subsequently, housing demand was maintained as a result of more people living alone. The effects on Western cities of changing household composition, size and organisation, is much underestimated. In Britain by 2001, 29 per cent of households contained only one person, and another 35 per cent only two people. In big cities households containing one or two adults make up a very large majority of the total. Large family households are a decreasing proportion of all households and are relatively rare in big cities. They are especially rare in gentrifying areas where, by comparison, single people, male and female, have a disproportionate presence. To some extent, then, gentrification reflects a change in Western household types.

One distinctive element of gentrifying households is the extent of the participation of career-oriented women in professional and managerial labour markets. The distinctive social attributes of populations of these areas include: an unusually high proportion of young and single women; very high proportions of women in professional and technical occupations; high levels of academic credentials; a high proportion of dual-earner households, but few children; presence of young single professional women: and the postponement of marriage and child-bearing (Beauregard, 1986; Smith, 1987; Mills, 1988; Rose, 1988; Bondi, 1991 and 1999). Reasons for this include increasing numbers of women in highest income jobs, with associated housing opportunities and constraints; minimising journey-to-work costs for households containing more than one earner; facilitating the substitution of marketed services for domestic ones; diversifying 'ways of carrying out reproductive work', partly because there is a 'concentration of supportive services' and 'a "tolerant" ambience' (Rose, 1988, p. 131). The living arrangements of the central city permit women to reorient their behaviour in the housing market to meet domestic and labour-market pressures. Gentrification is thus related to changes in women's career patterns, and has accelerated in parallel with the gradual extension of educational opportunities for women since the 1960s, wider employment prospects for married women in particular, and revised calculations regarding the integration of the activities of income generation and child-rearing. Among single households generally, access to commercial alternatives to services typically provided by women in family households can be readily obtained. For dual-earner households, living in the inner city is a solution to problems of access to work and home and of combining paid and unpaid labour. Thus, for utilitarian reasons, the life-course stage reached and the gender division of labour within households support the demand for inner-city residence.

Besides the use-value of inner-city location there are also cultural reasons for gentrification. The social marginality of first-stage gentrifiers has often been noted (e.g. Zukin, 1988) and their challenge to the model of cultural orthodoxy presented by suburban life was symbolic of a set of contested social values. Knopp (1998), among others, points to a connection between gentrification and expression of gay sexual identity, another instance of spatial preferences being associated with cultural alternatives to dominant norms of heterosexual family household formation. For example, the gentrification of some parts of the centre of Manchester in the 1990s went hand-in-hand with a growth in what is known as the gay village' and a strong assertion of sexual identity by the city's male and female gay community.

Gentrification, like other forms of segregation, is an expression of inequality and social closure. Its form varies from city to city, influenced by the differential histories of local economic and cultural development. It is governed as much by forms of household organisation as by capitalist logic. The rise of gentrification is also the story of the emergence of new forms of organisation of sections of the middle class, and thus shows how the formation of particular urban spaces is intimately tied up with the development of social groups themselves.

4.3.3   Negotiating the newly gentrified city

Of course, urban sociologists have long argued that the condition of, and the structure of, the city and the suburb are closely related. And as such, it should be no surprise that the processes of suburbanisation and gentrification are closely intertwined, with what happens in the outskirts of the city having an effect on the way the city centre is organised.

As some elements of the middle classes have returned to British and US cities as part of the gentrification, the way the centre – or in the US, the downtown – is experienced by those who live in it, or work in it, has changed. Urban managers have been under pressure on two fronts. First, as suburban shopping malls have rolled-out across North America and Western Europe, so the place of the city centre as the dominant area where people buy goods and services has come under threat. Despite still being largely an urban society, an increasingly number of the consumption needs of the British population were beginning to be met in the 1980s through visiting the new malls, in Sheffield (Meadow Hall), Birmingham (Merry Hill) and North London (Brent Cross). Although planning restrictions were tightened in the 1990s, the opening up of the Bluewater Centre in Kent and the Trafford Centre in Greater Manchester reaffirmed that suburban 'cathedrals of consumption' are here to stay, at least in the short term. In turn, as people began to spend more time and more money in visiting the new purpose-built shopping centres, so urban economies began to suffer. Shops and leisure facilities such as cinemas were closed down and public spaces became under-used. The movement of retailers to out-of-town malls also reflected the growth in the number of cars per household, and the increasing mobility that accompanies this, alongside other changes in society around patterns of consumption and expenditure.

Second, as part of the movement back to the centres of cities, residents and consumers have begun to make new demands on the urban economic and social infrastructure. Now accustomed to secure and sanitised places to shop and to carefully maintained open spaces, the experience of the mall has been recreated in the contemporary centres of British and American cities. Newly designed streets, well-lit arcades and comfortable seating have been introduced to improve the quality of the 'shopping experience' in Britain's cities. According to work in the US by Crawford (1992), Sorkin (1992) and Christopherson (1994), what we are witnessing is the emergence of 'the city as theme park'. An accompaniment to gentrification, the restructuring of urban space and of the social relations that dominate in these places is not restricted to either the suburban or urban mall. As Crawford (1992, p. 28) argues:

> The spread of malls around the world has accustomed large numbers of people to behaviour patterns that inextricably link shopping with diversion and pleasure. The transformation of shopping into an experience that can occur in any setting has led to the next stage in mall redevelopment: 'spontaneous malling', a process by which urban spaces are transformed into malls without new buildings or developers ... Today, hotels, office buildings, cultural centers, and museums virtually duplicate the layouts and formats of shopping malls.

As the middle classes have returned to the city, bringing with them their cultural values and consumption patterns, so the social fabric of the city has changed. New café bars and restaurants have opened up, to meet the needs of the new residents. And in order to ensure that people can shop safely – and mirroring the tight se-curity regimes in place in shopping malls – cameras have become regular fixtures on street corners, and on the entrances of restaurants and shops. The seminal work of Davis (1990, 1992) points to how this increasing emphasis on security and surveillance can lead to what he calls the 'destruction of public space'. In his rather dystopic account of the contemporary restructuring of the built environment and the socio-spatial relations in Los Angeles, Davis argues that the recreation of the city centre as shopping mall requires the 'militarization of city life'. By this he means the 'increasing arsenal of security systems and ... obsession with the policing of social boundaries through architecture' (Davis, 1992, pp. 154–5). And as is made clear, the emergence of a new urban built environment has serious implications for social inequalities:

> [In LA] the new Downtown is designed to ensure a seamless continuum of middle-class work, consumption, and recreation, insulated from the city's 'unsavoury' streets. Ramparts and battlements, reflective glass and elevated pedways, are tropes in an architectural language warning off the underclass Other. (1992, p. 159)

Although most extreme in the North American cities, such as LA and New York, the same patterns of social-spatial restructuring can be observed in the UK. Redevelopment in cities such as Glasgow, Manchester and Bristol has included the growth in new city-centre shopping malls, designer-strewn pedestrianised streets, and the introduction of CCTV and private security guards, connected to each other and the police through walkie-talkies. Those viewed as undesirable – what Davis refers emotively to as 'the underclass Other' – when not excluded are closely monitored.

4.4   Changing inequalities? Polarisation, exclusion and survival strategies

Segregation *per se* is not necessarily pernicious. If one section of the middle class prefers to live in suburbia while another selects a gentrified urban location there may be no apparent injustice. If, however, middle-class households systematically dispossess poorer ones, by fuelling house price inflation or, through neglect, causing the closure of shops and services that previously served local working-class people (a process which also occurs in the British countryside), then there are grounds for concern. For what will become of the displaced people? Because in general there is competition between individuals and social groups for access to urban spaces of different quality, such displaced people are in danger of being expelled into areas characterised by an inferior environment and poorer facilities. Such transitions are matters of social and political importance, and may become sources of social conflict if perceived as increasing absolute or relative deprivation.

4.4.1 Social polarisation

There is, thus, considerable debate about the changing urban map of poverty and privilege. The patterns of ethnic segregation which constitute the ghetto in the USA (see above) have remained fairly constant since the early twentieth century. More recently, since 1980 there has been a general tendency in Britain and the USA for income and wealth to become more unequal. The extent to which this takes a spatial form, such that it can be seen on the ground in the city, and through what mechanisms it might transpire, has been examined through concepts of social polarisation and social exclusion.

As Mohan (2000) points out, the concept of polarisation is often used loosely and it has associated measurement difficulties. Polarisation implies increasing inequalities between social groups and the existence or potential for tension or conflict between groups. There is a complex mix of processes which might determine the nature and extent of polarisation, from changes in job opportunities to adjustment to welfare regimes. Available evidence suggests that processes of polarisation can be detected in recent decades in countries including Britain, the USA and Canada (e.g. Massey and Denton, 1993; Dorling and Woodward, 1996; Hamnett, 1996; Walks, 2001).

The diagnosis of the social polarisation of the city was adumbrated with particular reference to the 'world city' (see section 3.1). Sassen's hypotheses, based on studies of New York and Los Angeles, have been particularly influential. She argued that the internationalisation of the world economy, the greater mobility of both capital and people, and the concentration of the headquarters of financial and business services in a few major cities across the globe had significant impact upon their social structures. In particular she noted the decline of manufacturing activity, along with its associated manual workforce, and their replacement with, on the one hand, an élite core of very highly paid professional and managerial workers and, on the other, a myriad of poorly paid workers, who were often immigrants, employed in the provision of routine services. Income inequalities in world cities thus became especially polarised, as middle-income jobs disappeared – though there is evidence of similar, if less pronounced, trends in other geographical locations too.

One empirical study providing support for Sassen's thesis, and also examining its detailed consequences for the spatial aspects of polarisation, is reported by Walks (2001). In this study of Toronto, Canada, a second-rank world city, the distribution of population, occupation and income in 1971 was compared with that in 1991. The comparison over time was argued to be particularly appropriate because this period experienced economic restructuring which constituted transition from a Fordist to a post-Fordist economy. In those years the Toronto urban region grew in population by 48 per cent, becoming 'the most important city in Canada'; manufacturing employment fell from 14 to 10 per cent; professional occupations increased from 30 to 42 per cent; and the percentage of its population foreign-born increased from 34 per cent to 38 per cent. Walks shows that several forms of polarisation occurred as a result. Whereas in 1971 the primary spatial line of division in the city was between the predominantly poor inner-city area and more affluent suburbs, the pattern was more complex by 1991. The central inner-city region was more sharply differentiated as a result of an influx of professional and managerial workers, with ex-manual-workers, low-level service workers and the unemployed shifting to peripheral inner-area locations and into the more mature inner suburbs. The inner city thus revealed high levels of income disparity within and between census tracts. The mature suburbs, built in the period after 1945, characterised by the largest increases in inequality and disparity between areas, were beginning to resemble a zone of transition, colonised, except for a few grander parts, by areas where the poor, including immigrants, were being located. The newer suburbs, which had scarcely existed in 1971, were more homogeneous in income levels though they housed people from a wide range of occupations. The most distant parts of the urban region had been home to agricultural and manufacturing workers but by 1991 professionals were the dominant occupational class. The overall pattern was, then, more highly differentiated, but with a perceptible polarisation, with occupational bifurcation, more segregation by occupational and immigrant groups, and more unequal income distributions among both households and local areas (Walks, 2001, p. 439). Those with fewest resources were, in other words, relatively poorer than before and highly concentrated on the edges of the inner city and in parts of the older inner suburbs.

When she first diagnosed polarisation in the world city, Sassen anticipated that one effect would be the emergence of a 'urban underclass' of people permanently excluded from good housing and secure employment. The term underclass' has most frequently been used to depict the condition of the inhabitants of the American ghetto (see section 4.2 above). Though the concept can be traced back to Victorian times, the current conservative version (e.g. Murray, 1990) sparked off political controversy by suggesting that there is a substantial minority of the population who share a common culture characterised by a lack of motivation to gain employment and who willingly depend upon the state for subsistence. It was argued that the emergent culture encouraged dependence, permitted avoidance of employment and sanctioned single parenthood – three primary features of an underclass. Portraying people in this manner suggests that they are personally responsible for their own unemployment, poverty and exclusion, rather than the unfortunate victims of structural economic change and inadequate institutional provision, and that they have become a very distinct and irredeemable section of the population by virtue of their values and behaviour.

The balance of argument militates against accepting the idea that there is an underclass in Britain (for a summary of the evidence in USA and UK, see Devine, 1997). Empirical studies tend to show that the unemployed are not significantly different in relevant respects from the rest of the working class and exhibit no sign of a culture of dependency. Moreover, there is considerable movement in and out of employment, as there is for poverty which affects a substantial proportion of the working class intermittently. Indeed, Berthoud and Gershuny (2000, p. 117) using panel data for the 1990s show that 46 per cent of people who were poor last year were no longer poor this year'. In this sense the concept makes a misleading appeal to the concept of 'class', because the condition is relatively unstable. The same is true for single parenthood, which in three-quarters of cases arises from divorce and separation, and is typically ended by a subsequent marriage. Thus, analysis suggests that the 'underclass' is not, conceptually speaking, a type of class at all. Marshall *et al.* (1996, p. 40) report from analysis of representative social surveys of the populations of Britain and the USA in 1991 that, like other researchers, they could not identify a stratum of people at the bottom of the social hierarchy with 'particular attitudes to work, job search behaviour, degree of social marginalization or participation'.

To deny the existence of an underclass in no way contradicts the observation that there is increasing concentration of deprivation among some groups in some parts of most cities. In contemporary European political debate it is more likely that concern for inequality will be expressed in terms of the more neutral but nebulous concept of social exclusion. Again, there is dispute about the nature and causes of exclusion (Silver, 1994; Levitas, 1998). The debates concern the restructuring of welfare states, and whichever diagnosis of the problem is preferred determines the relevant policy remedy. Significantly, however, this way of addressing the issue avoids use of the term 'class'. As Silver (1994, p. 572) points out, the notion of exclusion may 'distract attention from the overall rise in inequality, general unemployment and family breakdown that is affecting all social classes'. Then, if by separating out categories of risk, focus is placed on the 'more spectacular forms of poverty requiring emergency aid, policies to combat exclusion may make it easier to target money on smaller social categories, like the homeless or the long-term unemployed'.

One other topic of importance in assessing claims about the creation of an underclass concerns the extent of an informal economy. What is crucial here is whether it is possible for those excluded from secure formal employment to rely on informal work and household resources as compensation, or whether, by contrast, it is those who are already advantaged in the labour market who stand to benefit most (Williams and Windebank, 1998).

4.4.2 Getting by: households and their work strategies

While revenue from property and occupation is the most basic source of inequalities between individuals in capitalist societies, there are other kinds of resources that can be mobilised in pursuit of social survival. Urban sociology has always shown an interest in the contribution of reciprocal relations within communities and, more recently, has investigated the nature of the informal economy as a source of supplementary or alternative resources for those involved in appropriate social networks. The informal economy in some accounts (e.g. Pahl, 1984) refers only to communal economic arrangements – sometimes legal, sometimes not – which are beyond the scope of formal or state regulation. In other accounts (e.g. Harding and Jenkins, 1989) it also includes work done within households. We prefer the first usage, since the familial social relations typically involved in domestic work are significantly different from those of the communal exchange of labour and goods. Both work done at home and that exchanged with friends, neighbours and associates contribute to household standards of living and thus can affect the nature of inequalities. Many authors have seen these processes as particularly critical in the advanced societies in recent years as increased unemployment and cut-backs in welfare provision tend to reduce the resources of the poorer sections of the population.

This concern with the nature of the informal economy and household relations overlaps with the sociology of the family and there are some close connections between literatures on the family in industrial society and those on urbanism, as we suggested in Chapter 2. For instance, in the UK the studies of Willmott and Young in Bethnal Green and Woodford are much quoted as part of our understanding of social relations in neighbourhoods in the city. Community studies have also usually taken detailed note of behaviour inside households. One aspect of what we know about mining communities is that they are patriarchal, characterised by disparities of power between husbands and wives (e.g. Dennis *et al.*, 1956). Another key feature about family sociology is the exploration of levels of contact between members of different households, sometimes with other kin but equally often with neighbours, members of interest groups and associations, etc. Debates about privatisation of the family, the loss of community and the political consequences of owner-occupation hang on these inter-household relationships.

Feminist scholars in particular have insisted that we should use the concept of household rather than family partly in order properly to appreciate gender inequalities in heterosexual relationships and partly to register changing domestic arrangements. Indeed, concentration on households has produced a lot of new insights into change in the city and in everyday life, as well as throwing more light on gender relations.

Margaret Nelson and Joan Smith's (1999) *Working Hard and Making Do: surviving in small town America* is conceived as a study of the effect of deindustrialisation, and restructuring in manufacturing industry, on the lives and lifestyles of manual workers in north-east America. The research involved a survey and many in-depth interviews in 1991–2. Much is made of a contrast between the old and the new economy. The semi-rural area of Vermont (Coolidge County) saw the downsizing of the main industrial employer which had provided secure and reasonably well-paid jobs for several decades. The firm (Sterling Products) laid many people off. Replacement jobs were from new firms who offered poorer-quality contracts and less-skilled jobs. The argument hangs around the difference between households where at least one person still had a 'good' job, and those where there were only 'bad' jobs. Good jobs were defined as those which had five of the following six features: all year round, full time, permanent, had some benefits attached (health insurance and paid holidays), where layoffs were infrequent, and where there was some level of bureaucratisation (some number of employees). About half the households had at least one person in a good job, about half did not.

An important aspect of the study was its emphasis on the household as a unit. It depended not so much on an individual's location (if they lived in couple households – which was the basis of the study) as on the entire household. However, among the features was that having one person within the household in a good job often meant that the second earner was also in a good job. That is to say, there was a tendency for relative privilege to accumulate – for reasons as simple as that the security of one partner meant that other could spend more time looking for a job, or perhaps do some training, or start up some private business venture. One of the differences which was stressed was the kind of moonlighting' jobs that these different households had. Those with good jobs had better second jobs – motor mechanics, cutting grass, etc. – because they could afford the necessary equipment and were able to reinvest what they made. Those with poor jobs had more broken patterns of employment, and were not able to obtain enough to invest, and indeed 'investment' would often be at the expense of basic subsistence. And the consequences of this difference were clearly demonstrated in terms of self-esteem, for although both groups had rather similar aspirations to being self-sufficient, standing on their own two feet, and being independent, this was simply more achievable by the better-off group and they derived more satisfaction from their lives as a whole than did their counterparts in households with only bad jobs.

Pahl's (1984) study of the Isle of Sheppey drew very similar conclusions about the effects of deindustrialisation on household strategies in the UK. He discovered an enormous amount of work being done in the domestic mode of provision. Moreover, the more people in a household that were in formal, paid employment, the more work they did at home. It was this which suggested to Pahl that a process of social polarisation was occurring. Households with more than one earner had relatively high incomes but also produced more services for themselves – house improvements, home cooking, etc. As a result their standard of living was substantially higher than those households with little or no paid employment. What Pahl perceived was not so much a post-industrial, but rather a self-service, economy emerging, a trend illustrated by the explosion of expenditure in Britain on do-it-yourself products and domestic machines of all kinds.

Restructuring in America, as reported by Nelson and Smith, also produced different senses of masculinity – there being some interesting gendered effects demonstrated by the general change in the nature of the local labour market. There was a shift from the male breadwinner model, where men had a sense of the worth of their contribution to the household through their greater earning power, to a new situation where almost all people worked such that worth had to be demonstrated in other ways.

The informal economy is important to economic life in many cities, including in Italy and some of the American world cities (Redclift and Mingione, 1985; Mingione, 1987; Sassen-Koob, 1987). Its importance is even greater in the developing world and in the ex-communist states of Eastern Europe where the sudden transition to capitalism has led many people to adopt what Burawoy et al (2000b) describes as 'defensive' household strategies which involve increased dependence on extended kin relationships and much self-provisioning from family resources. But it is rarely a sufficient source of income or sustenance on its own, and makes rather more of a contribution to those households which also have 'good jobs' rather than to the unemployed and the poor.

4.5   Conclusion

This chapter has examined recent literature on social inequality in cities, much of which has been inspired by Weberian theorising about how cities act as a distributor of benefits. Urban sociology has for a long time considered such matters in terms of segregation, and one of the main spatial patterns, on the ground, has been the segregation of different categories of people in different areas of the city. Processes like gentrification, suburbanisation and ghettoisation remind us that patterns of segregation are dynamic and that urban development continuously reorders the socio-spatial mosaic of residential inequality. We are thus sceptical about whether there are any universal or necessary patterns of inequalities within cities.

The wing of the Chicago School using ecological analysis had long realised and described the extent of such segregation but had done little to explain the process. The more ethnographic wing of the School had been relatively little interested in inequality as such, being more concerned to give accounts of subcultural differences among groups rather than dwell on material inequalities. Marxist and Weberian scholars were prominent in bringing matters of explanation onto the agenda for urban studies and identifying the class and ethnic processes involved. In addition, feminists highlighted the gendered aspects of such inequalities. Savage *et al.* (2002) argue that it is important to retain the concept of social class as an explanatory tool. However, it is essential to recognise two constraints: that gender relations cannot easily be abstracted from social class and hence that classes are gendered (Savage 1992); and also that class relations are not only structured by the division between capital and labour, but also by cultural and organisational factors. Once this is done, changing forms of social inequality can be explored using the concept of class in the present period as in earlier historical periods.

Heuristically, it seems beneficial to see the generation of material inequalities primarily in terms of capitalist-market mechanisms for the distribution of rewards, regulated and coordinated through state policies for land-use, employment and welfare. Accounts of inequalities within cities have begun to make some progress in linking economic production to patterns of segregation. Emphasis on the role of capital in property development and its effect on urban form and the development of theories of the housing market, which consider both house construction and patterns of purchase and rent, have improved our understanding of processes within cities. But as yet, the theoretical connections to the more general theories of uneven development remain relatively weak. The ways in which cross-cutting social divisions of class, gender and ethnicity mediate the logic of capital accumulation are complex.

We still know insufficient about the texture and experience of the daily life of different groups of people in the city. Despite work like that of Wacquant, for example, information about the distribution of inequality remains greater than our knowledge of the varied experiences of urban living. There is still a need for repeated ethnographic studies that can tease out changes in everyday life, and that can place observations in a wider political economy framework. It is one of our main arguments that it is necessary to appreciate the dialectical relations between the mechanisms of capitalist production and the experience of modernity. The growing focus on the household is useful in this regard for it is, simultaneously, a unit of material resources, a site of work, a locus of the reproduction of labour power and a hub of everyday life. Survival strategies that encompass cooperation with other households as well as competition through impersonal market channels entail a complex embedding of households in their external environments. The patterns of sociation − reciprocity, conviviality, solidarity, competition and conflict − that routinely arise in and between neighbourhoods and subcultural groups remain critical to the experience of city life. Such matters have too often been addressed in terms of urban culture, divorced from questions of inequality. However, social inequality remains a foundation of the experience of everyday life in cities, and the recently renewed intellectual interest in urban culture should not be allowed to diminish its importance.

5 Perspectives on Urban Culture

The early urban sociologists, especially those associated with the Chicago School, were intent on probing the forms of social interaction found in cities. Borrowing the concept of sociation from Simmel they examined the informal social relations which existed in different parts of the city and which underpinned everyday life for various social groups and the processes of social organisation and disorganisation which they saw as typical of modern urban experience.

They bequeathed an interest in urban culture. But this legacy has proved a difficult one for later urban sociologists to utilise. Empirical studies suggested that urban cultures could rarely be distinguished from rural cultures. Conceptually, Manuel Castells (1977) dismissed the study of urban culture as ideological, as being incapable of rigorous theoretical definition. Other writers of this period denied that it was possible to discern a distinct urban culture (Smith, 1980; Saunders, 1981). Yet since the 1980s there has been a major revival in cultural studies of cities. There has been a striking number of studies examining the experience of urban living, in all its ramifications (e.g. Castells, 1983; Harvey, 1985b; Jukes, 1990; Sennett, 1996), and a distinct genre of urban biography has emerged (Davis, 1992; Ackroyd, 2000). The study of urban culture has returned to the agenda.

There are two contrasting approaches to the study of urban culture. The first attempts a generic definition, where writers discern common threads which apply to all cities. This project is usually concerned with delimiting an urban way of life. A second approach abandons the quest for a single form of urban culture and suggests that every city has its own specific culture, its own meaning. Here, the task of the writer is not to come up with statements about an urban way of life that holds, in some form, for all cities, but to identify the processes which give different meanings to cities. This chapter considers the value of generic definitions of urban culture. The next considers how we might think in terms of specific urban cultures.

There were two alternative classic attempts to establish a generic definition of urban culture. The first of these was developed by Louis Wirth in 'Urbanism as a Way of Life' (1938), which sought to generalise from the studies of his colleagues in Chicago. We will argue that this was largely concerned to distinguish between cities and rural settlements, thereby defining urban culture spatially. The second, and prior, approach was that of Simmel, who defined the nature of modern urban culture temporally, in relation to older social forms. Whilst Wirth contrasts the city with the countryside, Simmel contrasts the modern urban dweller with rural and small-town residents of an earlier epoch.

We begin by discussing Wirth's arguments, indicating some of the problems with his account which subsequent discussion has bought to light. We then contrast Simmel's account of metropolitan culture, taking pains to show how it differs from Wirth's. Simmel's work has recently experienced a major revival, leading to new lines of research on urban culture which we review. Nonetheless, we conclude that generic definitions of urban culture are bound to fail because they cannot deal with the variety of urban meanings tied up with cities.

5.1 Louis Wirth and the 'urban way of life'

Louis Wirth's 'Urbanism as a Way of Life', published in 1938, was one of the most influential sociological articles ever written. [In it he laid down a research agenda for examining how cities produced forms of social interaction different from those of rural settlements, and hence how urban and rural ways of life could be distinguished.]

Wirth (and Redfield, who also helped to develop an interest in urban and rural cultures) wrote at a time when the pre-eminence of Chicago was threatened by other American departments championing a more scientific brand of sociology. The Chicago School itself in the 1930s also reformulated traditional themes within a positivist framework, more congenial to the intellectual climate. Thus Wirth attempted to analyse urban culture by distinguishing three 'independent variables' – size, density and heterogeneity – which could be seen as causal factors behind urban cultural life. In order to tighten up the study of urban culture, it became more important to compare it with another, 'dependent', variable, in this case rural culture. In one important respect Wirth succeeded beyond measure, setting up an empirically testable hypothesis, which has sustained intense debate ever since.

Wirth's basic argument was that city life was characterised by isolation and social disorganisation, and that this was due to the fact that all cities were large, dense, and heterogeneous. In his own words:

 (1) Large numbers count for individual variability, the relative absence of intimate personal acquaintanceship, the segmentalization of human relations which are largely anonymous, superficial and transitory, and associated characteristics. Density involves diversification and specialization, the coincidence of close physical contract and distant social relations, glaring contrasts, a complex pattern of segregation, the predominance of formal social control, and accentuated friction, among other phenomena. Heterogeneity tends to break down rigid social structures and to produce mobility, instability, and insecurity, and the affiliation of the individuals with a variety of intersecting and tangential social groups with a high rate of membership turnover. The pecuniary nexus tends to displace personal relations, and institutions tend to cater to mass rather than individual requirements. The individual thus becomes effective only as he acts through organized groups. (Wirth, 1938, p. 1)

All three traits mentioned by Wirth were seen as being characteristic of urban rather than rural life: only cities had large numbers, and dense and heterogeneous social relations. Hence a distinct urban way of life could be distinguished. Wirth thus implied that there was some connection between type of settlement and psychic life, that certain sorts of personalities, psychological traits, and attitudes to life, were associated with being in the city. Strong social identities were eroded by urban life. In making this argument Wirth drew upon earlier sociological writers who had distinguished communities from more fragmented social relations. Most famously, Toennies's distinction between *Gemeinschaft* and *Gesellschaft* (usually translated as community and association) has often been interpreted in the same way – that different kinds of place, rural as opposed to urban, determine different kinds of social relationship. *Gemeinschaft* is often thought of as being 'community', where relationships between people were intimate and personalised. In small, rural communities, people formed close, intense and overlapping ties which bound them together into a coherent cultural whole. In modern societies, based on *Gesellschaft*, social relations of association predominate, people interrelating impersonally and instrumentally. In this situation actors encounter more other people than in a *Gemeinschaftlich* society, but they deal with them for specific purposes only, forfeiting the density of contacts which characterise *Gemeinschaft* (for further elaboration, see Lee and Newby, 1982, ch. 3). From this reading of Toennies comes a whole genre of work that considers urban culture as the experience of anonymity, loneliness, isolation, and fleeting relationships. The implicit contrast is with the security and warmth of the rural community.

5.1.1 The critics of Wirth

In the 1950s and 1960s a series of debates about the transformation of the American personality, the decline of community, the entrenchment of mass, individualised, society, and the existence of an urban–rural continuum, drew on Wirth's belief that as urbanism spread, so primary social relationships would weaken and decline. They were hence predominantly concerned with the idea of disorganisation, with the decline of secure and pervasive social bonds in an urbanised society. This was a continuation of the way in which the Chicago School presented cities as, essentially, disorganised and disorderly. But the other emphasis of Chicago writers – on the informal social bonding in urban areas – was neglected. The maelstroms of invasion and succession, of weak traditional ties, of competition between groups, etc., were seen to cause particular urban problems, a view that probably continues to have some sway over policy-makers.

The considered response, over fifty years, to Wirth's arguments and the debates they generated, has been to reject the idea of there being 'an urban way of life', largely because of the persistence of segregated, collective life in even the largest cities. More specifically the objections are threefold:

1. it misspecified the determining character of space;
2. empirical inquiries found communities in the city and conflict and isolation in the countryside;
3. the diversity of group cultures challenged the idea that there was one dominant urban way of life.

Let us consider these points in turn.

(i) Spatial determinism

There can be no doubt that there are many <u>lonely, isolated</u> <u>people living in cities</u>. What is in doubt is whether they tend to predominate there, and even if they do, whether cities themselves can be held responsible. One of the most important post-war writers on this issue is the American, Herbert Gans. He claimed that:

> Wirth conceived the urban population as consisting of hetero-geneous individuals, torn from past social systems, unable to develop new ones, and therefore prey to social anarchy in the city ... [This] ignores the fact that this [inner city] population consists of relatively homogeneous groups, with social and cultural moorings that shield it fairly effectively from the suggested consequences of number, density and heterogeneity. This applies even more to the residents of the outer city, who constitute a majority of the total city population. (Gans, 1968b, p. 99)

Gans admitted that there were some sections of the population in cities who were rootless, transient and anonymous, but he doubted their typicality, and also whether this loneliness was produced by cities. Much has been written about the concentration of the homeless in inner urban areas, for instance (Dear and Wolch, 1987). This however, is not due to city life itself, nor because of the three variables of size, heterogeneity, and density discussed by Wirth, but because of the type of people, the type of policy, and the type of facilities which exist in any given area.

Nor is it self-evident that the marginalised, isolated and lonely live in the inner cities. In some areas marginalised groups can be found living in other types of places, such as council estates situated on the outer rim of cities, or New Towns, well away from the centre of the urban milieu itself. Meegan (1990) has examined the way in which the most marginal groups of Liverpool's population are found in the outer council estates in Speke and Kirby. In a similar way, the movement of poor working-class residents away from the centre of Glasgow to the outer Clydeside council estates saw people move from an environment rich in cultural facilities and resources to a new environment with very few amenities (Savage, 1990). This was partly due to the fact that the Labour Council which commissioned the building of new council estates was dominated by a temperance lobby which did not want public-houses to be built on these outer estates. In other words, Wirth's stress on the effects of size, density and heterogeneity alone is misplaced; insofar as there is urban isolation it is linked to the types of social groups who typically – but not inevitably – live in central urban sites, the processes which cause them to concentrate there, and the types of urban policy which affect their resources and environment.

Gans also questioned whether the supposed isolation, individuation and autonomy of city life accurately described more than a small proportion of people. He pointed out that the inner cities also contained groups of people of common ethnic origin and cosmopolitan types, such as gentrifiers. Studies of the moral order of the slum have usually suggested that all the necessary properties of a predictable subcultural way of life (norms, values, ties, rituals, reciprocities, etc.) are present, though these are substantively different from those of a dominant culture. The city was not a place of incipient anarchy. Let us develop this point in more detail.

(ii) The urban–rural typology
A second source of discontent with the urban way of life model was the fact that sociological investigations threw up endless counter-examples to the supposedly anonymous and anomic pattern of urban life and to the integrated community of the countryside. Sociologists and anthropologists who carried out research on parts of large cities found neighbourliness, tradition, moral order and even strong ties of 'community' in inner-city areas like Bethnal Green in East London or Boston's West End.

'Urban villagers' – people living in cities, identifying with their particular neighbourhood and having close ties with their neighbours – abounded.

Young and Willmott (1962) conducted a survey of the Borough of Bethnal Green in inner London and a series of in-depth interviews there between 1953 and 1955. Bethnal Green was a poor, inner-city area which might have been expected to exhibit features of the urban way of life and the atrophying of family relations. On the contrary, Young and Willmott 'were surprised to discover that the wider family, far from having disappeared, was still very much alive in the middle of London' (Young and Willmott, 1962, p. 12). The frequency of kinship contact of people in Bethnal Green, with brothers and sisters, aunts and uncles, and particularly with parents, was prodigious. As regards married people with a parent still alive, 'More than two out of every three people ... have their parents living within two or three miles' (ibid., p. 36). About 30 per cent of those married women lived in the same street as their parents. Moreover 55 per cent of married women with a mother alive had seen her within the last 24 hours. The centrality of the mother–daughter link and the extent of mutual aid was probably the most notable feature of all. However, the picture, generally, was of intense kinship contact which in turn fostered dense social networks throughout the community. Young and Willmott remarked that:

> far from the family excluding ties to outsiders, it acts as an important means of promoting them. When a person has relatives in the borough, as most people do, each of these relatives is a go-between with other people in the district. His brother's friends are acquaintances, if not his friends; his grandmother's neighbours so well-known as almost to be his own. The kindred are ... a bridge between the individual and the community. (ibid., p. 104)

Thus was discovered a set of strong extended kin and neighbourhood ties in the very centre of the city, completely confounding any generalisation that social bonds had evaporated. Bethnal Green was like a village, where long residence and dense social networks had produced 'a sense of community, that is a feeling of solidarity between people who occupy the common territory' (ibid., p. 113). When they compared a new London County Council housing estate built at Greenleigh, 20 miles east on a greenfield site, Young and Willmott found far more isolated and privatised ways of life.

Subsequent criticism has contested the sense of community said by Young and Willmott to exist in terms of the difference between public and private accounts of social life. Cornwell (1984) argued that East Enders' public accounts tend to give a rosy impression of the past, whereas private accounts, collected using oral life-history techniques, tell of jealousies, competition, conflict and violence as well. While realising the popular attractions of a garden and some control over the fabric of a house, effectively unattainable in Bethnal Green but a feature of Greenleigh, she nevertheless found people who had moved back into its very low-grade housing because they missed the companionship or preferred the social connections of the inner city.

Gans in another celebrated study also described as an urban village the West End of Boston – a mixed area, with many nationalities, but predominantly Italian; not quite a slum, though often thought of as such. It was ugly, noisy, had poor facilities, and bad housing, but nevertheless was convivial and socially highly organised, mostly through peer groups and through kin. Gans examined a whole range of local institutions of everyday life – family, associations, caretakers, political bosses, etc. – and argued that ethnic groups do very similar things in different countries, and that this is because of class location rather than specific ethnicity. Accordingly he isolated the features of what he called lower-class subculture, which included a central role for women who usually had working-class aspirations, while a significant proportion of the men were drifters and seekers of exciting action. Nevertheless, Gans showed, this inner-city area exhibited tight social bonds and strong institutional forms.

In recent years some studies of globalising cities (e.g. Eade *et al.*, 1997) have emphasised the rising significance of long-distance communication and have argued that small-scale communities have been eclipsed (Giddens, 1990; Beck, 1992). It is possible to exaggerate the extent of global change: international migration flows, for instance, have not risen significantly despite impressions to the contrary (Papastergiadis, 2000). However, Castells (1996) has noted that even mobile populations have to be fixed in particular places, and he has shown that globalising forces can in fact lead to an increase in communities that are based on turf loyalty. Recent research in parts of the Greater Manchester area indicate that there are still some neighbourhoods marked by dense social ties, and close contact between members of the extended family (Savage *et al.*, 2002). In one area of inter-war housing, two-thirds of households had at least one parent or child within a ten-minute drive.

Furthermore, while such studies showed that parts of cities exhibited characteristics of 'community', inquiries in rural areas challenged romantic views of social life in the countryside. Studies initially indicated that although in villages people knew their neighbours and met many of them regularly, life there was neither harmonious nor necessarily highly integrated. Lewis's re-study of the Mexican village that had been Redfield's model for his influential ideal type of 'the folk society' was often cited because it showed high levels of real and latent conflict (Redfield, 1947; Lewis, 1951). The post-war British community studies similarly showed conflict and resentment emanating from inequalities of class, status and participation (Frankenberg, 1957; Littlejohn, 1963; Williams, 1963). Subsequent studies, like Newby (1977) on East Anglian farmworkers, relied not at all on models of rural life or community. Observed deferential behaviour by farm labourers was shown to be situationally specific action, their concerns and practices being in most part similar to those of other working-class occupations. Moreover, by the 1970s, the proportion of the population of rural areas employed in agriculture had diminished to such an extent that villages were inhabited by urban 'off-comers' who bought second homes for holidays or commuted daily to the city. This caused appreciable social divisions, pushing the poorly paid rural labourers into enclaves, within or beyond the village, which Newby termed 'encapsulated communities', that separated them geographically and socially, partly for purely financial reasons. Recent concern in Britain about the state of rural communities emphasises the degree of isolation which is current in rural areas, with the relatively high suicide rate of farmers being attributed to their lack of contact. Insofar as 'rural institutions' are preserved, it is often the in-migrants who play key roles in rural social life.

Of course, Britain is a very highly urbanised society. In states with much greater land mass, and/or where agricultural production remains a significant source of employment, rural settlements may be less fragmented. Thus Dempsey's (1990) study of Smalltown, Australia, a township and hinterland containing fewer than 4,000 people, 250 kilometres from Melbourne and 110 kilometres from 'the nearest town of any size' (Dempsey, 1990, p. 23), showed a strong sense of belonging, an attachment to the place and a high degree of social cohesion. Class inequalities existed between farmers, state professionals often employed in state welfare agencies, local working-class households and some marginalised people. There are considerable and visible differences of power between men and women. Yet high levels of social interaction, a strongly held view that life in Smalltown is clearly superior to that in a city, and the exigencies of getting along in a small and isolated place, produces a way of life that does have strong elements of *Gemeinschaft*. However, the conditions for the existence of such settlements are such that they face constant pressure from external forces that have, over time, reduced their number.

Despite its widespread use, the concept of 'community' has often proved to be troublesome because of its vagueness. Hillery (1955), for example, in a much-quoted observation, distinguished ninety-five different senses of the term used in sociological literature. More usefully, Bell and Newby (1976) distinguished between three analytically different connotations of the concept:

1. It is used as a purely topographical expression, to describe finite, bounded areas, such as a village, a tract of land within a city, a housing estate, or whatever.
2. It has a sociological expression, characterised by the degree of interconnection of local people and their social institutions, implying some level of mutual social involvement or integration, a phenomenon conceptualised by Stacey (1969) as a local social system.
3. Community describes a particular kind of human association, a type of social relationship, which has no logical connection with places or local social systems. This kind of relationship Bell and Newby usefully prefer to call communion, indicating warmth of feelings, personal ties and belongingness. However,

this is not necessarily secured by geographical proximity: modern city-dwellers may obtain this sense of communion through churches, clubs, social movements, gangs, and the like. They entail face-to-face interaction, but may be obtained through more or less formally organised meetings.

In sum, there is only a contingent link between area, local social system and the hallowed sense of communion. No doubt there are geographical areas with relatively complete local social systems that generate a sense of communion. There are also places where people hate their co-residents. It is a mistake to imagine that settlement type produces specific qualities of social relationship.

Research into communities became bogged down in a series of intractable problems of a conceptual and methodological character. These problems finally undermined the use of the term 'community', as it was recognised that its use was ideological – that is to say, that it reflects widespread cultural assumptions and biases, rather than reality. The idea of community itself is much revered, regret being widely expressed about the loss of the intimate, face-to-face relationships of small rural villages. A myth of an idyllic rural way of life has had pronounced effects on British society at least for 200 years. The myth has been dissected many times in informative ways (see Williams, 1973; Newby, 1979) and has been shown to have important consequences for the declining profitability of British industry (Wiener, 1981). The attraction of the country-side in the British imagination has been a conception of the special kind of social relationships thought to be present in the rural village. This has very often missed the oppressive and restrictive character of life in small, preindustrial communities. Ethnographic studies of rural areas have begun to pick out conflictual rather than cooperative social relations (see Gasson *et al.*, 1988, for a survey). In the urban planning literature, nostalgia for an imagined lost community has obscured the way in which architects of new urban settlements have conceived of the restoration of community life as a strategy for control of subordinate social groups (see Bell and Newby, 1976).

By the 1970s the community studies were denounced as scientifically flawed, though they were appreciated as interesting ethnographic accounts. They were, and still are, fascinating and absorbing reading, describing the minutiae of everyday life, mostly of the working class, as seen voyeuristically by social scientists. Their failings were that they were non-cumulative, since it was difficult to compare them systematically, as they were written by different people in varying ways. They made no contribution to theory, often preferring to stick close to their empirical investigation. Also they gave unsatisfactory explanations because they were concerned only with processes internal to the community. In the late 1970s these problems led Wellman and Leighton (1979) and others to champion the value of network methods as ways of empirically measuring people's social ties. The basic idea of Wellman's network analysis was to avoid assuming that a particular space was characterised by particular kinds of social ties. Rather, by measuring the contacts between people in diverse locations, it was empirically possible to adjudicate whether some places were richer in ties than others. Community thus becomes an empirical question. As network approaches have been utilised over the past two decades, they have demonstrated the difficulty of revealing any clear spatial patterns to communities. Researchers have shown that even nineteenth-century urban communities were not as bounded and cohesive as might have been once thought (Scherzer, 1992). The most significant differences in the organisation of social networks are not based on urban residence so much as class, with working class areas being characterised by closer, stronger ties, and middle-class areas by weaker ones (see also Adams and Allan, 1998). The result of this long line of inquiry was therefore to dismiss the idea that the countryside was full of communities, whilst cities were not. It proved, however, remarkably difficult to research communities in such a way that Wirth's expectations could be rigorously tested. Since strong social ties, based upon subcultural affiliation, existed in the city, the evidence for the urban–rural contrast was found unconvincing.

(iii) The proliferation of subcultures
Wirth's view that there was an urban culture always sat somewhat uncomfortably with the Chicago School's recognition of the existence of varied practical cultures in the Western city. If the practices of the Gold Coast and those of the slum were so very

different, as charted by Zorbaugh (1929), then in what sense was it possible to maintain that there was some generalised 'urban' culture? The objection was that responses to the opportunities of urban life largely depend upon the social group to which someone belongs – defined in terms of lifecycle stage, generation, class and ethnic group (see Gans, 1968b). The implication of this position is that the 'urban' ceases to be a first-order cause of particular social practices, and is replaced by central sociological variables (demographic and socio-economic) as the way to explain differential experience within the city.

We have emphasised that the Chicago School depended on urban ethnographies for their arguments. The sheer variety of subcultures to be found in any city makes it impossible to identify some dominant type of urban social relations. There are certainly strong forces making for competition, individuation and personal difference; but there are counter-tendencies in shared interests, sociability, friendship and kinship, membership of organisations, etc. that induce cooperation and communality. What studies of urban villagers, of Bethnal Green, of ethnic groups, etc., have constantly shown, is that heterogeneity is in part an illusion, behind which integrated, homogeneous groups are involved in high levels of interaction. This also weighed heavily against Wirth's theoretical synthesis.

Recent ethnographic studies have been framed in rather a different way from that of Wirth. It is striking that despite theoretical interest in issues of globalisation, there is no evidence that urban ethnography is on the wane, though its tools and perspectives are undergoing change. (For an overview of the history of such studies, see Hannerz, 1980; and for the tradition of community studies, see Bell and Newby, 1974; Allan and Crow, 1993). In the US, the 1990s saw a remarkable wave of urban ethnographies of black communities, ranging from Duneier's *Slim's Table* (1994), an account of how under-privileged black male customers of a local café in Chicago sustain their pride in difficult circumstances, to Loic Wacquant's (e.g.1999a) studies of ghettos in Chicago (and comparisons in France). There is a similar number of innovative ethnographic studies of suburban cultures (Baumgartner, 1988; Dempsey's (1990) studies of suburban Australia). In the UK, Crow (2002) talks about the 'rejuvenation' of ethnographic community studies after a period of relative quiet in the 1970s. Admittedly, urban ethnographies have changed their focus: no longer is there marked interest in localised subcultures, but rather the concern is to use a local lens to explore processes of wider theoretical and social relevance. In the UK, this has led to local enthographies of musicians (Finnegan, 1989), cultures of crime and fear of crime (Hobbs, 1987; MacKay *et al.*, 1997) and virtual communities (Wakeford, 2002).

These studies recast the purpose of local ethnographies. Rather than centring on local areas as self-contained communities, they explore the interface between global social processes and their instantiation in specific social and physical spaces. In some ways this is a different rendering of urban ethnography from that used by the Chicago School since it imparts no particular causal role for urban processes as such. Rather, such studies lead away from issues of urban personality or urban culture towards the identification of a variety of different modes and patterns of everyday life. These new ethnographic studies do not, then, rely on Wirth's framework, nor do they rely on a conception of the distinctiveness of urban space. However, it may be premature to write off Wirth's contribution. Some, mainly American, writers have recast Wirth's framework in somewhat different terms.

The most significant writer here is Claud Fischer, and especially his studies of southern California (1982). Fischer explored the social networks of urban and rural residents, and develops an argument that offers an interesting revision of Wirth's. Fischer argues that urban living allows the proliferation of subcultures, and identities, since people can choose a variety of bases on which to identify. Urbanism allows such subcultures to proliferate since a critical mass for the formation of a distinct culture is often only possible in a city of a certain size. Thus only when the number of potential members of a given group rises above a threshold can they form a collectivity. Furthermore, once it is known that a subculture exists in a certain city, selective migration takes place as people choose to move to that area in order to join. Subsequently, conflict or interaction with other social groups may reinforce a sense of shared identity.

Fischer discusses the emergence of homosexual subcultures in urban areas in precisely these terms. In some urban areas, such as San Francisco, selective migration of gay men to the city over a long period led first to them becoming a large group able to sustain their own social and cultural life. Other gay men, often moving from more repressive rural areas and small towns, were encouraged to migrate, reinforcing the gay subculture. Frequent conflicts with homophobic public authorities have served to strengthen the subculture. Subsequent writers, notably Bellah *et al.* (1985), have developed the idea of 'lifestyle enclaves' to refer to the creation of communities of interest, where those sharing a similar 'enthusiasm' develop shared communities which are not based directly on Wirth's triad of size, density and heterogeneity. Nonetheless, Fischer's emphasis on the need for a size threshold, and the significance of communication through various kinds of transport and media to allow like-minded people to come together, still suggests that urban areas continue to be advantaged because their population size allows more like-minded people to live in close proximity. In his more recent re-evaluations of his perspective, Fischer (1995) insists on the sociological significance of the rural–urban divide. He is sceptical of claims that new forms of virtual communication make actual spatial proximity irrelevant for subcultures (as argued, for instance, by Wellman, 2001), and instead insists that urban dwellers in advanced capitalist societies tend to be more 'unconventional' than rural residents. He thus paves the way for a partial reappraisal and reinstatement of Wirth's arguments.

5.1.2   Reappraisal of Wirth

This three-pronged critique of Wirth's notion of an urban way of life made a considerable contribution towards better understanding the city. Many defects of Wirth's synthesis were identified and laid aside: for example, notions of the urban personality, the urban–rural distinction, the uniformity of the urban temperament, the idea that cities *per se* had effects, and the belief that communal and community networks had atrophied. Nonetheless, recent re-evaluations have shown that whilst Wirth's arguments cannot be sustained in their entirety, they contain important insights into the nature of life in modern cities. In three important areas it can be argued that the critics have overstated their case.

First, older ethnographic and community studies demonstrating the persistence of social bonds tended to look for coherence and interconnections. This is partly because it is easier to carry out research in communal settings than on specific private households. Persuasiveness in traditional anthropological work has typically come from giving a coherent and understandable picture of some network of social interaction. The analysis of such interaction systems need not exclude conflict; the best anthropology has a lot to say about dispute, negotiation and conflict, as was apparent in community studies. However, such research has focused on particular groups of people in contexts where there are high levels of interaction and some recognisable moral order. The method itself tends to enhance the impression of coherence. This has been appreciated by modern anthropology and current best-practice guards against such misrepresentation. The recent emphasis in anthropology to recognise the reflexivity of the researcher, and the need to guard against intellectual closure (Clifford and Marcus, 1986), has led to different kinds of research. Certainly, many of the key empirical studies in the debate from the 1950s to the 1970s upon which the critique was based probably overemphasised the coherence of social groups. The fact that urban communities were discovered in cities may partly reflect the methods used by researchers.

Second, recent ethnographic studies continue to demonstrate that local context matters. The contextual aspects of human interaction, the sense in which configurations of co-presence are an important part of the construction of distinctive group subcultures, got lost in the most thoroughly aspatial theoretical critiques of Wirth (e.g. Saunders, 1985). Although settlement type does not directly generate particular types of social relations, the frequency, density and context of personal contact does have effects on sociation. In Bethnal Green and in Smalltown, widespread face-to-face interaction was one precondition of communal practice and a sense of belonging. Repeated interaction encourages more intense interpersonal sentiments, whether of belonging or antagonism. Often the specific features of the local environment – its layout, the memories it invokes, the public spaces that it contains – frame a distinctive context that supports particular forms of interaction. Distances, boundaries and configurations between sites for association restrict some and enable other types of joint and collective behaviour. That spatial arrangements do not determine the quality of social interaction does not mean that they should be ignored altogether, a point that recent research on space and place has increasingly appreciated.

Third, the critique tended to reinforce the sense that sociation should be explored as an antinomy: *Gemeinschaft* or *Gesellschaft;* rural or urban; cooperative or competitive; communal or anonymous. In fact, these characteristics usually exist together; more of some and less of others in particular groups or situations, for sure, but the texture of life in late capitalism is a mixture. Both competition and cooperation are required in a society with a division of labour and private ownership, an insight from Durkheim of which Wirth was fully aware. These antinomies are not alternatives; almost everyone has both in their social repertoires for use in different circumstances. Nor are they spatially determined. Rather, they are supported or undermined by particular types of social interaction situation and material contexts. These last are more appropriate objects of study.

Urban sociology after 1945 tended to generalise unacceptably from Wirth's model of an urban way of life without necessarily doing the kind of research that would corroborate or refute its key tenets (see Fischer, 1975). In addition, statistical approaches to segregation failed to depict sociation satisfactorily. Demographic and material characteristics as identified through census-type variables are insufficient to understand everyday life. Groups in similar socio-economic circumstances may have quite distinct lifestyles. Ley (1983) quotes a comparative study of two affluent social areas in Vancouver. Both were among the richest 10 per cent of neighbourhoods by socio-economic status, but exhibited enormous differences in terms of settledness, background, respectability, leisure activities and friendship patterns. Residential distribution generates different social milieux. Case studies, those with a historical component as well as ethnographies, which often take a territorial area as a convenient unit for studying social relationships in context, are essential to understanding the diversity of urban living.

5.2   Simmel and metropolitan culture

Wirth failed to sustain the idea of a generic urban culture differentiated from rural culture. But an alternative approach is possible, thinking in terms not of its spatial differentiation from a rural way of life, but of its temporal distinctiveness from older, traditional cultures. This is the line of argument which Simmel developed.

Thirty-five years before Wirth published 'Urbanism as a Way of Life', Georg Simmel had produced another classic essay on urban culture, 'The Metropolis and Mental Life' (see Simmel, 1964). It is common to see these two essays as part of the same tradition, with Wirth elaborating and systematising some of Simmel's ideas (e.g. Smith, 1980; Saunders, 1986). However, Wirth misunderstood Simmel's essay in important respects, for his project was rather different. Simmel was primarily concerned to establish that urban culture was the culture of modernity.

In 'The Metropolis and Mental Life' Simmel rehearsed many of the themes which crop up in Wirth's later essay: the metropolis as the site for the lonely, isolated individual, shorn of strong social bonds: 'the relationships and affairs of the typical metropolitan usually are so varied and complex that without the strictest punctuality the whole structure would break down into an inextricable chaos' (Simmel, 1950, p. 412). More specifically, Simmel argued that there are four distinctive, but interrelated, cultural forms which are characteristically found in urban settings. These are:

1. 'intellectuality', where the urban dweller 'reacts with his [*sic*] head instead of his heart' (Simmel, 1950, p. 410).
2. urban dwellers are 'calculative' (*ibid.*, p. 412) – instrumentally weighing up the advantages and disadvantages of each action.
3. people are blasé.
4. urban dwellers retreat behind a protective screen of reserve, rarely showing emotion or expressing themselves directly to others.

These traits all seem consistent with Wirth's account. There, however, similarity stops. Unlike Wirth, Simmel did not claim that cities *per se* caused these cultural forms. Although Simmel has frequently been interpreted as positing a causal link between cities and cultural life, so that the mere fact of population density itself produces the effects he discusses, this claim is dubious. The belief that Simmel was showing how size of settlement affected cultural life – a view similar to that of Wirth – is often justified by evoking Simmel's interest in the sociology of numbers, and the way in which the formal properties of quantities affect patterns of social interaction (Mellor, 1977, p. 184; Saunders, 1986, p. 89). Yet although Simmel did write extensively about this issue in his earlier work, by the time he wrote 'The Metropolis and Mental Life' he had abandoned his rather formalistic treatment and rarely mentioned the significance of size alone, and was careful to qualify any statements relating to it: hence his observation that 'it is not only the immediate size of the area and the number of persons which ... has made the metropolis the locale of freedom' (Simmel, 1950, pp. 418–19). Rather, Simmel's concern had become the correlation between quantitative and qualitative relationships. In this context, he emphasised the sociological significance of money whose 'quality consists exclusively in its quantity' (Simmel, 1978, p. 259). Numbers only became sociologically significant because they were premised on a money economy, and it was this which Simmel regarded as most important.

Hence Simmel did not, in this paper, seek to establish any clear causal links between cities *per se* and these cultural traits, and he was certainly not interested in contrasting the city-dweller with the rural-dweller. What is striking, on a careful reading of Simmel's paper, is that his point of contrast was generally not between cities and rural areas, but between contemporary cities and towns in earlier historical periods. Indeed, the usual contrast is with the 'small town', especially in antiquity (e.g. Simmel, 1950, p. 417). Simmel rarely compared the city-dweller with the rural-dweller directly, and on the few occasions that he did, it is unclear whether he was referring to the rural-dweller in earlier historical periods or the contemporary era. Generally Simmel was not arguing for a distinction between urban and rural cultures, because he believed emphatically that in the modern world the metropolis's influence spreads throughout the whole society, including its rural hinterland:

> the horizon of the city expands in a manner comparable to the way in which wealth develops ... As soon as a certain limit has been passed, the sphere of the intellectual predominance of the city over its hinterland grow(s) as in geometrical progression ... For it is the decisive nature of the metropolis that its inner life overflows by waves into a far-flung national or international area. (Simmel, 1950, p. 419)

Simmel also did not explain the specified cultural traits in terms of the causal effects of cities *per se,* but it is the role of the city as centre of the 'money economy' that he developed at greatest length, and it is consistent with the overall tenor of his mature social theory (see Frisby, 1985, especially pp. 77ff). Since the money economy is most highly developed in cities, so too are the cultural traits. The decisive evidence for this argument is that Simmel himself thought the *Philosophy of Money* (see Simmel, 1978) his most important work, noting at the end of 'The Metropolis and Mental Life' that 'argument and elaboration of its major cultural-historical ideas are contained in my *Philosophy of Money*' (Simmel, 1950, p. 424). His book analysed many of the same cultural traits discussed in the shorter essay, and he was happy to explain them in terms of the dominance of the money economy. He thus spent two pages discussing the blasé attitude without mentioning cities once (Simmel, 1978, pp. 256–7). He argued that money is by its very nature instrumental, a pure means to something else. Hence the dominance of the money economy in modern societies explains the associated calculative attitudes. From time to time in *The Philosophy of Money* Simmel referred to cities, but merely to illustrate the effects of the money economy. A typical observation is that 'our whole life also becomes affected by its remoteness from nature, a situation that is reinforced by the money economy and the urban life that is dependent upon it' (Simmel, 1978, p 478)

In short, Simmel's arguments cannot be used to justify the idea that an urban way of life stands in contrast to a rural way of life. Simmel's main stress, like that of Toennies, was a historical one, in which modern societies, based on the dominance of the money economy, exhibited very different cultural traits from traditional societies. Cities were interesting because they exhibited these new emergent features most clearly, not because cities themselves possessed some generic causal power.

Simmel's contribution to the analysis of urban culture was thus rather different from that suggested by many of his interpreters. As his most perceptive advocate, David Frisby, has hinted, the importance of Simmel's work lies in his arguments that the nature of modernity makes it virtually impossible to pinpoint any coherent way of life at all. Frisby has argued that Simmel should best be understood as a sociologist attempting to develop an account of 'modernity' – 'the modes of experiencing what is "new" in "modern" society' (Frisby, 1985, p. 1). In this context Simmel's constant refrain is the fragmentation and diversity of modern life. As Simmel stated:

> the essence of modernity as such is psychologism, the experience and interpretation of the world in terms of the reactions of our inner life and indeed as an inner world, the dissolution of fixed contents in the fluid element of the soul, from which all that is substantive is filtered and whose forms are merely forms of motion. (quoted in Frisby, 1985, p. 46)

For Simmel, modern life saw a rupture of inner, spiritual life and feelings from outward behaviour – in Simmel's terms 'the separation of the subjective from objective life'. In order to protect ourselves from the potential instability and chaos, given the diversity of stimuli which bombards the senses in the course of everyday life, we are all forced to retreat into an inner, intellectual, world which acts as a filter on our experience. This account is not without problems, for he appears to have used an empiricist theory of experience, in which the outside world is able to affect our senses of their own accord (see Smith, 1980). Even if we adopt a weaker version of Simmel's thesis, that we need to control our perceptions intellectually in order to maintain identity and personality, it is clear that the implication of Simmel's argument is still to deny that we can specify a distinct way of life at all. The very concept of 'way of life' suggests a fusion between thought and practice, social position and individual action, which he regards as absent in the modern world. If we recognise that our activities are context-specific (i.e. we behave in different ways in different settings) and that each person may interpret or intellectualise the same actions in a different way, then it becomes very difficult to accept a notion of 'a way of life' – implying as it does a certain coherence to people's activities, and a fusion of culture and practice.

Simmel's real significance is that he problematised the very idea of urban culture, if by this is meant a single and unified urban way of life, based upon axes such as urban alienation or loneliness. Ironically, one of the most powerful critiques of Wirth can be found in Simmel's own, earlier account, which offers a more sophisticated notion of contemporary culture. There are four major differences between Simmel and Wirth:

1. Wirth made what had been a largely historical claim, about traditional communities turning into modern societies, into a spatial one about the difference between cities and villages.
2. Relatedly, he made the study of urban culture part of a comparative project with rural cultures, in an unprecedented way.
3. He claimed that the three defining characteristics of the city were causal forces behind urban cultures, whereas Simmel made no such claim.
4. He used a concept of culture as a 'way of life', which diverged from Simmel's more aesthetic and fragmentary definition.

In all these ways Wirth's innovations proved unhelpful.

5.3   The culture of modernity

Recently, urban culture has again become a focus for study, mainly by writers from outside the terrain of urban sociology. Many are associated with literature and literary criticism, some with the visual arts. In this section we show how Simmel's account of urban culture as the culture of modernity has been used to explore aspects of urban culture. Simmel's work is indeed the best starting-point for the analysis of contemporary urban cultures, and recent writers have interestingly applied his account. We develop this argument by considering the merits of recent writing which draws upon Simmelian themes in four main areas, namely: the visual, modernist aesthetics, sexual identity and the nature of street life.

5.3.1   *The visual*

Several authors have developed Simmel's arguments that the 'eye', or the visual, gains particular prominence in modern urban culture. Simmel saw the urban as characterised by the dominance of the visual sense over all others. Clark (1985) echoes this stress on the dominance of the visual when arguing that the rise of French Impressionist painting in the mid nineteenth century was associated with the development of the modern urban form. The painting of Impressionists such as Manet, Monet, Dégas and Seurat did not 'fix' images to known social referents. Instead they marked the proliferation of visual signs and symbols which the new urban spaces had brought forth (see also Hannoosh, 1984; Reff, 1984). In contrast, earlier painting – for instance, British eighteenth-century landscape painting – was organised through literary forms. For Pugh, 'the discourse of the "landscape" and the "rural" was first negotiated through verbal modes of represen- tation ... the verbal interpellates the visual' (Pugh, 1990, p. 3).

John Urry (1990a), in examining the construction of the tourist 'gaze', also stressed the visual. The construction of particu- lar vistas, the development of viewing points, and so forth, can be seen as a major element used to draw people to particular sites. In a similar way post-modern architecture of the 1970s and 1980s is designed to elaborate and enhance the visual imagery used in ar- chitecture (Harvey, 1989; Connor, 1989); grand ornamentation contrasts with the functional plain style favoured by modernists.

Recent cultural theorists (Jay, 1993, 1996) have explored Simmel's emphasis on the interrelation between modernity and the visual. Modernist thinkers have situated their accounts of the modern through either endorsing, or denigrating, the role of the visual. The most critical analysis of the development of the visual sense in modern urban cultures comes from feminist writers who relate it to the voyeuristic male gaze (e.g. Pollock, 1988). It is only men who are able to cast their wandering eye freely around the urban landscape, and furthermore, it is often female bodies which are the target of such gazes. The ambivalences of the visual can, then, be seen as one of the contradictory features of modernity itself.

5.3.2   Modernist aesthetics

A second recent issue in the analysis of the city and modernity idea has been the connecting of Modernism – as a cultural move- ment affecting literature, the visual arts, and music in the first part of this century – with the urban experience. Modernism seems, in many ways, to be an artistic elaboration of many of the themes which Simmel developed in 'The Metropolis and Mental Life'. The most celebrated modernist works – for instance Proust's *In Remembrance of Things Past*, T. S. Eliot's *The Waste Land,* and James Joyce's *Ulysses* – all developed a form of 'high aesthetic self-consciousness and non-representationalism in which art turns from realism and humanistic representation towards style, technique, and spatial form in pursuit of a deeper penetration of life' (Bradbury and McFarlane, 1976, p. 25). This is linked to the 'intellectualisation' of life in response to psychic overload emphasised by Simmel (Sharpe and Wallock, 1984).

Bradbury observed, 'Modernist art has had special relations with the modern city, and in its role both as cultural museum and novel environment' (Bradbury, 1976, p. 97). In part this simply reflects the growth of a Bohemian artistic culture in the metropolises of Paris, London, Vienna and New York as young avant-garde artists moved into the big cities. At another level, however, it reflected the way in which modernism was a reflection upon the urban experience as such. These new immigrants to the city saw it as strange and wonderful, in contrast to their often rural or small-town upbringing, and hence it became the source of artistic inspiration (Williams, 1989, p. 45). Urban sights and sounds became the topic of modernist work:

> in the early part of this century, for painters like Chagall, Stella, Mann and Severini, being modern meant coming to terms artistically, with the juxtaposition of urban sights and sounds, the compression of history and modern technology on a single street. (Sharpe and Wallock, 1984, p. 11)

According to Berman (1983), cities such as St Petersburg offered remarkable scope for modernist work since the contrast between old and new, tradition and modernity, could be most directly observed in street life. The Nevsky Prospect, for instance, a modern consumer street in a city still dominated by a feudal social order, was a frequent source of inspiration for the Russian modernists.

Associating the modernist sensibility with urban experience has however led to disagreement over one vital matter. It remains unclear whether the links apply to modernist art, narrowly defined, in a small number of 'great' metropolitan cities in a small time-span between, say, 1890 and 1930, or whether there is a more general association between urbanism and particular forms of cultural production. Berman (1983) argued that the experience of 'modernity' is a generic feature of all social life in the nineteenth and twentieth centuries, and continues to see the urban experience as the wellspring of creative art. Perry Anderson (1984), however, claims that Berman's arguments do not apply after the 1920s, since modernist art was effectively a commentary on the slow transition from an aristocratic landed order to an advanced industrial capitalist order, and so, with the triumph of capitalism after 1930, modernism lost its distinctiveness. In his recent work Frisby (2001) has further developed Simmel's arguments to emphasise the urban specificity of particular kinds of modern urban cultures, in his exploration of the diverse modernisms of Vienna, Berlin, and Paris. This account recognises that modernism itself is diverse because the manner of its development varies in specific historical contexts (see further, Kahn, 2000). Here, we see how Simmel's emphasis on the temporal nature of modernity can lead to a further elaboration of urban difference.

Feminists have also been critical of claims about the universality of the experience of modernity. Pollock (1988) and Wolff (1987) argue that writers such as Simmel, Benjamin and Berman do not recognise that the experience of modernity as they define it is primarily a male one. Indeed, the same process whereby men moved into the public sphere, enjoying the excitement and insecurity which that involved, depended on a parallel process by which women were confined to the domestic, private sphere. Yet, as Pollock (1988) shows, there were female modernist painters, using experimental techniques similar to those practised by men. However, unlike men, their chosen subjects were frequently domestic and familial. If female artists are given proper recognition, then artistic modernism cannot simply be seen as a commentary on urban change.

Thus, while there is clear evidence for a specific association between particular cities and particular cultural movements, it is altogether more difficult to claim a generic association between cities and cultural life. Particular types of modernist culture may have had close ties to Vienna, New York and Paris, but not to Rome, Birmingham or Copenhagen. Some forms of modernist art, often that by women, were denigrated even in 'modernist' cities.

5.3.3   Sexual identity

The third development concerns the relationship between sexuality and modern urban cultures. Simmel, as we have seen, saw the intellectualisation of life as a typical feature of modern urban culture. The process of developing a sexual identity, interrogating intellectually the nature of this identity, and forming specific sub-cultures based upon it, exemplify his view. Recent research, some of it drawing on Fischer's work discussed above, has pointed to the way in which the urban milieu has a prominent role as a site in which subversive and non-conforming forms of sexuality may take root. One example of this is the siting of gay and lesbian cultures in large urban areas, such as San Francisco and New York (Fischer, 1982, ch. 18; Castells, 1983). Feminist writers (e.g. Benstock, 1986), have also noted the greater potential for women to find alternative, less patriarchal ways of living in urban contexts. This is also an aspect of gentrification (see Chapter 4).

Wilson (1991) argues that urban living threatens patriarchal, fa-milial ways of life characteristic of smaller towns and rural areas. She sees the disorder and potential subversion inherent in the culture of modernity as threatening to men, but as enhancing options for women. 'The city offers women freedom. After all, the city normalises the carnivalesque aspects of life' (Wilson, 1991, p. 7). Their power challenged, men find ways of clamping down on the licence and 'freedom' of urban living – through such devices as planning. As a result, urban culture is a complex interplay between male and female principles: 'urban life is actu-ally based on this perpetual struggle between rigid, routinised order, and pleasurable anarchy, the male–female dichotomy' (Wilson, 1991, pp. 7–8).

Wilson's view, however, is romantic. One might object that the heightened significance of fashion and appearance in urban environments increases the pressures for rigid sexual identities to develop. Similarly it is not self-evident that unconventional forms of sexuality can only find a haven in the city: there is a long tradi-tion of retreating to rural environments where the public gaze is thought less intense – for instance, in Utopian communities (Taylor, 1980). Furthermore, despite Wilson's claims concerning the possible development of subversive forms of sexuality in cities, they are also the sites for sexual activities that reinforce and sustain patriarchal sexuality – most notably, prostitution. Interestingly in this regard, Simmel attributed the concentration of prostitution to the dominance of the money economy typical of modernity (Simmel, 1978, pp. 376ff). As with the case of artistic modernism, it seems unwise to generalise: some cities such as New York and San Francisco may be homes for gay subcultures, but other metropolises may not. Single women may be able to create their own alternative culture in some inner cities, London for example, but not in all.

5.3.4   The nature of street life

A final development of Simmel is by Marshall Berman who examined the way in which encounters on the street are linked to the culture of modernity. Working within a largely unacknowledged Marxist elaboration of Simmel's framework, Berman explored the double-edged nature of modern life by arguing that people's freedom to develop and change goes hand in hand with the insecurity caused by the resulting lack of certainty. Hence:

> to be modern, is to experience personal and social life as a maelstrom, to find one's world in perpetual disintegration and renewal, trouble and anguish, ambiguity and contradiction … to be a modernist is … to grasp and confront the world that modernisation makes, and strive to make it our own. (Berman, 1984, p. 115)

Berman sees the street as a microcosm for modern life and the battle for public space as at the heart of the modernist quest: 'I've come to see the street and the demonstration as primary symbols of modern life' (Berman, 1984, p. 123). He connects the role of the street to wider concerns by arguing that street encounters are unpredictable and unknowable. We are never sure whom we will meet, or with what consequences. At one level this gives us unparalleled potential – to meet the love of our life, a potential employer, an old friend – but at another level it is deeply worrying – we may be robbed, attacked, or slighted. This general insecurity reinforces the role of the visual in urban cultures – as we scan passers-by in order to assess their risk or value to us. This in turn leads us to highlight the visual imagery we wish to emphasise to others, hence the significance of fashion and style. These kinds of issues are reasons why thinkers such as de Certeau (1984) regard walking in cities as having the potential to develop a different kind of knowledge from that based on academic detachment. This call to celebrate knowledge emerging from urban milieux has been made by others, such as the geographer Derek Gregory (1994).

Such contributions deepen Simmel's analysis of how the 'psychic overload' of modern urban life is related to the culture of modernity. However, it is by no means clear that tensions which Berman sees as characteristic of the street are unique to it. Given the relative instability of family, household and personal relationships in contemporary societies it might very well be argued that household life is composed of the very same blend of promise and danger as the street. Feminists might argue that the street fails to possess any excitement at all given its status as male territory, where women are under constant threat. His view might also be said to adopt a male perspective by locating both promise and danger in encounters with strangers. Women might object that they are more usually endangered by men known to them, often fathers or lovers, since the majority of sexual violence takes place within the family. Equally there seems no reason why one cannot see promise or excitement in relations with people one knows very well. Furthermore, to take only one well-known aspect of street life – its potential dangers – recent studies in criminology, echoing the Chicago School, have shown that there are highly localised differences in the incidence of crime within large cities. Not all streets are the same. Berman recognises this implicitly, since he plays particular attention to some types, such as the central-urban shopping street. It is better to recognise the specificity of street cultures, rather than to generalise about the street *per se*. Finally, we spend only a relatively small part of our time – even if we live in cities – walking around them. In short, the stress on the 'sociology of the street', cannot bear the theoretical weight placed on it by Berman or Jukes (1990).

5.4   Conclusion

Urban sociology has learned much from its various attempts to depict the key attributes of a culture of the city. An elaborate understanding of sociation – neighbouring, kinship, friendship and association – has emerged from the concern with the quality of life and social relationships in cities. We can also appreciate the proliferation of subcultures in contemporary society, the contexts of their development and the structured social divisions transposed through them. Moreover, the attention devoted to urban culture recently has expanded further the interdisciplinary contributions to urban studies as the techniques of literary criticism and art history have been brought to bear.

Nevertheless, attempts to develop an understanding of the generic meaning of living in cities have had only limited success. Relatively little can be said in general terms about the meaning of urban life in the contemporary world. It seems that a good deal of what has been valuable in explorations of urban culture could more appropriately be grasped as illumination of the experience of modernity. The culture of modernity, which in Simmel's time found its clearest expression in urban life, is now virtually universal throughout developed countries. The problems, dilemmas and potentials of modernity are of the utmost importance, but they cannot be consigned to the category of urban culture. Cultural differences emerge between and within cities. Different cities and different quarters support alternative, and sometimes competing, patterns of cultural existence. Insofar as sociologists continue to note the existence of urban and rural differences, their arguments are cautious and contingent to particular kinds of societies. To some extent it is unique combinations of attributes that make places recognisably different the one from the other. It may be better, then, to explore how cities take on their own specific meanings and how these are communicated and interpreted, rather than to refer to urban culture as a whole. This does not imply that we should be content with merely describing the particular cultures of individual cities. Rather, a more analytic approach recommends itself, considering how urban experience can be analysed in more particular and specific ways. This is the subject of the next chapter.

6 Urban Culture and the Regeneration of Urban Meaning

In this chapter our focus is on understanding how urban cultures are constructed, maintained and re-constructed. Over the past two decades, and especially in the 1990s, there has been a dramatic growth of interest in the generation of urban meaning, and an astonishing growth of urban cultural analysis. The aim of this chapter is to explore different ways of interpreting urban cultures, and to examine how urban cultures have undergone reinvigoration even at a time when globalising processes have exercised a powerful effect. The main theme of the chapter is to consider how to reflect sociologically on the built environment in order to understand how urban meanings are constructed in complex interplay with it.

In section 6.1 we begin with the influential work of Henri Lefebvre, in which the social construction of space is related to the commodifying forces of capitalism. This leads on, in section 6.2, to the work of the Marxist cultural critic, Walter Benjamin. We briefly outline some of his ideas and explain their relevance to the study of urban culture. He addressed urban meaning as an interface between personal memories and experiences and the historical construction of dominant meanings and values. The city, for Benjamin, was a site where cultural contradictions could best be revealed and dominant cultures criticised. Finally, section 6.3 explores how globalisation can go hand in hand with the regeneration of urban cultural meaning.

6.1 Urban meaning

It is a striking contemporary paradox that urban specificity seems to be prized at the very same time that globalising processes mean that places are becoming more similar. One influential approach to this puzzle was developed by the French neo-Marxist, Henri Lefebvre. His starting-point is that in capitalist society, space is used instrumentally, as a commodity. Space is no longer defined in terms of its geographical and physical attributes, but is increasingly the product of capitalist forces: it becomes 'abstract space'. He proposed that industrial capitalism gives way to what he terms the 'urban revolution'. As the world becomes subordinated to the capitalist global market a counter-movement takes place in which spaces become increasingly differentiated symbolically. As leisure industries spring up, and since capital's mobility means that enterprises can shift, so a battle occurs over the images of places, that they might appear attractive and desirable.

Lefebvre is particularly concerned with the relationship between three elements of space: spatial practices, representations of space and spaces of representation – or as he has also termed them, the experienced, the perceived, and the imagined. He argues that these are dialectically related, so that the social construction of space involves not just a purely discursive process whereby places are valued differently, but also the alterations in people's actual experiences of places. By examining the social production of space, Lefebvre sought to surmount dichotomies between structure and agency, discourse and practice.

Lefebvre's work remains rather arcane and abstract. His influence, however, is profound. One central feature adopted both by David Harvey and Anthony Giddens is the idea of 'created space'. In Harvey's words, 'created space replaces effective space as the overriding principle of geographical organization' (Harvey, 1988, p. 309). As real geographical differences between places are eroded in a global system, so symbolic differences become more important: 'the signs, symbols and signals that surround us in the urban environment are powerful influences' (Harvey, 1988, p. 310). Giddens echoes Harvey in seeing one of the distinctive elements of contemporary societies as the dominance of created space, one result being a problem of developing a sense of 'ontological security' in a world where even spatial settings cannot be treated as fixed or permanent (Giddens, 1981).

Lefebvre reorientated analysis of the construction of spatial imagery through linking practice with discourse. A point of contrast is Raymond Williams's study, *The Country and the City*, which surveyed literary constructions of the city and countryside by English writers as diverse as Oliver Goldsmith, William Wordsworth, Thomas Hardy and T. S. Eliot. He showed that they all tended to present a picture of the countryside as an 'image of the past and the common image of the city as an image of the future ... the pull of the country is towards old ways, human ways, natural ways. The pull of the idea of the city is towards progress, modernization, development' (Williams, 1973, p. 357). He insisted that the images so constructed were misleading, since the myth of country as rural idyll failed to correspond with the countryside as the actual site of exploitative capitalist relations in agriculture. However, though extremely influential, Williams's emphasis on the cultural construction of places tends to lose Lefebvre's insistence on the dialectic with experience.

Early sociological studies of the symbolisation of places also suggested that symbolic processes defined experience, rather than there being a reciprocal relationship. Anselm Strauss, for instance, explored the use of urban symbols as synecdoches, where one specific symbol would come to stand for the whole city: 'thus the delicate and majestic sweep of the Golden Gate Bridge stands for San Francisco, a brief close-up of the French Quarter identified New Orleans, and most commonly of all, a New York skyline from the Battery is the standing equivalent for that city' (Strauss, 1961, p.9). Given the inevitable diversity of ways of seeing any one place, the symbolisation of cities involves selecting a small number of symbolic representations and marketing them as the city itself. These may be buildings, as in Strauss's examples, or they may be social types, such as the Beefeaters, often used to symbolise the Tower of London, which might typify London itself. Strauss, however, like Williams, retained a strong distinction between images and 'reality', emphasising the frequent disjunctures between them. Thus he discussed the phenomenon of disappointment, where the real experience of seeing a city does not live up to its promise. In the case of New York, 'the imaginative impact of that skyline is sometimes so conclusive, so overwhelming, that to see the city in normal perspective, and in detail, may be anticlimactic' (Strauss, 1961, p.11). Strauss suggests that the complexity of modern urban experience needs to be simplified into discrete images and sights in order to gain popular currency. Yet he does not elucidate on how these images are developed or sustained, nor does he explore popular experiences of place. Shields (1991) has offered the most ambitious remedy. Also indebted to Lefebvre, he developed the notion of 'social spatialisation', 'to designate the ongoing social construction of the spatial at the level of the social imaginary (collective mythologies, presuppositions) as well as interventions in the landscape (for example the built environment)' (Shields, 1991, p. 31). Social spatialisations define particular places as good or bad, sites of danger, work or whatever; for Shields, places are constructed meaningfully through social spatialisation.

Shields developed his position by dissecting the construction of place-myths around a number of sites. He examined, for instance, the way in which the North–South divide in England was culturally constructed and sustained in the British realist films of the 1960s (for instance, *Saturday Night, Sunday Morning*), in soap opera, and in newspaper reporting. More generally he claimed that place-myths are constructed in novels, popular publishing, the mass media, advertising literature and the like. Shields's study illustrates some of the advantages and disadvantages of working in the vein of Lefebvre. The advantages include a sophisticated appreciation of the construction of places in cultural media, an awareness of the reworking and re-evaluation of these images over time, and a powerful rebuttal of architectural determinism. However the organising concept of 'social spatialisation' is ultimately rather slippery. Theoretically it is designed, after Lefebvre, to encompass both representations of place and how people use these images in everyday life. But in practice, the actual experience of urban living is entirely ignored in favour of discussions of the place-myths themselves, with Shields asserting that 'the actual presence or absence of the activity is beside the point ... the question ... is about the power of social spatialisation and myths to overrun reality' (Shields, 1991, p. 106). A concept originally designed to overcome the polarity between discourse and practice ends up by giving priority to the former.

Nor can Shields explain types of place-myth. He provides detailed descriptions of the development and reformulation of place-myths over time, but without saying why these social spatialisations are changing, or at whose behest. In this respect his analysis is retrogressive since earlier writers concerned more explicitly with architecture were much more sensitive to the causal role of social forces. Shields's work has further inspired a number of contemporary accounts of space. Hetherington (1997) argues that modernity produces greater attentiveness to spatial specificity, through the moralisation of space, and through the embedding of both past and future hopes in particular locations. The utopian visions that are endemic to modernity have an inherently spatial form, as they depend on constructing places appropriate to such visions. Hetherington's work is also influenced by the actor-network theory of Latour and others, which has moved away from its origins in the sociology of science to become highly influential in geography and urban studies (see Thrift, 1996; Urry, 2000). Actor-network theory attempts to resolve tensions between technological determinism and social constructionism in novel ways. It criticises humanist accounts that assume only humans are agents, and shows that various technologies (including, for our purposes here, the built form) can themselves affect social change. The focus is on showing how various technologies are 'enlisted' into stable networks that allow them to exert influence. Social relations do not exist over and above the material objects of everyday life but are rather instantiated through them. In Latour's famous words, 'technology is society made durable'.

Adapting this work to urban studies leads us away from Lefebvre's emphasis on abstract space as a defining feature of capitalist modernity. For Latour, networks depend on processes of circulation, which in turn depend on objects being able to 'translate' and organise networks. Globalisation, for instance, rather than being a kind of general social process that abstracts from fixed space, actually depends on a range of day-to-day technologies – mobile phones, computers, airports, etc. – that allow global networks to be multiply organised. Linking this argument to that of Sassen (1991) and King (1990) it becomes possible to argue that globalisation produces and is dependent on fixed urban spaces, especially those urban spaces of the world cities that are fundamental for modern capitalist business.

Whilst this approach is undoubtedly interesting, it marks a significant move away from Lefebvre's project to find a bridge between experienced space, representations of space, and spaces of representation. The radical anti-humanism of actor-network theory entails an eclipse of human experience that leaves no obvious place for the traditional concerns of urban sociology. It is in this context that the complex humanism of Benjamin's work commands interest.

6.2   Urban meaning and the power of 'aura'

Over the past decade there has been a remarkable explosion of interest in the work of Walter Benjamin and its urban dimension (Gilloch, 1997; Thrift, 1996; Caygill, 1998; Pile, 2000). Much of Walter Benjamin's writing in the last years of his life, from around 1925 to his death in 1940, constituted an attempt to learn how to 'read' cities. Benjamin's point of departure was resolutely the urban form as it is experienced and viewed by its observers. For Benjamin the crucial issue is how an urban landscape can be interpreted and its meanings located in the context of the individual's experience. He began his autobiographical 'A Berlin Chronicle' by reciting how he was brought up in Berlin's streets, recounting how he came to find his way around them. His concentration on how individuals gain a sense of the urban from their own experience, with the help of 'guides' and maps, posits the sense of places as integral to personal experiences and feelings, such that urban meaning is interpreted through one's life happenings.

Benjamin's conceptualisation of the individual's experience of the city took a distinctive form. Usually dissections of people's experiences of urban living have had either positivist or existentialist roots. Positivist geographers charted people's cognitive awareness of their physical landscape, by asking questions about the types of mental maps people have of their environment, their knowledge of place-names and the like. Existential approaches, such as that of Lowenthal (1961), explored people's imaginative understandings of place. Benjamin sought an unusual fusion of the humanist and environmental view, where he was preoccupied by the human dimensions of urban life, yet aware also that human awareness is never transparent or complete. Benjamin argued that the city is a repository of people's memories and past, and is also the receptacle of cultural traditions and values. Whereas Simmel had emphasised the separation of the culture of modernity from that of previous eras, Benjamin concentrated on what Frisby (1985) calls the 'prehistory of modernity', recovering the past buried in the built form. Simmel thought that urban life caused us to intellectualise and develop forms of reserve; Benjamin postulated the primacy of unconscious and dream processes and their association with the urban environment. Hence, reading the urban text is not a matter of intellectually scrutinising the landscape: rather it is a matter of exploring the fantasy, wish-processes and dreams locked up in our perception of cities. Benjamin revealed his general aims thus:

> I think of an afternoon in Paris to which I owe insights into my life that came in a flash, with the force of an illumination. It was on this very afternoon that my biographical relationships to people, my friendships and comradeships, my passions and love affairs, were revealed to me in their most vivid and hidden intertwinings. I tell myself it had to be in Paris, where the walls and quays, the places to pause, the collections and the rubbish, the railings and the squares, the arcades and the kiosks, teach a language so singular that our relations to people attain, in the solitude encompassing our immersion in the world of things, the depths of a sleep in which the dream image waits to show the people their true faces. (Benjamin, 1978, p. 318)

One way of indicating the novelty of Benjamin's approach is to contrast it with those urban and architectural historians who see the urban form as the embodiment of social values embedded in architectural styles and forms. The distinguished American urbanist, Lewis Mumford, thus wrote that 'The city, as one finds it in history, is the point of maximum concentration for the power and culture of community ... the city is a form and symbol of an integrated social relationship ... the city is also a work of art ... mind takes form in the city and in turn urban form conditions mind' (Mumford, 1938, pp. 3, 5). But for Mumford, the relationship between human subject and the built environment was largely passive.

For Benjamin, by contrast, people's memories lay bound up in their experience of built forms, so that specific buildings can take on very different meanings from those intended by their builders. Yet Benjamin was also an objectivist. He did not see meanings as the result of subjective processes alone – as a relativist might do – but as objectively located in specific cultural phenomena (Wolin, 1983; Buck-Morss, 1989). He insisted that architecture, for instance, did not just exist in the mind of the beholder, but also as 'the most important evidence of latent "mythology"' (quoted in Frisby, 1985, p. 192). These objective meanings could not be grasped conceptually, through a process of intellectual analysis, but only by imaginary and dream processes. Understanding involved unlocking the hidden, obscured meanings by undermining – (shattering) – received accounts, placing fresh images and fragments together in a new combination to disclose their meaning. The resulting allegories (Sontag, 1978) offered insight into objective meanings which were otherwise obscured.

Much of Benjamin's work is therefore concerned with the complex relationship between individual and collective memories, objective meanings and the forms of cognition – mythologies, ideas, symbols – which cloud true knowledge. The interface between individual experience and cultural traditions is at the heart of Benjamin's concerns, and whilst recognising that every city is unique, he also provided insights into the peculiar nature of urban interpretation, in relation to other forms of artistic appreciation. Thereby he delineated some central forces constructing urban culture. Benjamin's intention was to recognise that objective meanings can be located in cultural forms, but also that people interpret these cultural artefacts themselves. But how does this translate into method? The key concept is that of 'aura'. Aura concerns the relationship between an art work and tradition. For Benjamin, before works of art could be mechanically reproduced – through printing, photography, recording, and so on – each piece was uniquely located in time and space, and hence retained a distinctiveness and distance from the viewer. Once art works are mechanically reproduced, however, they lose this specificity and perceptions of them change.

> The uniqueness of a work of art is inseparable from its being embedded in the fabric of tradition. The tradition is alive and extremely changeable ... the existence of the work of art with reference to its aura is never entirely separated from its ritual function ... in the age of mechanical reproduction ... for the first time in world history, mechanical reproduction emancipates the work of art from its parasitical dependence on ritual. (Benjamin, 1973, pp. 225–6)

The rise of mechanically reproduced art released it from a specific tradition and allowed it to be deployed in other, more political ways. This both liberates and weakens it. Liberation comes from expanding the uses of art, and from its use in non-traditional ways. But by removing the art work from its own specific tradition it is deprived of its context and unique meaning. Benjamin was fascinated by the way that cities were simultaneously auratic and not auratic. Benjamin regarded film as the archetype of mechanically reproduced art, but literature (mass production of books, etc.) and painting (prints) are also susceptible. The city, by contrast, cannot be mechanically reproduced. Specific buildings might be copied but entire cities cannot: London is London, Paris is Paris. While people might claim some knowledge of most art-forms without having seen an original, it would be inconceivable in respect of cities. It would be curious if someone described Istanbul (for instance) as an attractive city without ever having been there. The uniqueness of cities in space marks them out from other art-forms, and gives them distinctive qualities vis-à-vis each other. Yet in another way cities lack aura. Their location within specific traditions is tenuous. Cities have spatial, but not temporal distinctiveness. Whilst virtually all other art forms were composed at a specific moment in history, and hence can be located within a tradition, cities are generally the product of centuries of construction and deconstruction, as new buildings turn to ruins. Their buildings originate in different historical periods, and exhibit many styles. They are frequently marked by evidence of sharp ruptures as was the case in Paris with Haussmann's reconstruction in the 1870s, and in the redevelopment of Vienna in the same period. Rather than being related to an external tradition, cities are their own tradition: that is to say, the specific historical mixture of styles, forms and functions characterising a city defines its own distinctive tradition. Cities therefore have specific textual properties compared with other forms of art. Spatially unique and unreproducible, they range across time, each with its own aura.

Benjamin saw this distinctive aspect of urban landscape as having certain qualities in relation to other cultural forms. Benjamin was concerned with the potential of different forms of art to challenge received traditional views of history which propagated a conservative view of social evolution. He saw history, and historical knowledge, as fundamentally conservative, a celebration of the victors in battles between oppressors and oppressed. 'There is no document of civilisation which is not at the same a document of barbarism; barbarism taints also the manner in which it was transmitted from one owner to another' (Benjamin, 1973, p. 258). This is because only cultural artefacts used and developed by the historically successful are preserved. To give one example, the city of Troy, for instance was virtually reduced to rubble by the Greeks, and hardly a trace survives, whilst there are extensive ruins of most classical Greek cities. In a similar way architectural styles which grow out of fashion may be pulled down, but those which endure do so because they are preferred by powerful groups. Because of the complicity between enduring cultural artefacts and the powerful, to reveal the possibility of political change in the present necessitated the disruption of orthodox historical knowledge so as to expose the perpetual possibility of social change. This notion fascinated Benjamin. Even dismantled buildings may leave traces, and frequently buildings lie derelict after being abandoned. By exploring the ruins of the urban landscape, as much as the celebrated urban centres, it is possible to reveal the range of possibilities which existed in other periods, and to disclose the dreams and hopes implicit in now neglected urban forms. Hence, for Benjamin, exploring the city as a cultural form allows the force of tradition to be disrupted.

Disruption of the urban text was also facilitated by another feature of artistic perception. Benjamin argued that art can be absorbed either through concentration or distraction (Benjamin, 1973, pp. 240ff). Buildings are usually perceived in distraction:

> A man who concentrates before a work of art is absorbed by it … in contrast the distracted mass absorbs the work of art. This is most obvious in regard to buildings. Architecture has always represented the prototype of a work of art the reception of which is consummated by a collectivity in a state of distraction. (Benjamin, 1973, p. 241)

People usually perceive buildings in passing, on their way to other business – a marked contrast to engagement with paintings or literature. This 'distracted' perception of the urban form was a positive feature, since it, too, helped to disrupt conservative cultural traditions based upon concentrated perception of auratic art. Benjamin's 'Arcades project' (see Buck-Morss, 1989) explored the modes of experiencing urban landscapes, in the hope of recovering ways of experiencing buildings which might disrupt received cultural traditions and expedite social change. The site was nineteenth-century Paris. He elaborated the distracted nature of perception by focusing on social types with distinct ways of experiencing the urban. The most famous of these was the *flâneur*, or stroller, who wandered in an unsystematic way around the city, especially its shopping centres. The *flâneur* was 'above all, someone who does not feel comfortable in his own company' (Benjamin, 1969, p. 48), someone who sampled aspects of urban life in an unpremeditated and voyeuristic way. The distracted nature of urban perception allowed 'involuntary memory' to operate and the present to be incorporated into the past. Drawing upon Proust, Benjamin argued that in a state of distraction memories from the past could be ignited by a current event, so that the present and past united. This was not possible where perception was concentrated, for the attentive frame of mind ruled out the remembrance of involuntary thoughts.

Benjamin's ideas are complex and at times obscure. However, a number of general points emerge:

1. Because each city is unique in space it retains a degree of aura, and therefore the extent to which we can talk about urban culture in general is restricted. For Benjamin, each city has its own traditions and values, and the particularities of urban cultures are as important as any generic traits they may possess.
2. Urban culture is rooted not only in famous sites (the city centre, the monuments, the tourist attractions) but also in the 'interstices' of urban life – the run-down subway station, the children's playground, the shopping centre. Here people are most likely to perceive the city in distraction and conjure up the images which permit the appreciation of objective meaning.
3. The city is an interface between individual experience and cultural representation and, hence, the site where received cultural values can most easily be displayed, and therefore subverted. The urban experience is especially conducive to the shattering of cultural aura because it can happen as we go about our daily business.
4. Urban cultures are grasped not purely by cognitive or intellectual processes – in the way supposed by positivist geographers – but also through fantasy and dream processes.

6.3   Globalisation and urban meaning

We are now in a position to take stock and explore more fully debates about urban meaning and their relationship to globalisation. We have used the arguments of Walter Benjamin to suggest that it is possible to examine urban cultures without relying on a generic notion of urban culture, and without completely banishing urban sociology's traditional concerns with urban experience. Such a perspective allows urban sociologists to recognise the salience of urban specificity even amidst global change. This involves conceptualising the significance of globalisation as involving the transformation of place. As Morley (2000, p. 14) puts it, 'it is ... the transformation of localities, rather than the increase of physical mobility (significant though that might be for some groups) that the process of globalisation has its most important expression'. As Tomlinson (1999) says, the 'paradigmatic experience of global modernity for most people ... is that of staying in one place but experiencing the "displacement" that global modernity brings them'. This indicates the salience of what Augé (1997) calls 'non-places', functional sites from which the mobility of people and commodities takes place: airports, shopping malls, motorway intersections, and the like. Indeed, it is this bland architecture of uniformity and functionality rather than the glamorous post-modern architecture of corporate office blocks and prestigious development, that have been striking in the past two decades.

David Harvey, for instance, sees the development of these sites as the by-product of the condition of post-modernity, made possible by the 'time-space compression' of contemporary global capitalism (see Chapter 3). For Harvey (1987), the most important development brought about under conditions of flexible accumulation is the growing ease of spatial mobility of people and artefacts. In this situation the condition of post-modernity is largely concerned with the development of a new 'placeless' urban environment. Harvey's argument is elaborated by his analysis of 'new urban spaces'. These are the characteristic sites of urban development in the 1980s and 1990s. The out-of-town hypermarket, the shopping mall, and the motorway network have gained new prominence in urban living, appearing to herald a new 'placeless' city. Once inside a shopping mall, or on a motorway interchange, one could be almost anywhere in the world; links to others parts of the urban fabric seem tangential and haphazard.

Shopping malls are particularly interesting examples. Most widespread in North America where they have largely eclipsed central shopping venues, but also found throughout Europe, they offer a self-contained, roofed and enclosed environment in which shoppers move off the city streets and enter an environment geared exclusively to the selling of products. In some malls, such as one of the world's largest at West Edmonton in Canada (Shields, 1989), references to other countries and cities are made inside the mall itself, so that the visitor is wrenched even further away from the culture of the specific city in which it is located, into a new, imaginary realm.

Shopping malls are only one instance of emerging interchangeable urban spaces divorced from local context. Similar architectural styles – based on the manipulation of concrete and glass – are used in most cities. Many British and North American cities sport 'waterfront' developments, in which leisure facilities and middle-class housing – sometimes in the form of warehouse conversions, sometimes newly built – intermingle. Where high streets continue to flourish, each contains branches of the same major retailers. Private housing estates on the outskirts of large conurbations seem indistinguishable from one another, as do motorway systems.

These new urban spaces have been seen as distinctive, not simply in terms of their architecture, but also in terms of the cultural values they embody. Perhaps the most important of these are concerned with the redefinition of social boundaries, such as the clouding of the distinction between inside and outside. Frederic Jameson (1984, 1991) claims that post-modern architecture has a number of distinct features: 'the strange new feeling of an absence of inside and outside, the bewilderment and loss of spatial orientation in Portman's hotels, the messiness of an environment in which things and people no longer find their place' (Jameson, 1991, pp. 117–18). Shields makes a similar point, that 'post-modern spatialisation' means that

boundaries may be becoming more than lines defining the enclosed from the unenclosed, the ordered from the unordered, the known from the unknown. Boundaries have marked the limit where absence becomes presence. But such boundaries appear to be dissolving. They appear less as impermeable barricades and more as thresholds, limen across which communication takes place and where things of different categories – local and distant, native and foreign, and so on – interact. (Shields, 1992, p. 195)

This is rather similar to Latour's idea of the 'immutable mobile', the need for certain centres in networks to be able to be of a kind that are transposable with those elsewhere: hence they can be circulated. Yet the extent to which there has been such a dramatic change in the nature of urban boundaries is questionable. For although some areas may have lost a clear boundary between the inside and outside, others have gained it. This is indicated by increasing securitisation of urban space, with the rise of walled communities (Castells, 1997a; Davis, 1992), and urban zoning. We might be better off thinking that cities have always had mobile spaces (train stations, markets, etc.), and that we are only witnessing the reworking of urban space in rather different economic and social conditions. Many examples of new built forms in which boundaries are blurred are in fact high status developments, built for wealthy individuals or corporate clients. Perhaps behind these new forms is the tendency for an ostentatious display of wealth, partly in order for it to function as cultural capital. This is the line of argument taken by Mike Davis (1985) who sees post-modernism as the architectural product of a laissez-faire political regime. In this context Shields's argument that 'presence and proximity is no longer an indicator of inside status, of citizenship, of cultural membership' (Shields, 1992, p. 195) seems erroneous. As we saw in Chapter 4, there is very little evidence that social segregation is in decline, and the rise of gentrification appears to mark the rezoning of cities to accommodate specific groups defined both by gender and by class.

Benjamin saw the precursors of today's shopping malls – the Paris Arcades – as an allegory for the modern city. The shopping mall can simply be seen as their development. Equally, Benjamin recognised that the experience of being lost in vast and complex urban space characterised our perception of the modern city. Paris, for Benjamin, 'was a maze not only of paths but also of tunnels. I cannot think of the underworld of the Metro and the north-south line opening their hundreds of shafts all over the city without recalling my endless flâneries' (Benjamin, 1978; p. 299; see also Frisby, 1985). In this line of thought the shopping mall is simply the last in a long line of tunnels, which need to be reconnected, by the wanderer, back into the urban landscape. If the shopping mall appears new and placeless today, this is because it has not yet been integrated back into its surrounding urban fabric, either by wear and tear, by feats of imagination, or by reputation. Urban-dwellers of the nineteenth century regarded innovations such as the subway as heralding a new, placeless realm. Today these have been moulded into their contextual environments. We should therefore be cautious about assuming that the shopping mall has revolutionised urban culture.

Sharon Zukin (1992) attempts another way of formulating the distinctive meaning of post-modern cities. She has identified two types of post-modern spaces: gentrified areas and the new fantasy theme-parks such as Disneyland. She claims that these new developments mark a major break from older urban structures. In traditional and modern cities, landscape – the city spaces of the culturally and politically dominant – stands opposed to the vernacular – the spaces of the dispossessed and powerless. Zorbaugh's (1929) contrast between the Gold Coast and the slum is perhaps the perfect example. In the post-modern city, Zukin argues the distinction between landscape and vernacular breaks down. Gentrification implies the revaluation of formerly run-down areas of the city – the vernacular becomes part of the landscape.

More generally, Zukin depicts the post-modern city as increasingly commodified and as the site of consumption. This relates to a broader conception of the contemporary city developed by Harvey and others, which sees it as primarily the site for a new consumerism, in contrast to the modernist city – such as Chicago – which was primarily defined by its role in industrial production. The idea that post-modernism can be seen as the culture of consumerism has been developed by Frederic Jameson (1984) and echoed by Harvey (1989), Featherstone (1987), and many others. One way of developing this argument in relation to urban development is to apply it to the expansion of tourism. Tourism also has a long history, but it has grown markedly in recent years, and places are increasingly forced to sell themselves in order to attract trade (Urry, 1990a).

The significance of tourism in urban space can be interpreted through Benjamin's arguments about the distinctive nature of 'aura'. As art forms become increasingly mechanically reproduced, so people search out those auratic objects that remain. Although some forms of tourism offer resorts that are 'placeless', in that their beaches, pools, bars and shops could be anywhere, other forms of tourism invite people to visit distinctive and unique urban sites. Although in order to attract tourists these unique cities develop the touristic infrastructure of chain hotels, fast-food chains and the like, it would be wrong to assume that aura can ever be fully eradicated. After all, Benjamin argued in his reflections on the Paris Arcades that the commodity was the clue to the lost dream-worlds of the inhabitants of the modern city. Berman likewise maintained that the experience of modernity suffused the shopping streets of the Nevsky Prospect. Similarly, while tourism has expanded massively in scope, it seems in many ways simply to represent the extension of the flâneur's role which Benjamin again saw as symptomatic of modernity (see Urry, 1990a). As Buck-Morss (1989, p. 344) writes, 'the Utopian moment of flânerie was fleeting. But if the flâneur disappeared as a specific figure, the perceptive attitude that he embodied saturates modern existence, specifically the society of mass consumption.' Hence, even contemporary global cities demonstrate continuity with modern cities.

Notwithstanding the major interest in new forms of urban development, whether high-prestige office-blocks, shopping malls, warehouse conversions or whatever, many older parts of the urban fabric remain – and decay. Benjamin laid particular stress on the importance of these sites of dereliction and his lead has been taken up by a number of cultural critics who search for meaning amongst the rubbish. The foremost of these is Patrick Wright (1991), who has shown how it is possible to read contemporary social change through the scrutiny of our urban ruins.

In general, then, globalisation tends to accentuate rather than undermine urban distinctiveness. Our position is close to that developed by Giddens who argues for the persistence of modernity. In *A Contemporary Critique of Historical Materialism* Giddens used an analysis of the changing role of the city to understand everyday life. He observed that 'life is not experienced as "structures", but as the durée of day-to-day existence ... the continuity of daily life is not a "directly motivated" phenomenon, but assured in the routinisation of practices' (Giddens, 1981, p. 150). He then argued that tradition loses its capacity to routinise practices for three reasons: the commodification of labour; the 'transformation of the "time-space paths" of the day' (ibid., p. 153); and the commodification of urban land which results in 'created space', the manufactured environments of the modern world. In such societies, the routinisation of day-to-day practice is no longer bound by tradition and is therefore not strongly normatively embedded: 'the moral bindingness of traditionally established practices is replaced by one geared extensively to habit against a background of economic constraint' (ibid., p. 154). The modern condition of personal anxiety and insecurity emerges from a deficit of legitimacy which appears as normative uncertainty. This condition emanates from the normative disembedding of the routine practices rather than from control over labour, reification or material aspects of commodification. For Giddens, cities are not fundamentally the products of capitalist economic forces, but rather those of a search for meaning.

In Giddens's more recent work (1990, 1991), these themes recur as central to his understanding of modernity. The existential and social problems of the age are concerned with developing sufficient trust in others to allay the fears inspired by the ever-present risks of life in an uncertain world. Thus he explores the dynamics of personal intimate relationships and addresses the risks posed by nuclear war and ecological catastrophe. He argues, nevertheless, that the present is better grasped as high modernity rather than as post-modernity. There is no abrupt transformation. The tribulations of the 1990s represent perhaps an intensification of the paradox of modernity but no qualitative break.

6.4   Conclusion

In this chapter we have emphasised the persistence of urban distinctiveness and urban meaning. In developing this argument, we have considered the views of social constructionists who wish to remove the 'human' aspect of urban meaning, but our preference is for a version of Benjamin's complex, agonistic account of urban experience. Benjamin's formulation of the way that personal experience and dominant meanings grate upon one another provides an axis for the appreciation of the role of the symbolic in urban social conflict.

Observing the diversity and plurality of images of place reminds us that imagery is created and can be manipulated. Many actors, from estate agents to local authorities, have vested interests in presenting places in their most favourable light. Increasingly, local authorities try to present their own area as appealing, sometimes to tourists, sometimes to affluent households. If people generally can be persuaded to think a neighbourhood 'good', an old town 'historic', or a downtown 'exciting', then a place may attract residents who can pay higher local taxes, new commercial opportunities may arise, and additional jobs may be generated. A reputation for distinctiveness and quality is beneficial. The economic strategies of the local state represent the reassertion of the dull compulsion of economic life even in the sphere of memory and the imaginary. Indeed, in the urban manifestations of the consumer culture may be discerned the coincidence of the relentless impulse of capital accumulation and many of the dreams and aspirations of personal life.

As Lefebvre appreciated, urban meaning is a political instrument. The next chapter indicates many of the ways in which contemporary urban politics is infused with the presentation and representation of people's sense of place. For Castells, as also for Lefebvre, urban meaning may be contested politically by the oppressed who seek to define 'belonging' in particular ways. For other citizens, identification with place or region may be becoming a more significant element in their political calculations. For urban élites, the management of image has become a vital aspect of economic policy and political success.

7 Urban Politics

Sub-national political authorities with territorial jurisdiction are ubiquitous in Western societies, though their forms vary considerably. Urban politics has traditionally referred both to what local state agencies do and to the external, mobilised social groups, which try to influence their policies. More recent theoretical development in the study of urban politics has turned to studying its role in light of on-going debates over globalisation. Local states make decisions that affect life in cities; and at the same time, sections of the populations of those cities, through their attempts at influencing local government, in elections, movements and campaigns, reciprocally affect the state and its policies. Often it is difficult to disentangle clearly the effect of local, regional, national and global, agencies. Understanding politics has always been an essential aspect of a satisfactory urban sociology. Under the contemporary era of global state restructuring, this centrality is perhaps even more important to stress, particularly as it shapes the lives of citizens.

Urban and regional politics continue to change rapidly, and urban sociology has responded through reconsidering its analysis in the light of new economic and political practices. In the UK, from the Second World War to the 1970s most political forces worked within a 'social democratic consensus', which supported extensive national state welfare services and economic-planning agreements. The rise of the 'New Right' from the mid-1970s challenged assumptions of the benevolence of the welfare state and campaigned for the replacement of state involvement by market provision wherever possible. This was probably the most far-reaching political controversy of the era. It caused intense debate within urban sociology over the relative benefits of 'states versus markets': socialists defended the achievements of the welfare state, while sympathisers with the New Right position avowed that privatisation of services and a popular capitalism, whose emblem was home-ownership, offered real individual empowerment. The 1990s witnessed a convergence across the Western world in political thought amongst elected officials, around what became termed the 'third way' (Giddens, 1998), although there was less agreement of what it meant *in practice*. The involvement of the market in the provision of, and delivery of, services became an accepted part of political life, a new political orthodoxy. The 1980s and 1990s also witnessed a second bitter dispute, between central government and local authorities about their respective powers and jurisdictions. The increasing role assigned for the market in central government policy and the creation of new local and regional institutions had a number of ramifications for everyday political life. These included the nature of democratic accountability, the proper powers of local government and the capacity to which local politics could arouse the interest of citizens in local affairs in a world where most important economic and political decisions were taken at the national or increasingly the international level.

Over the past 20 years urban political analysis, and the conceptualisation of local political practice, developed in a rather mechanical way, mostly trying to isolate the functions or purposes of local governance. Four different views of the local state can be distinguished:

- as provider of welfare;
- as regulator of the local economy;
- as intermediary in the formation of collective identity;
- as coercive agent of social order and discipline.

This chapter is organised as a review of the literature and issues occasioned by each of these approaches. We seek to argue that these might be better integrated if considered not as alternative theoretical accounts, but as the systematic and unintended outcomes of contradictions inherent in on-going capitalist economic arrangements and the condition of modernity. Each of the four theses about the local state contains internal tensions that produce political dilemmas that have themselves then to be managed. The welfare and economic interventionist roles of the local state arise from problems of managing capitalist development; those of identity and order are more matters of dealing with the consequences of modernity. The contrary demands, imposed upon local states by the operations of these conflicting roles, produce permanent fluctuations in the nature of political problems and what might be appropriate solutions. In many respects, solving one set of problems makes another set worse, what Offe (1982) refers to as the 'crisis of crisis management'. For instance, the fiscal crises of states, national and local, since the 1970s, emanate from the contradictory requirements of reconciling policies for economic growth with those for social maintenance.

Most Western governments in the 1980s and the 1990s sought to reduce public expenditure, particularly on social welfare. Demand for services was said to be inexhaustible – no matter what level of service was provided, organised groups of potential beneficiaries would campaign for improvement and extension. The effect was 'overload', the incapacity of state revenues to meet escalating demand. Moreover, it was argued, funds made available for welfare diminished expenditure directed to productive economic activity, hampering the economic growth that eventually had to finance social services. In the late 1990s the logic of welfare provision changed quite fundamentally. Quasi-markets were introduced into the state apparatus, in order to reduce costs and to increase the efficiency of service provision. Indicative of this new way of thinking about welfare delivery is welfare to work: borrowed loosely from the US workfare model of dealing with the unemployment, this system requires the unemployed to perform work for their benefits. Yet as many authors continue to argue, welfare provision is essential to societal reproduction, both for humanitarian reasons tied up with the legitimacy of Western societies and in order to educate and maintain the health and efficiency of the labour force (see O'Connor, 1973; Offe, 1982). Welfare provision, even in its current contested form, contains contradictions.

Economic management itself also contains specific tensions. Capitalist states are obliged to encourage the operation of markets and the investment of capital in specific locations. Yet, being part of a world system, investment is increasingly switched from one country to another; totally free markets pose problems for national governments since essential new investment may be lost abroad. At the same time mobile capital can be attracted by inducements and subsidies, whether by direct grants, efficient cheap urban infrastructure, a highly skilled and educated labour force or sophisticated efforts to market the locality. Inducements require state intervention, however, which entails raising revenue through taxation and, in important ways, interfering with market mechanisms. The logic of this process is contradictory: the state must preserve and facilitate market mechanisms, but must supplement market mechanisms by offering subsidised provision. This dilemma occurs in many spheres.

Capitalism has profound social implications. It structures work experience, forms of industrial organisation, it leads to uneven development and above all it causes an unequal distribution of rewards and privileges. However, it is neither intrinsically orderly nor disorderly. Certainly, the capitalist economy is highly dynamic, pushed on by competition between firms and conflicts between social classes with antagonistic interests in the process. But as corporatist and social democratic forms of the state have shown, and contra the neo-liberal variant, these matters can be handled in a highly orderly way. Other capitalist regimes exhibit, by contrast, more markedly unruly, lawless and disorderly social relations. By the same token, the condition of modernity is not necessarily or inherently one that produces divisive inequalities. It is, as recent authors propose, a world of individual competition, a condition in which people are compelled to assert their individuality, exercise personal autonomy and in the process create their own selves (see Bauman, 1988, 1998, 2000; Giddens, 1991; Beck, 1992; Christopherson, 1994). These activities of the presentation of self entail only that people construct themselves as different; it does not necessarily follow that differences are hierarchical, that some have more prestige or power than others. That this is usually the case is a function of the fact that people enter this process with unequal resources. Difference gives way to distinction. The dilemma specific to the condition of modernity arises from the paradoxical nature of its dominant mode of experience.

Modernity is double-edged. It displays a paradox of self-development, where the potential for change is both welcomed as exciting and shunned as threatening. It promises much – fun, novelty, stimulation, improvement; but change may be for the worse, implying risk and anxiety. Modernity leads to desire for both freedom and security, but these are also mutually exclusive. Savage (1987a) argued that much political campaigning of the twentieth century was concerned with reducing insecurity, typically through entitlements to multifarious welfare provision. However, at the end of the twentieth century and the beginning of the twenty-first, political emphasis switched to unburdening the individual, to empowering them in everyday life and at work, reinforcing the point that what for one generation was security for another becomes burdensome and compromises personal autonomy. There is again a dilemma for the state that whether it gives priority to security or enterprise will disturb many of its citizens. If anything, the 1990s saw the mainstream political parties continuing to walk the empowerment-insecurity tightrope.

Modernity is intrinsically disorderly because it obliges individuals to experiment, to hope, to gamble and to be ambitious. Its social life lacks the predictability and the certainties that characterise societies governed by tradition. Individual creativity is exchanged for the security of calculable social obligations and the sense of belonging that emanate from fixed social bonds. Recent accounts of the paradoxes of modernity have concentrated unduly on individual self-identity to the neglect of understanding the foundations of collective identity in the contemporary world: for while individual and collective identities are practically inseparable, analytic attention has been devoted to how individuals create 'a self' (e.g. Giddens, 1991). This is not helpful in understanding political behaviour because political agendas and effective political mobilisation are conditional upon collective action. Political demands are presented as the concerns of social categories – citizens, businesses, local ratepayers, conservationists. Individuals *per se* do not make claims. Yet modernity renders collective identity problematic: indeed it corrodes collective identities to the same degree that it enhances individual choice. Attaching people to a collectivity, organising them, becomes a key political task. The labour movement exemplified this at one time by organising people around class identity, thus providing a sense of belonging that was supported by an ethic of cooperation and a programme of enhanced collective security. It provided a basis for orderly belonging and hope in a world of individual anxieties.

Governments in recent years have tried to influence the formation and organisation of collectivities of citizens – whether based on characteristics like class, ethnicity and gender, or on campaigns over single issues. On the one hand, it is desirable to reduce the effectiveness of these groups for they are sources of claims for resources, rights and services – one cause of 'overload'. There are thus reasons for seeking to disorganise such people, to fragment and individualise the social body. Yet such disorganisation also has negative consequences, causing apathy and disaffection with political processes and the sort of individualistic instrumentalism that is expressed as criminal behaviour. There is, hence, a need to encourage reorganisation in different collectivities, but again these cannot be prevented from formulating and expressing their joint interests and bringing pressure to bear on the state. Thus, for example, to the extent that class identities waned in the late 1980s, environmental, ethnic, sexual and local ones flourished.

One final politically relevant aspect of the condition of modernity is its effect upon those who fail to make a success of the opportunities it presents for self-development and autonomy. In many respects the categories of people who are presented as socially problematic – for instance, the homeless – are, from one point of view, just those who have been unable to benefit from a competitive personal freedom for self-growth, whether because of insufficient resources, ill-health, poor education or bad luck. Modernity, an ethic for restlessness and insecurity, itself produces disorderly failed selves. It also produces the disorganisation associated with the excluded – people who are not integrated into acceptable institutions or conventions of behaviour. For most of the time they are treated as problematic pathological individuals, called delinquent or deviant as they deploy the personal options offered by modernity in ways unacceptable to established authorities. However, in some circumstances the socially disconnected, who are almost always simultaneously the socially underprivileged, express resentment collectively, not in the organised ways of pressure groups but through sporadic, demonstrative, sometimes violent, protests. From this arises one further role for the state agencies – to control the dispossessed in the name of law and order.

This framework allows many of the debates concerning urban politics to be put into fresh perspective. Section 7.1 considers the changing form of state welfare provision through a brief reconsideration of the 'new urban sociology' of the 1970s (see Chapter 2).

This placed the question of the state at the forefront of urban sociology. It established the shifting emphasis from the apparent inevitability of state intervention in urban welfare services in the 1970s to arguments concerning new forms of privatised consumption that allow some social groups to by-pass public provision. Many of the more general contradictions in the way the state deals with the tensions of capitalism and modernity are revealed through this debate.

Section 7.2 considers how the local state affects economic development and urban economic fortunes. We explore first the emergence of the 'new urban politics' of the 1980s, with its emphasis on competitiveness between places and on growth, and then set out the 'entrepreneurial city' approach, which seeks to capture the increasingly innovative discourses and practices of the local state. We show how the global scope of capitalism has forced political agents to develop increasingly sophisticated strategies for attracting inward investment, which have wider implications.

Section 7.3 examines place, political identification and urban participation. We examine the formation of identity through an attachment to place, and the growth in the last two decades of the different ways individual citizens define themselves. Fincher and Jacobs (1998) talk of 'cities of difference' to capture the many factors that lie behind how individuals identify themselves in the contemporary city. The section begins by examining the methods of formal representation and the geographies of voting. It then moves on to examine local political cultures and the range of factors that shape how and why individuals involve themselves in formal politics. The second half of the section explores the role of the local state in the regulation of law and order. The losers in the distributive stakes in urban conflicts, the unemployed, the homeless, the poor, the drifters – precisely the same social groups with which sociologists in the early twentieth century were concerned – also pose issues of political management. In part they were people whom Castells thought would join urban social movements – squatters, disgruntled tenants, people oppressed by the conditions of congested cities. But often discontent appeared in more rudimentary outbursts of disobedience or riots. The 1990s saw a series of 'local' uprisings, whether poor people's movements, environmentalist protest or concerted class- or gender-based movements. Often these discrete examples of mobilisation are

linked across space through common causes, as in the May Day
demonstrations in Berlin, London and Sydney that attract the attention of the global media. All are activities by means of which
citizens try to bring pressure to bear on the state and government
in order to improve the quality of their lives.

7.1   States, markets, welfare and workfare

7.1.1   Collective consumption

Classic works of the Chicago School, investigating the world of
the transient urban poor, saw cities as a maelstrom of social disorder. The Chicagoans themselves were involved in local reform
politics devoted to expanding state support to remedy the problems they diagnosed. In succeeding years, not only in the USA
but also throughout the developed capitalist world, an increasing
range of state welfare provision began to be directed at the urban
population. Public housing, state educational and health agencies,
planning and zoning controls, and public leisure facilities appeared to transform the urban landscape into one regulated by
state welfare provision.

It was thus unsurprising that when urban sociologists in the
1960s and 1970s turned to the city they were increasingly struck
not by the chaotic urban life dissected by Simmel and the
Chicagoans, but the planned, regimented and controlled life apparently ushered in by the welfare state. British urban sociologists
following Rex and Moore (1967) developed an approach sometimes termed 'urban managerialism' which argued that 'gatekeepers' – key managers in bureaucratic institutions – played a vital
role in distributing resources to different groups within the city.
Rex and Moore (1967) emphasised the way that housing managers, housing visitors, planners, building-society managers and
the like could affect people's lives. One example concerns the
way in which building-society managers could 'red-line' an area;
by deciding that a particular part of a city was disreputable and
hence a bad financial risk, they could refuse to give mortgages on
property in it. As a result these areas were starved of new investment and fell into greater decay, so realising a self-fulfilling
prophecy.

Urban managerialism was much debated in the 1970s (see Saunders, 1986), and seemed to offer a new way of seeing the city as the product of bureaucratic action. Increasingly, however, this interest dissolved into an obscure debate about whether urban gatekeepers had real autonomy in their decision-making or whether their actions were the inevitable product of the bureaucratic structures in which they worked. Ultimately it was the new urban sociology developed initially within French Marxism in the 1970s that took up some of the useful emphases of urban managerialism in a more rigorous way. The new urban sociology may be seen as a theoretical reflection on the significance of state welfare provision both for capitalism as a system and also for urban politics and conflict. Its importance lies not so much in its specific ideas and arguments, most of which have now been undermined, as in its role in developing a concern with the role of the state and market in organising processes of consumption. If anything, these ideas have gained in intellectual purchase in the 1990s, if not in urban sociology then certainly in cognate disciplines such as urban and economic geography.

The key book of the 'new urban sociology' was *The Urban Question*, which was written by Manuel Castells and was published in English in 1977. It was a critique of older urban sociology *and* an attempt to reformulate urban sociology around the issue of state welfare provision. Castells maintained that the distinctive social function of the city in late capitalism was as the principal site for the reproduction of labour power. Cities had become central to processes of 'collective consumption' rather than production or exchange (in the way Harvey might argue, for instance). Castells's two most distinctive concepts were reproduction of labour power and collective consumption.

The idea of the reproduction of labour power pointed to the fact that capitalism does not simply rely on physical resources, but also depends upon the existence of a healthy labour force, able to work effectively in order to produce commodities for their employers. Hence, capitalism can only survive if the labour force can be reproduced – clothed, kept healthy, educated, and such like. Castells's argument was that the reproduction of labour power depended upon state intervention, since in many areas it is not profitable for capitalists themselves to provide the welfare services necessary for the reproduction of labour. Thus the state organises and subsidises housing and transport, it runs a health service, and it provides a huge complex of educational, training and research facilities. In general these services play a vital role in the maintenance of the existing workforce and the creation of the next generation of healthy, skilled and socialised workers. In this way, the state guarantees certain essential functions for the continuance of effective capital accumulation.

Castells claimed that the fundamental characteristic of the city was that it was the spatial unit within which collective consumption was organised in monopoly capitalism. He suggested that the city is the most efficient and convenient form of collective consumption since the concentration of the population around centrally located services minimises the costs of reproducing labour power. For Castells this process was the basic cause of spatial form in the contemporary city. It was not the only function of the city, but the distinctive current one. Castells argued that the spatial form of the capitalist city depends upon the period in which it develops.

Castells went on from his analysis of collective consumption to a discussion of the way that it led to urban contradictions, primarily that of fiscal crisis, and 'urban social movements'. As the state pays for the services that the private sector will not touch because they are unprofitable, so it is forced to raise revenues to finance them. There are, however, limits to how much can be raised through taxation without causing popular unrest or undermining the profitability of capitalist firms, and there are also limits to how much financial institutions are prepared to lend. As a result the state faces constant pressures to cut back spending. As it does so it runs the risk of raising opposition from the urban dwellers who rely on state-organised welfare provision, and this can lead to 'urban social movements', as they band together to campaign for improvements in public services.

Thus, Castells offered a rudimentary (and here much simplified) account of the role of the city in contemporary capitalist society. He identified a major function, the organisation of collective consumption; he showed that it related to industrial production and the accumulation of capital but that the city is now less important in this respect than before; and he suggested that this gave rise to urban problems and to resistance from urban movements. In short, Castells proffered a theoretical account of contemporary urban change.

Despite his research triggering a series of studies on the significance of public welfare in cities (Dickens *et al.*, 1985; Pinch, 1985; Lowe, 1986), Castells's general framework has been heavily criticised. Orthodox Marxists, like Lojkine (1976), argued that Castells underestimated the continuing importance of the city to the process of production, an objection that also underlines the work of other Marxists emphasising the continuing centrality of production processes, such as David Harvey or Doreen Massey. A further critique came from feminist scholars who objected because the concept of the reproduction of labour power tends to confuse biological, physical and social reproduction. More pertinently, it also tends to explain the practices involved in reproduction solely in terms of the logic of capital, hence ignoring gender inequalities inherent in the ways reproduction of labour power is socially organised. Castells's notion of collective consumption is contrasted to individual consumption assumed to be based on buying services on the market, whereas in fact the domestic arena is a third, highly important, way of obtaining services which is completely neglected in this schema.

Finally, the implications for city politics were also criticised. Castells equivocated about the relationship between urban social movements and the labour movement (Castells, 1978, ch. 8). In his writings in the 1970s he clearly expected urban movements (squatters, tenants' groups, opposition to planning proposals for urban renewal and new roads, demands for better urban services, etc.) to succeed in transforming the political system, but only in association with labour movements based on old-established social classes. In particular, as a supporter, he thought that the Communist Party needed to play a leading role if urban social movements were to succeed. He envisaged some sort of alliance between urban movements, trade unions and left-wing parties because he believed that the urban movements could not succeed alone.

But perhaps the major problem with Castells's analysis is that it seems no longer applicable in an age when the social democratic consensus has all but disappeared. There is a dated ring about arguments concerning the inevitability of state welfare and their functional value for capitalism following a decade of major restructuring and considerable diminution of welfare provision, both in Britain and the USA. Castells did not appreciate sufficiently the contradictory nature of state intervention. He assumed that people have a vested interest in always struggling for more state services, when in fact they might prefer to obtain services in other ways. People might also prefer to trade off security against personal excitement.

7.1.2   *From collectivised to privatised consumption*

If Castells's work was an attempt to theorise urban politics from the perspective of the significance of state welfare, that of Peter Saunders approached the subject via privatised consumption. What Castells was to the 1970s, Peter Saunders was to the 1980s. The rise of 'popular' capitalism, the growth of home-ownership, privatisation, the expansion of market provision of services, the decline of planning and so forth were the pressing issues on the contemporary political agenda raised forcefully by Saunders in his contributions to the analysis of urban politics.

The progress of Saunders's work reflects how the agenda for urban politics changed during the 1980s. More influential in Britain than elsewhere, since his empirical research and the political issues he addresses arise immediately from British experience, his importance derives partly from his willingness to reject central assumptions of British sociology. His early research on Croydon (Saunders, 1979) was primarily an attempt to refine Castells and to explore the local politics of consumption, but he was already concerned with home-ownership. His essay, 'Beyond Housing Classes' (Saunders, 1984), advanced the claim that home owner- ship brought about far-reaching social change, offering a powerful critique of prevailing social-democratic assumptions about housing. In subsequent years he has become more absorbed by the politics of the New Right and expressed increasingly critical views of the dominant liberal and left standpoints of British soci- ology about social justice, equality and citizenship. This has sometimes led to his incorporating reactionary themes about the biological basis of human behaviour, and on many other occa- sions it has produced defiant defences of the market mechanism against state planning. His critiques have usually been framed as a repudiation of Marxism and Marxist influences: thus in *A Nation of Home Owners* (Saunders, 1990) theoretical preambles and chapter summaries are almost always framed as refutations of Marxist scholarship, though the actual contents of the chapters are much more nuanced. He thus offered a glimpse of an intelligent sociology written from a free-market liberal perspective.

While Castells had very little to say about services not provided by the state, Saunders insisted that privatised consumption was of increasing social importance, and – contra Castells – that there is no inevitability about the state provision of services. Saunders maintained that there is a new division between those people who can afford to purchase their own services individually, on the market, and those who are forced to rely on state welfare. This new division, or 'cleavage', tends to lead to the decline of social class and its replacement by consumption-based divisions as the main axis of political conflict.

For Saunders, analysis of urban inequality is particularly bound up with the social and political importance of owner-occupation, with access to housing unable to be linked in any simple way to social class or other economic divisions. He maintained that owner-occupation is a superior tenure to public (and private) renting. It allows money to be made through capital gains, it gives greater control to its owners, and provides greater psychological security: it allows the 'expression of personal identity and [is] a source of ontological security' (Saunders, 1984, p. 203). Furthermore, Saunders postulated that we increasingly derive our satisfaction not from work, but from consuming goods and services, so that our enjoyment of housing is of major significance. He therefore sees the increase in owner-occupation in Britain as having almost revolutionary implications, allowing the majority of the population to gain a 'stake in the country'. Certainly owner-occupation in Britain has expanded rapidly. The number of council houses has reduced sharply in Britain, as councils first sold off their stock and then entered into ever-more elaborate partnerships with the private sector to provide new housing. While levels of owner-occupation in Britain are now almost as high as those of USA, Canada and Australia, and are significantly higher than in many European countries, what is less clear is whether this process has the widespread social and political implications claimed by Saunders.

Saunders suggested that divisions in housing relate to the development of a wider 'cleavage' between those reliant on public provision and those who enjoy private provision. People

Table 7.1 Privatised and collectivised modes of consumption

Mode	Privatised	Collectivised
Property rights	Ownership	Non-ownership
Access	Purchased	Allocated
Control	Consumer	Bureaucratic
Sector	Market	State
Quality/satisfaction	Good	Poor

Source: A. Warde, 'Production, Consumption and Social Change', *International Journal of Urban and Regional Research*, 14, 2 (1990).

consume in two broadly different ways: some use 'privatised' modes, others 'collectivised' ones. There is in Saunders's work an implicit ideal-typical opposition between these two modes that looks something like Table 7.1.

This schema is deemed applicable to other consumption practices besides housing, such as health care, education, transport, and so forth. Privatised consumption involves consumers purchasing what they choose through the market and this generally provides a good service. Collectivised consumption denies people ownership, and they become clients of the state, receiving bureaucratically allocated, poor-quality services. This is the basis of consumption-sector cleavages. As collectivised services become fewer, and poorer people make most use of them, they will deteriorate further in quality.

Saunders's work has proved highly controversial (see Harloe, 1984; Burrows and Butler, 1989; Hamnett, 1989; Warde, 1990, for critiques). There are a number of initially attractive features of his account. First, he correctly challenged the assumption that there is no alternative to direct state provision of services and registered the importance of private service provision. Second, his propositions appear to gain credibility from developments in political alignments. There has been much discussion in Britain about class de-alignment, the idea that political division is less based around social class than in the 1950s and 1960s. This debate is immensely complex (see Crewe and Sarlvik, 1981; Heath *et al.,* 1985; Marshall *et al.,* 1988; Dunleavy, 1990, amongst others). The inability of the Labour Party to win office during the 1980s and early 1990s and the desertion of many skilled manual workers to the Conservatives – precisely the group who are likely to own their own homes and cars – seemed *prima facie* to support Saunders's contentions. Third, he also offered a rationale for explaining the strong anti-statist culture that the Conservative Party – and other right-wing political forces throughout the developed world – adumbrated in the 1980s and 1990s. However, what the New Right were rejecting was a particular form of state structure, as they set about replacing the Keynesian state with a neo-liberal state type.

Over the 1990s, it became clear that Saunders's analysis drew too much on the particular circumstances of the 1980s and did not necessarily apply more generally. Saunders's arguments relied on the one-off experience of deregulation of finance that was tied up with the globalisation of financial services. During the early 1990s a severe slump in the housing market led to increasing risk and insecurity for home-owners, and whilst the later 1990s saw significant house price increases, the extent of these was linked closely to the status and desirability of local areas. Saunders's own study of the privatisation of the water industry in the later 1980s (Saunders and Harris, 1994) showed that there was no clear relationship between privatisation and improved services to consumers. Indeed the rapidly increasing prices paid by consumers for services provided by privatised amenities became a matter of major public concern as the decade wore on. Research in the 1990s has emphasised that privatisation does not entail the reduction of state power or regulation (Feigenbaum *et al.*, 1999). Privatisation of state-owned industry also became important in the mid 1980s when many of the largest and potentially profitable companies, like British Telecom and British Gas, were sold. However, whilst the Conservative government reduced state involvement in some areas, its intervention increased in others. Rather than there being any move towards individualised consumption, it can instead be argued that the nature of collective consumption has changed, from it being provided predominantly by the state, to it being provided by a hybrid of state and the corporate sector. Monbiot's (2000) polemical analysis of *The Corporate Takeover of Britain* argues that the crucial development has been the increased role of the private sector in providing core services for consumers, in ways that ensure they can obtain a secure profit from the process.

Saunders's mistake, it can be argued, was that he read too much into the social and political implications of home-ownership. Yet housing is a distinctive commodity. It is not, in its form, mode of delivery or relation to human need, directly parallel with medical, educational or transport services – the other major means of consumption analysed. Individuals can buy entire houses but not entire hospitals or roads. Saunders conflates the control that people have when purchasing their houses with the control which people have when purchasing specific services on the market. But this is not a useful comparison. Indeed many people who are committed owner-occupiers strongly support the state provision of educational and medical facilities. Similarly, houses are distinctive, as Saunders has shown, in that they can be bought and sold at a profit, and he makes much of the money that people can accrue in this way. Leaving aside the question as to whether such gains are as widespread as Saunders suggests (see Chapter 4), it is important to recognise that few other artefacts, for instance motor cars, have this potential.

Ultimately, Saunders failed to develop a viable analysis of the way in which states and markets are related. He operated with a sharp distinction between state provision of services and provision by the market even while recognising that the state cannot currently be divorced from regulating the provision of services on the market. Owner-occupation, for instance, is crucially affected by state policies ranging from tax relief on mortgages, through planning controls, to inducements to buy council houses under 'Right to Buy' legislation. It is true that the dominant political rhetoric in the 1980s in Britain concerned 'rolling back the frontiers of the state' and 'releasing market forces'. In the early years with Margaret Thatcher as Prime Minister strategic emphasis was on cutting state expenditure, particularly on welfare services. The selling of council houses was one of the most prominent policies.

Thus, as with Castells in the 1970s, perhaps the ideas of Saunders are products of the experiences of one decade. Many of the trends that fascinate Saunders – house price inflation, the decline of the Labour Party, and privatisation – are probably unrepeatable. While Saunders diagnosed well some of the problems in the state provision of services, he should not have assumed that the market provision of services is without contradiction. Indeed, according to his argument, it was the problems of market provision of services that initially led to the rise of the welfare state earlier in the twentieth century! The uneasy balance between market freedom and state regulation is an inherent feature of capitalist societies, not amenable to any permanent resolution.

7.2 Local states and economic development

Castells saw urban politics as the structurally determined politics of collective consumption. We showed in section 7.1 that the main flaw of this was to generalise a theory of the state in advanced capitalist societies from specific types of state welfare provision of the 1960s and 1970s. Initially in reaction to structural Marxist accounts, attention shifted to questions of the autonomy of local politics, and the role of the local state in economic development rather than consumption. Most recently, work on the 'entrepreneurial city' has focused on non-material efforts by the elected and the non-elected urban élite to redevelop local economies in light of on-going economic and social change brought about by globalisation and the responses of central government.

One development was the recognition of the immense diversity of forms of local governance. It was clear, for instance, that the forms of urban politics in the USA differed from those in Britain (Harding, 1991 and 1994; Stoker and Mossberger, 1994). Gottdiener (1987 and 1989; see also Cox, 1991) argued strongly that the experience of the USA is very different from that of European states. Moreover, there are differences within the European Union. The nature of local government, or of political units with internal territorial jurisdiction, varies from country to country. Hence the scope and powers of local governments vary, as do the sorts of political and administrative positions that are elected or appointed. There are also different systems for financing local government, as the proportion of local expenditure paid for grants from central government varies. In Britain, local government is unable to introduce local taxes, unlike their US equivalents, but it receives more generous funding through central resources. In the US, by contrast, local government grant-aid is relatively small. Nevertheless, local government as multisystems throughout the western world, usually have responsibility for some mix of public services – like education, roads, policing, fire-fighting and garbage collection – and also have the right to raise taxes locally to pay for those services, and to fund efforts to increase inter-urban competitiveness.

Action by local authorities is, importantly, a result of what they are empowered to do. This varies according to the institutional structures. In Britain, for instance, local governments traditionally have had an 'executant' role, with considerable discretion about how to implement central government policies (Pickvance, 1990). A considerable proportion of public employees have as a result been employed by the local rather than the central state (38 per cent as compared with 10 per cent in the more centralised France). This effectively allowed local authorities more autonomy, as witnessed by at least their temporary room for manoeuvre in the face of early Thatcherite attempts to exert more control over them. In the longer term, however, the privatisation of the local state through central budget cuts, and policies such as first Compulsory Competitive Tendering (CCT) and then Best Value, undermined the ability of local government to stop the creeping intervention of the central state.

Simultaneously the presumption that urban politics was concerned primarily with welfare issues was challenged. Attention shifted to the politics of local economic development, mostly inspired by American writers, where the role of the local state in encouraging investment was the orthodoxy, as was the involvement of local capital in the formulation of strategy. American writers' theoretical inspiration tended to come from one of two starting points. The first was Harvey, with his emphasis on the way in which capital accumulation in the built environment was a crucial element of capitalist economies, and they hence developed an interest in the ways by which such investment took place (see Chapter 3). The second was Dahl with his emphasis on 'who governs?' and the organisation and the exercising of community power. However, American political economy approaches of the 1980s, which Cox (1993) terms the 'new urban politics', were at pains to tread a thin line between economic determinism and individual voluntarism. Instead they stressed the role of local political processes in formulating locally differentiated policies. This ran in parallel with the increasing favour found by neo-Weberian approaches in urban politics, which insisted that the state apparatus – bureaucrats and their organisations – have interests at stake too in local politics.

7.2.1 New urban politics

According to Leo (1997, p. 77):

> local politics has long been subject to influences originating in the global economy but it is only lately that students of urban political economy have begun to appropriate a language and set of concepts intended to comprehend that reality.

In light of this increasing *global turn* in urban political studies, two key conceptual developments emerged in the US in the 1970s and 1980s in order to make sense of the urban political economy. The first was Logan and Molotch's 'growth coalition' concept (Logan, 1976; Logan and Molotch, 1987; see also Jonas and Wilson, 1999). The second was Stone's 'urban regime' concept (Stone and Saunders, 1987; Stone, 1989; see also Stoker, 1995; Ward, 1996; Lauria, 1997). In each case it was argued that local political regulation and intervention for reasons of economic development is of major importance in contemporary urban politics.

Growth coalitions are defined as groupings of influential actors who seek local growth at almost any cost. Borrowing from Harvey, *rentiers* were identified as standing to gain from more intensive use of their land and property, and therefore as tending to form coalitions to apply pressure through local government in support of their interests. This entails encouraging urban expansion that will lead to the more intensive use of their natural monopoly, land. This may be achieved by attracting mobile capital (and the in-migrants who follow), securing amenable planning decisions, or subsidising new buildings and urban infrastructure. The interests of such *rentier* groups, who, according to Logan and Molotch, aim to pursue increases in 'exchange-value', may not coincide with the interests of most existing residents, who might seek use-values like a non-congested city. However, political forces and the political machinery work generally in favour of growth coalitions. Members of the coalition tend to take an active part in local government, partly because they have more to gain directly than most other people (Ward, 2000a). But they generally also manage to persuade others that growth is in everyone's interests. Trade unionists and workers are likely to be persuaded that growth brings jobs, though in fact, as Molotch (1976), demonstrated, rates of unemployment are not correlated with rates of increase in city size. Consensus on the value of growth is shared not only by local government, but also by local newspapers that have the material incentive that they can only improve their sales if there are more people around locally (Imrie and Thomas, 1995). The implication is that only a small proportion of the population gains from growth, while environmental amenities may deteriorate for many residents. Within any place, some residents, usually already the more privileged, get a better deal than others – for example, when the costs of growth have been the destruction of inner-areas working-class communities. This has indeed recently created degrees of resistance among local populations, with 'no-growth' movements emerging. Another effect has been to reinforce what Harvey (1985a) refers to as 'inter-urban' competition between Western local governments for footloose investment..

An 'urban regime' is, according to Stone (1989, p. 6), 'the informal arrangements by which public bodies and private interests function together in order to be able to make and carry out governing decisions'. A 'regime' is said to exist where and when different economic, social and political forces combine around, and articulate, a clear strategic agenda. This conceptualisation of USA urban political economy was underpinned by the belief that elected officials cannot govern cities without the involvement of other institutions (Stoker and Mossberger, 1994). Hence

> governmental conduct is constrained by the need to promote investment activity in an economic arena dominated by private ownership ... This political economy insight is the foundation for a theory of urban regimes. (Stone, 1989, p. 9)

Through the use of *selective incentives* – trading of favours, benefits, etc. through negotiation between different agencies – elected government is able to steer development. Informed by a rational-choice understanding on how individuals make decisions, urban regime theory emphasises the longevity of governance arrangements. Distinguishing the approach from the earlier community power debates, the emphasis is on *social production* rather than *social control*. That is, on the achieving of agreed outcomes through coercion and negotiation, rather than through mechanisms of control. Unlike the 'growth coalition' concept, the emphasis in urban regime theory is not on growth *per se*, but is instead on the assembling of typologies that reflect the different types of policies pursued by the regime (Ward, 1996). So, work by writers such as DiGaetano and Klemanski (1993) and Stoker and Mossberger (1994) seeks to sharpen the analytical edge of urban regime theory through the widening of the different regime types. These ranged from 'entrepreneurial' and 'instrumental' pro-growth regimes, to 'growth management' and 'progressive' caretaker regimes through to 'organic' and 'social reform' regimes.

Both approaches have been subject to criticism, often on their own, although sometimes grouped together under the rubric of the 'new urban politics'. Logan and Molotch's ideas were first criticised effectively by Cox and Mair (1989; see also Clark, 1988; Clarke, 1990) who argue that it contains a number of ambiguities. First, in the course of analysis the category of *rentiers* tends to dissolve, discussion covering an amorphous mass of all sorts of property interests. Logan and Molotch cannot consistently identify a fraction of business with a primary interest in increasing land-rent as opposed to other forms of capitalist investment. Second, the key distinction between use-value and exchange-value is insufficiently subtle to sustain the argument. Owner-occupiers, for example, also have interests in exchange-values and these seem more often to be the basis of political conflict with developers than the protection of use-values. Cox and Mair assert that the origin of these defects is to be found in the idealism and voluntarism of a neo-Weberian theoretical framework and an associated simplistic account of capitalist accumulation.

Stone's 'urban regime' concept has also been subject to critique since it was introduced. First, it is held to over-emphasise the importance of local factors in the formation and continued existing of urban regimes (DiGaetano and Klemanski, 1993). It fails to pay sufficient attention to the wider economic and political context, such as the important role that government reform or economic globalisation might play in the emergence of urban regimes (Jessop *et al.*, 1999). Second, urban regime theory exaggerates the agency of urban politics. Individual government officials or business leaders only play a role in the formation of urban politics because they are licensed to through other reforms, such as those bound up in the restructuring of the state (Peck, 1995; Peck and Tickell, 1995; Ward, 2000b). Third, urban regime theory fails to theorise why local business actors involve themselves with local government in the governing of localities.

Cox and Mair (1989) offer an alternative explanation of the existence of growth coalitions, which can be also used as a means of augmenting the urban regime framework. It is primarily geographically immobile capital, rather than just anyone with an interest in land-rent, which provides the core of local coalitions. These groups are 'locally dependent' and hence have distinct interests in developing the local area. In America where banks are legally prohibited from operating in more than one state, and where gas and electricity utilities are local, and privately owned, the expansion of their business does indeed depend on encouraging other enterprises (and subsequently more people) to locate in the area. All agree that in the USA, 'boosterism' – support for economic development through urban growth – has been a fundamental driving force in urban politics, given extra impetus under contemporary global economic conditions, as Leo (1997) has argued. Moreover, local politics are about advancing the material interests of different sections of the population. Logan and Molotch (1987), while giving considerable weight to political machinations at the local level, argue that the outcome is usually to favour the interests of a small group. As such their argument knits with the older community-power debate that Stone (1989) draws upon in his work on urban regimes. This work was also concerned with examining whose decisions held sway, whether power was in the hands of a small unrepresentative élite, or whether there were a number of effective interest groups in the community.

As the community-power debate of the 1950s and the 1960s revealed, formal representation through electoral channels does not necessarily coincide with effective power. The extent to which organisations or groups exert influence behind the scenes through other channels is a key issue, both practically and methodologically (Harding, 1995). Which issues are admitted to be political, and which are placed on the agenda for discussion and decision, are key questions in understanding the operation of local power. Crenson's (1971) account of Gary, Indiana, where US Steel had such a reputation for power that the pollution from their factories was neither regulated nor contested, was a much-quoted case-study of the operation of covert power (see Lukes, 1974). This was a case where the dominant local employer, without formal representation in local politics, pursued commercial policies that negatively affected the local population but without creating opposition or resistance. This may have been an extreme case, though one which has often been repeated in communities where the economic power of a dominant employer renders local people so dependent that they are effectively powerless to offer overt resistance. This has been demonstrated especially in geographically isolated industrial sites, as with the miners of the Appalachian Mountains (Gaventa, 1980) or the textile workers of Manchester, New England (Hareven, 1982). These extreme cases are useful for indicating clearly that power can be exercised informally and covertly; the extent to which it is so exercised will vary with local conditions.

If we place Logan and Molotch's, Stone's, and Cox and Mair's arguments within the context of this wider debate, it is noteworthy that Cox and Mair by implication suggest that local politics is reverting to a much older pattern where leading local capitalists play a crucial role in urban governance. The players may have changed – from the textile and engineering employers to the corporate banks and utility companies – but the processes are similar. In the same vein, Logan and Molotch's emphasis on the part of property capital has historical parallels with the political significance of the urban *petite bourgeoisie* (Hennock, 1973).

All these writers emphasise the role of economic motivations behind political processes. Mollenkopf (1983) by contrast advances a rather different argument that links together the political strategies of national parties and the ways in which cities have pursued urban development. Extensive federal urban development programmes in the USA, emerging from the New Deal, were a conscious attempt by the Democratic Party to establish a new social base and new political alignments. What Mollenkopf (1983, p. 9) insists upon is that 'Politics runs on votes as well as money'; the need to win electoral support also affects the types of policies that local states could develop.

The most recent theoretical innovation in the realm of the local state and economic development is that of the 'entrepreneurial city'. Drawing upon the economic principles espoused by Joseph Schumpeter, Jessop's (1997 and 1998) work on the restructuring of the local state in Britain during the late 1980s and 1990s attempted to explain the wider logic of a series of discrete changes in the development strategies pursued by local coalitions. He isolated three interlocking shifts in how the local state was involved in economic development and the type of policies it pursued. First, he sets out the process through which localities are re-imaged. Here, places engage in a range of efforts to market themselves through the use of images and the language in a form of narrative. By narrative, Jessop (1997, p. 300) means:

> (a) a selective appropriation of past events and forces; (b) a temporal sequence with a beginning, middle, and end; (c) and a relational emplotment of the events and forces and their connection to some overarching structure which permits some causal and moral lessons to be drawn.

Key events, such as the hosting of major sporting or musical spectacles or the securing of state funding are linked together through an entrepreneurial narrative, which stresses the successfulness of these strategies. Linked to this shift is the redesigning of governance, Jessop's second theme. Here he seeks to capture both the ranges of changes in the internal structure of local government, and its increasing propensity to work in partnership with external agencies, alongside the growth in business-led and voluntary-based organisations that participate in a place's redevelopment. This growth in those agencies involved in urban politics has implications for how urban politics is performed. Jessop argues that the local state is increasingly characterised by élite networks that regulate economic development, replacing the previous methods of management, which tended to centre on more bureaucratic forms of decision-making. Jessop's third element to the entrepreneurial city framework is the restructuring of capital. In this he tries to place the first two trends in a wider context. Since the 1970s new forms of global economic activity, and the intensification of pre-existing links between economies, have challenged the capacity of nation-states to govern their own economies, and led to the growth in sub-national governance arrangements. In Jessop's (1997, p. 33) terms this has been interpreted for cities to mean that:

> the post-war [national] economic and political regime has failed and, if cities and regions are to escape the consequences of this failure, it is essential to modify economic strategies, economic institutions, modes of governance, and the form of the state.

Taken alongside the growth machine, the urban regime and local dependency, the entrepreneurial city represents the most recent example in on-going efforts to explain the general tendencies in how Western local states are involved in economic development. While, unlike the first three conceptual apparatuses, the entrepreneurial city was developed in the UK, its most recent refinement points to some wider explanatory power (Jessop and Sum, 2000). Certainly, the last decade in urban politics has been characterised by almost as much theoretical transfer as the policy transfer these theories often seek to explain.

7.2.2 Urban economic development at the end of the twentieth century

The American concern for the urban politics of economic growth was not reflected in British research until the late 1980s. Triggered by an apparent convergence in policies between the two countries, academics from the two countries began to indulge in the process of theoretical transfer (DiGaetano and Klemanski, 1993 and 1997; Harding, 1994; Stoker and Mossberger, 1994). Urban development has been an objective of local authorities in Britain since the middle of the nineteenth century, where it was embedded in competing notions of Civic Virtue and Municipal Socialism. The emphasis was on providing services and facilities for residents, from gas and water to parks and roads. However, local authorities until recently had almost no role in specifically economic development. There are though some interesting exceptions. Seaside towns developed a tourist infrastructure and advertised the delights of holidaying in Morecambe or Bridlington, while Leeds city council sought to attract inward investment by advertising itself in the 1970s as the 'Motorway city of the seventies'.

Attempts to intervene to counteract uneven economic development in the UK began to be formulated in the 1930s, largely at the instigation of central government, and these spawned regional rather than local policies. Various forms of policy for regional aid and development were tried after the Slump and again in the 1960s and 1970s when the reappearance of unemployment showed strong regional variations. Only since the 1960s, however, have local authorities in Britain begun to be seriously involved in economic development, providing land for industry, sometimes producing promotional literature and even less frequently industrial premises or financial assistance (Pickvance, 1990). Their activities expanded more quickly from the late 1970s, due to worsening levels of unemployment and to the desire of Labour-controlled local authorities to resist the imposition of Thatcherite central government economic policies. The slogan, 'restructuring for labour', rather than for capital, identified the political motivation involved among the radical Labour administrations of some metropolitan counties like Sheffield and the Greater London Council. These attempted to implement on a local level some of the features of Labour's national *Alternative Economic Strategy* (1973), with planning agreements covering working conditions and types of product in exchange for financial assistance (see Wainwright, 1987). More moderate Labour councils, like Swindon (see Bassett *et al.,* 1989; Bassett and Harloe, 1990) or Middlesbrough (Hudson, 1990), formed growth coalitions but with much less direct involvement by business than in the US. These have been understood in the British urban politics literature as 'spatial' or 'territorial coalitions', the cross-class, consensual, social bases for local economic regeneration (Quilley and Ward, 1999). The differences between the two countries are probably due to the fact that the extent of 'local dependence' by capital is much weaker in Britain than in the USA, because of the greater likelihood that firms are controlled from outside any specific place.

One of the main differences between Britain and the USA is that it is difficult to find any evidence in Britain that there are local social forces pressing for development. In Britain, policies appear to be largely developed by political parties, or by local state professionals (Urry, 1990b). One of the most interesting demonstrations of this point is Susan Halford's analysis of women's initiatives in local government (Halford, 1989). In the 1980s a number of local councils developed a series of feminist-inspired initiatives, including women's committees, equal opportunities policies, women's training schemes, and grants to women's groups. Some of the strongest of these – especially in central London – were found in areas with powerful traditions of feminist politics, and in particular where there were large numbers of women in professional and managerial jobs. Yet, Halford (1992) argued that their extent and success were not due to the character of local social relations, but to the internal politics of the local councils, and especially bureaucratic processes within differing local authorities.

The implication is that local policies should be seen not only in the context of the wider urban social structure, but also in terms of internal politicking, both between different interest groups within the state and between local and central government. Pickvance has developed this idea in his analysis of the changing relationship between central and local government in Britain. In Britain there was a major restructuring of local government in the 1980s (Cochrane, 1988, 1991 and 1993). Pickvance (1990) summarises concisely the policies designed to reduce local authority autonomy during the 1980s. Central government began by trying to reduce local spending, to control the amount of income generated (by rate-capping), to insist that local services were contracted out rather than provided by local authority employees and to sell assets like council houses. These policies had both an economic rationale – to reduce public expenditure – and a political rationale – to reduce the power of local authority trade unions, to privatise economic activities and to penalise Labour councils. That these projects largely failed, because of local authority resistance, Pickvance sees as indicating the considerable strength of local autonomy. That power was based partly in the expertise of the local authorities with a strong executant role – their officials had the knowledge essential to the implementation of government policies such that the central state was incapable of directly imposing its policies. In addition, as local government has become fully partisan (there being few Independents elected to councils since the 1970s), the threat of electoral unpopularity at the local level could have consequences for fortunes in Parliament.

In the 1980s and 1990s successive Conservative governments, and then after 1997, a Labour government, introduced a series of institutional reforms in order to exert greater control over local government. Altering the system of local finance, from rates to the poll tax, was one way of trying to reduce local discretion, though one that backfired when its enormous unpopularity had highly negative effects for the then national Conservative government. The abolition of the GLC and the other six large metropolitan authorities in 1986 removed one focus of significant political opposition, for they had been amongst the most recalcitrant of authorities. However, they tended to have legitimacy locally and the overtly political reasons for abolition were unmistakable. A third strategy was to try to by-pass local authorities, often through more opaque methods. On the one hand this involved the introduction of the market into the provision of public services. Compulsory Competitive Tendering (CCT) most embodied this initiative under the Conservative governments, while Labour introduced Best Value when it first came to power nationally. Both policies set up local government departments to compete with external service providers in community care, school meals, park management, etc. Alternatively, sometimes this has meant removing existing institutions from local authority jurisdiction. In the educational sphere, polytechnics were removed from local control in 1988, City Technical Colleges were set up that were funded centrally, and schools were permitted to opt out of local control and become self-governing under the 1988 Education Act. Circumventing local authorities has also been significant in the field of economic policy where the creation of Urban Development Corporations (UDCs), Enterprise Zones and Training Enterprise Councils (TECs) instituted new authoritative bodies, not subject to local electoral control, designed to encourage private investment in areas with economic problems. Finally, and in addition to the more formal creation of new centrally licensed bodies, central government restructured its grant programmes. Local authorities had to form 'public–private partnerships' and to assemble bids in order to secure money from central government. This introduction of the 'challenge fund model' (Oatley, 1998) represents the latest in a long line of central government efforts to change the context within which its relationship with local government is rooted.

Urban Development Corporations were set up in twelve places in Britain, the first two in Liverpool and London Docklands in 1981, the rest in two subsequent waves in areas including Tyneside, Manchester and Glasgow (Imrie and Thomas, 1999). Each one had its own shelf life, and they began to be wound up in the mid-1990s. The creation of UDCs was one of a still on-going series of initiatives for resolving some of the problems of inner-city regeneration faced particularly by old industrial manufacturing centres. UDCs had appointed boards, mostly composed of local business people, and without any direct representation from local councils or trade unions. The brief was to encourage private capital investment, and incentives include making large tracts of land available (through compulsory purchase where necessary), financial investment by the UDC in infrastructure and the abolition of normal planning restrictions (the UDC is its own planning authority). In most instances the outcome has been that any inward private capital investment has taken the form of property speculation, with large cleared and prepared sites offering opportunities for the construction of shopping centres and new up-market dwelling. Little new employment has been generated. In such places the public costs have vastly outweighed the forthcoming private investment. The only instance where extensive private investment has emerged has been in London Docklands where not only has the economic prognosis been gloomy, but the environmental and social consequences have been profound. Disinherited local working-class communities lie alongside new gentrified enclave; the congestion incurred by situating new plant and offices has required enormous, unanticipated public investment in transport infrastructure; and considerations of social welfare, arguably the core of inner-city problems, are completely neglected since this is not a UDC function. Despite this gloomy analysis and a lack of formal means of local populations influencing their programmes, there is some evidence of some UDCs taking on board the voice of local communities or local authorities (Deas *et al.*, 1999).

The experience of UDCs has several wider implications that continue to resonate amongst contemporary policy frameworks. The first is the extent to which local authorities, elected or appointed, can effectively intervene to manage or attract flows of private capital in a global economy. Local authorities dare not cease to advertise their attractions, cajole mobile capital and provide limited incentives, largely because other places are doing these things (Philo and Kearns, 1993). Indeed, during the 1990s, efforts to market the city became increasingly aggressive, sophisticated and widespread. Whether in the form of billboard advertisements on foreign shores or in the creation of a designer web-site, the result has been expensive, essentially futile, competition. The location decisions of capital are not much influenced (most accounts of regional economic policy suggest this), and anyway success mostly means taking investment that would have gone somewhere else in the UK, thus not increasing national economic production or national employment. Second, it alerts us to the existence of non-democratically accountable, spatially defined, agencies of the state. This might lead to reconsideration of the concept of 'the local state'. For as Cox (1991) argues, there are many state agencies that have localised but non-coincident (ad hoc or arbitrarily defined) jurisdictions. Indeed, one element of the increasingly sophisticated activities of local coalitions is their capacity to manipulate scale in order to secure external funds. Local authorities, together with business representatives, have through marketing efforts attempted to insert themselves into global systems of economic and political power. There are also regional bodies and many local quangos (quasi-autonomous non-governmental organisations) whose policies are neither democratically accountable nor coordinated. The recent creation of Regional Development Agencies (RDAs) mirrors the earlier creation of UDCs, both in terms of the mix of institutions involved and the type of policies delivered. It is then perhaps best to think not in terms of a local state, but a plethora of state institutions with different spatial scopes, comprising a complex geography of state involvement in economic development.

In Britain, for part of the 1980s, local authorities used their accumulated powers, resources and expertise to frustrate attempts to impose central control over their behaviour. In the 1990s, however, they nevertheless lost control over a range of economic development and welfare functions. But they did gain some new economic functions, as they became more involved in trying to encourage new capital investment. The 1987 Local Government Act granted each local authority the ability to form its own economic development department. However, during the last decade, central government became ever more adept in usurping control, despite often couching reform in terms of granting localities greater say over their own economic futures

Similar patterns can be found in the USA. There, Gottdiener (1987) dates the decline of urban politics from the 1960s. It is often believed that local politics was an arena for active citizen participation and control of the affairs immediately affecting them. According to Gottdiener, while this might have been true once, by the 1950s suburban dislocation and the emergence of regional metropolitan growth, increased affluence, a new preparedness to commute, and the changing size and shape of living quarters ended the dominance of the city as a locus of politics. The role of the federal state was considerable in the creation and sustaining of urban growth, through awarding suburban defence contracts, mortgage tax relief, interstate highway building and so forth. Three crises finally upset old city politics: first, the ghetto riots of the early 1960s, which rendered apparent ethnic inequalities of income and power, induced federal policies for amelioration and alleviation; second, urban fiscal crises also required federal intervention; and third, deindustrialisation, the decline of manufacturing, hit the cities hardest. A mixture of federal involvement and disillusionment with political outcomes led to a decline of confidence in local representation. As non-democratically (locally) controlled authorities proliferated and redistributive policies failed, political participation, at least as measured by turnout in elections, reduced.

The nature of urban politics, then, has changed enormously in the last decade. Conflict between central and local government has intensified, and the emphasis on the local politics of service provision has been supplemented, and at times been replaced by, an interest in the politics of investment and urban development. But there is a danger that new accounts have exaggerated the variability of local state activities and their autonomy in relation to their environments. While local politics cannot be reduced to the local social structure in any deterministic way, the conflict between central and local government does have its roots in the nature of on-going uneven development under capitalism. Duncan *et al.* have developed this argument, by showing that

> Because social relations are unevenly developed there is, on the one hand, a need for different policies in different places and, on the other hand, a need for local state institutions to formulate and implement these variable policies. Local state institutions are rooted in the heterogeneity of local social relations, where central states have difficulty in dealing with this differentiation. But ... this development of local states is a double-edge sword – for locally constituted groups can then use these institutions to further their own interests, perhaps even in opposition to centrally dominant interests. (Duncan *et al.*, 1988, p. 114)

The implications of this are twofold. First, and despite the best efforts of central government to circumvent local authorities, they continue to perform an essential role both in the delivery of uneven development and in the management of its effects. This is bound up with the fact that local political bodies have legitimacy, and an efficacy, that inevitably leaves them with a degree of discretion in certain matters. It is unsatisfactory, therefore, to see them simply in terms of the working-out of the logic of capital accumulation. However, it is a moot point whether and to what extent, given the globalisation of production, local political intervention can have any profound impact, over and above meeting the needs of capital. That at the beginning of the twenty-first century urban development is a growth sector in and of itself, does not necessarily point to increased autonomy for local governments. There is indeed a danger of romanticising local differences and local autonomy. Despite this fetishism of the local, as Logan and Molotch (1987) make clear, cities with existing advantages tend to maintain them in relative terms. Urban and regional authorities have to be seen to be acting, but even for the most successful the gains are relatively minor. Economic cycles, national policy and the power of large organisations usually mean that local initiatives are operating on the margins, steering the system rather than rejecting it.

Second the process of uneven development remains of major significance for politics. As we have seen, globalisation, while reducing local economic control, in some respects heightens the significance of spatial difference. And this is not merely an empirical concern. Cochrane (1999, p. 122) argues:

The urban politics of the twenty-first century will be both a local politics and a global politics: the challenge to be faced by those seeking to analyse it effectively, will be to hold aspects together at the same time, without allowing either to dominate as a matter of principle.

For example, firms make heavily researched location decisions on criteria that include the quality of the urban environment and the character of local industrial relations. This implies the need to recognise local political differentiation, including an anticipation of political responses by local communities to industrial restructuring. Uneven development renders places politically distinctive, while at the same time appearing to tie them into similar fates. Indeed, this is one of the ironies of the last decade in terms of the relationship between local states and economic development. What has been termed the 'new localism' (Lovering, 1995), through which the role for local coalitions in economic development is increased, rests on an alternative logic to that upon which more traditional forms of involvement are predicated. Far from seeking to manage uneven development, strategies to secure inward investment or to promote the city seek to build upon existing inequalities. Involvement is about the construction and exploitation of local difference in order to gain an economic advantage over others.

These points suggest that the separation of urban politics from its economic and social context can be exaggerated. Every now and then politicians and bureaucrats do have to take notice of popular politics, in the form of votes, protest, or even violence. It is to a consideration of popular participation in urban politics that we now turn.

7.3   Place, political identification and urban participation

We have argued that theories of urban politics have to be dynamic in the sense of recognising the historical and spatial specificity of various state activities and policies. In this section we show how state agencies exhibit a problematic relationship with social groups and political forces outside its own confines. As we proposed earlier, the state has good reasons both to organise and disorganise social groups. In the contemporary period the continued disorganisation of nationally coordinated class-based political movements organised through workplace institutions, such as trade unions, enhances locally based groupings and increases the pressure on local states from their constituents. This encapsulates what Agnew (1987) refers to as the 'politics of place'.

7.3.1   Formal representation and geographies of voting

A political orthodoxy of the 1950s and 1960s was that as societies modernised, local differences in political affiliation gave way to primarily national divisions. Modernisation theory maintained that places became more alike as industrialisation and urbanisation developed. Ways of life, culture and politics would become more homogeneous with a more developed division of labour, centralisation of state functions and the growth of the mass media. As a consequence, political cleavages typical of early modern and pre-industrial societies, those based on religion, region, clan or ethnic group, would subside and industrial divisions, essentially of class, would replace them. Those earlier cleavages might survive to a greater or lesser extent in different nation-states, but the tendency was for spatial homogenisation around a politics that was shaped by economic groups. This became apparent in, for example, voting behaviour – the most common, perhaps because requiring the least commitment, of ways of participating in official politics. The UK, with the dramatic exception of Northern Ireland where religion determines the vote, was thought to be a classic case of the tendency toward the modernisation of politics. Though there were some regional differences in support for the two main parties, this was considered to be largely attributable to the differing social composition of the regions. With more working-class people in the North, more salaried workers in the South East, it was unsurprising that more Labour MPs came from the former. Region was not an independent source of variation in support, though there have always been some national differences between Scotland, Wales and England.

In the 1980s there was a strong reaction against this view. The reason for this is that the politics of territory – in its various forms – has refused to die away. In virtually all areas of political activity local issues have commanded attention in recent years. That people may become attached to places, and can be mobilised to defend 'their' spaces, is witnessed by activities as different as the organisation of gangs to defend their 'turf', the activities of football supporters, the creation of local political movements, and wars between nation-states.

Sources of collective identity in such cases are many – ideologies of patriotism, the logic of group formation, ethnic and sexual identity, shared interests, attachment to certain symbols and myths specific to particular territories. This is particularly well attested in studies of voting behaviour. Here, evidence shows that spatial variation increased in British electoral behaviour in the 1980s (see Savage, 1987b; Johnston, Pattie and Allsopp, 1988), a tendency also identified in the USA (see Agnew, 1987). During the 1990s, and especially as the Labour Party increased in popularity and won seats outside its urban heartlands, this pattern of spatial polarisation was to some extent broken though not eliminated (Johnston and Pattie, 1998). However, its gains in so-called 'middle England' and in and around London may prove temporary.

Survey evidence has demonstrated the salience of neighbourhood effects (MacAllister *et al.*, 2001). The 1997 General Election was not marked by particularly strong spatial divisions. Nonetheless 29 per cent of the working class who lived in high-status constituencies voted Labour, compared with 53 per cent who lived in low-status ones. The proportion of the professional and managerial classes who voted Labour rose from 19 per cent in the low-status areas to 41 per cent in the high-status ones. It is clear that the voting patterns of individuals from different social classes were affected by the kind of area they were living in. However, the reasons for these patterns are much disputed. One of the most frequently invoked causes is that local variations are related to the social context in which voters find themselves. The best-known contextual effect is the so-called 'neighbourhood effect' – whereby people tend to be affected by the politics of their neighbours (Miller, 1977). Hence, a working-class person living in a strongly working-class town is more likely to vote Labour than an equivalent worker living in a middle-class suburb. But why? Historically, there is good evidence that coercion has been put on people to adopt certain political views. Shopkeepers, for instance, used to be pressurised by their clients to follow their political beliefs, and on some occasions were boycotted if they did not (Savage, 1987a). In Victorian Britain employers used their influence over their workers to encourage them to vote for chosen candidates (Joyce, 1980). However such strong forms of coercion are hardly ever, if at all, found today, for voting is secret and social cohesion weaker. Another possible reason is everyday interaction and discussion of political affairs in the neighbourhood and its institutions, which may, without coercion, encourage people to support the dominant politics of the area. However, this is unlikely too, since people from different social classes rarely converse even if they live on the same street, and so it is not clear what arenas exist for political discussion.

One plausible way of resolving this question is to suggest that the neighbourhood effect exists not because of communication processes within the neighbourhood, but because people living in a certain area tend to have certain shared interests which might dispose them to vote the same way, even if they never talked to each other about politics, nor had the slightest knowledge about the political alignment of their area. Indeed perhaps the most in-stantly plausible explanation of local variations in voting patterns is that it reflects the state of the local economy. So, Johnston and Pattie (1989) argue that voter satisfaction with governments' economic policy and the voter's degree of economic optimism was probably the major influence on changing patterns of voting, 1979–87. Heath *et al.* (1991), pursuing such a hypothesis, found that regional differences in voting are not the result of differences in regional income, but are correlated with unemployment. This led them to suggest that 'perceptions of the community's economic situation' (Heath *et al.*, 1991, p. 112) is the basis of regional difference. The suggestion is that part of the voting calculation is a consideration, by members of all classes, of the economic predicament of most other people in a certain town or region, rather than a simple individual calculation of economic advantage. This calculation is especially prominent among the working class, perhaps the result of their lower levels of geographical mobility and hence greater dependence on the fortunes of the local economy.

However, this formulation raises a difficult problem, for it might well be that rather than people's degree of optimism or pessimism about their local economy determining their vote, their political affiliation determines their beliefs about how the local economy is changing for the better or worse. Discovering an association between one's feelings of optimism or pessimism and one's vote is simply redescribing people's political beliefs, not explaining them. Another way of accounting for the local variations in political alignment is therefore to stress the significance of local political culture. The idea here is that different places develop distinct traditions of political affiliation, which tend to mark them out both to their inhabitants and to outsiders. Thus in the UK in the inter-war years some industrial towns became labelled as 'Little Moscows' because of the peculiar strength of the Left within them (see MacIntyre, 1980). During the 1980s Sheffield became popularly known as the Socialist Republic of South Yorkshire because of its radical policies (such as cheap, subsidised public transport, and municipal intervention in economic policy). To its Conservative opponents, Sheffield, along with other Metropolitan and old industrial Labour-controlled districts, were branded as 'loony left' authorities. Other examples might include the Welsh Valleys and Glasgow with historically strong socialist traditions, and Belfast characterised by religious sectarianism. Johnston and Pattie (1998) argue that the long-term association with the industrial working class and the Labour movement in the North of England continues to be salient. This draws attention to the idea that local political culture offers an explanation of local variations that does not rely purely on instrumental assumptions about the reasons for people's votes, but also considers how people's expressive and emotional attachments to places might affect political partisanship

Some applications of this concept are problematic. It runs the risk of assuming a degree of cognitive awareness of local politics that most people do not possess. Survey research suggests that most people gain their political knowledge from national events, notably the performance of political parties and their leaders nationally. It is also the case that political alignments can change dramatically quickly, in a way which contradicts the idea of local political cultures where the emphasis is upon the perpetuation of local traditions as successive generations are socialised into prevailing beliefs (Savage, 1987b). In Britain, for instance, Liverpool, notorious until the 1960s for the depth of its working-class Tory support, became one of the most left-wing cities in Britain in the

1980s; Glasgow, the centre of 'Red Clydeside', and historically the most militant, socialist area in the UK, became the centre of pragmatic, moderate Labour politics in the 1980s and although the Labour Party retains control, it faces frequent challenges from the Scottish Nationalist Party (Savage, 1990); areas around the Home Counties which embraced Thatcherism in the 1980s now elect Labour MPs.

Therefore, we need to consider how local political cultures can be sustained *alongside* the globalisation of culture and cultural media (Chapter 6). The last twenty years have seen a series of anthropological and ethnographical works on the changing nature of local cultures (Cohen, 1983; Burawoy *et al.*, 2000a). This shows how local identity is rooted symbolically in the processes by which local boundaries are culturally constructed and outsiders and locals distinguished. In Cohen's words:

> it would be inadequate to say that a television programme or an EEC directive or a political statement are the 'same' for all those who experience or are confronted by them. They are experienced differently in different circumstances: their meanings differ. (Cohen, 1983, p. 2)

In this context the new media actually allow symbolic markers to proliferate, so possibly enhancing people's sense of communal identity, even if this is of an imaginary kind. To be 'European' might mean something quite different if you live in an inner-city estate in east Manchester as compared to a rural village in the South-West of England.

There is another general factor of major importance underlying the growing significance of local variations in voting. One way by which the Labour Party came into prominence in the early twentieth century, and more recently the Conservative Party sought to prolong its period in office during the 1980s and 1990s, was to create an institutional infrastructure that spanned different areas. In the case of the Labour Party, it put in place trade unions, the creation of national collective bargaining systems, and so forth. The 1970s and 1980s saw the erosion of working-class organisation at the national level. In its place, the Conservatives created business-led institutions to introduce their pro-market reforms. In addition to creating national institutions, the Conservative Party also introduced regional and local agencies.

This trend is not symptomatic of the replacement of national-level organisations, as some have claimed (Lash and Urry, 1987), but reflects the complex geographical configuration of contemporary economy and society. The implication might be the greater salience of community and locality as axes of political identification as national cohesiveness subsides. This does not mean that social class itself becomes less important, rather that it becomes important in a different way, combining with other factors that shape how people identify themselves. In place of political alignments being orchestrated by nationally coordinated groups they increasingly rely upon the symbolisation of place and space – with the social class and lifestyle imagery used in depicting places being of major importance.

7.3.2   DIY politics and urban movements

The extent of popular interest in and action over issues of local politics has increased in recent years. Local democracy seems appealing because, being close to home and on a relatively small scale, it is possible for the citizen to be involved and to influence outcomes. Yet as it appears to be the case in contemporary Britain that voting turnout is low and involvement in local politics is decreasing, then we need to think about alternative methods of representation. And a good deal of urban politics literature has indeed been concerned with more direct forms of mobilisation. Building upon this work, recent research has sought to hold together an analysis that is sensitive to issues of local citizen *and* explores how some issues bond together groups from quite different parts of the world.

Different social groups tend to intervene in different kinds of ways. Means of participating in urban politics include lobbying councillors, joining residents' associations, mass movements and rioting. The sort of strategy adopted depends upon what resources – economic, cultural, political, social, etc. – are available to particular groups. One type of political movement that has attracted increasing interest is the 'new social movement' in which groups of people combine to press for specific, usually single-issue goals. Examples include the Green movement, conservation politics, gay rights, and anti-racism. Much has been written on whether these 'new social movements' are forms of middle-class

politics, for instance because the middle classes have the knowledge, time, skills and connections which make its protests more
effective. 'Poor people's movements', by contrast, are likely to
rely on occasional outbursts of protest, like a demonstration or a
riot, their lack of resources making it difficult to mount a sustained campaign of any other kind. Moreover, the extent of
grass-root participation itself varies from country to country, with
direct local participation in movements, like that of the Greens,
very high in Denmark but low in Britain, where organised, pres-
sure-group methods are more usual (Halkier, 1991). Recent
efforts to resist globalisation by organising from below, points to
mobilisation through the Internet and at the very least the tran-
scending of national differences, as 'new social movements'
mirror in terms of organisation those corporations whose actions
they are opposing (Klein, 2000).

Participation in informal movements is uneven. Women tend
to participate more in informal and neighbourhood-based actions,
a result of the unequal gendered division of labour that leaves
them with less time and less resources for attending meetings.
Middle-class people join more formal associations and vote rather
more often; ethnic minorities, the elderly and the unemployed
are less involved. Middle-class presence in social movements is a
result of them typically having more flexible time-schedules, organising and campaigning skills and different values. Sometimes
their involvement stems from their own material interests:
ratepayer and housing associations representing owner–occupiers
are usually channels through which middle-class residents claim
more services or privileges. As many studies have shown, such
groups are likely to be effective in mobilising to achieve planning
decisions that will protect their property values (Saunders, 1979;
Logan and Molotch, 1987). On other occasions, though, middle-
class people (or rather certain fractions of the middle class) are
likely to be principal actors in Green, feminist or peace movements, where, as Offe (1985) puts it, they promote 'the politics of
a class but not for a class'.

The role of urban movements in causing change is con-
tentious. In his early work, Castells envisaged a grand role for
urban movements which, in contesting issues around collective
consumption, might profoundly alter the social relations of contemporary societies. He believed that the multitude of protests

that persistently emerge in cities over housing, transport, access to public facilities, planning decisions and so forth, might be coordinated through alliances with labour movement organisations. In his scenario, urban protest might be elevated to an urban social movement with the potential to transform fundamentally the urban structure. However, despite high levels of protest in the cities of the advanced societies in the 1970s, such radical urban social movements directed towards the alteration of the material inequalities associated with the organisation of collective consumption did not transpire. Critics concluded that Castells's analysis was wrong. He was considered too tied to a Marxist interpretation of the centrality of class struggles. He was oblivious to the gender and ethnic bases of urban discontent, ambivalent about the relationship between urban protests and the class politics of the labour movement, and insufficiently appreciative of other political issues besides those arising from material inequalities.

Castells's later work, especially *The City and the Grassroots* (1983), acknowledged many of these criticisms and abandoned many elements of his structuralism. He acknowledged that:

> although class relationships and class struggle are fundamental in understanding urban conflict, they are not, by any means, the only primary source of urban social change. The autonomous role of the state, gender relationships, ethnic and national movements, and movements that define themselves as citizen, are among other alternative sources of urban change. (Castells, 1983, p. 291)

Castells reinterpreted urban politics as conflict over 'urban meaning'. Urban meaning is concerned with the role that the city is assigned at different periods in history, that role being fought over between dominant and subordinate social groups. Such a concern allows much greater flexibility in interpreting what is at stake in urban protest, for people may want quite different things from a city. While *rentiers* and property-developers might want opportunities for investment, the unemployed want work, the young excitement, the homeless adequate housing and mothers suitable child-care facilities. What constitutes a good city to live in is an issue that engenders multifarious conflicts of interest. For that reason urban protest remains fragmented. Take the protest against the poll tax in Britain in the 1990s. This was a tax that a great many people refused to pay, which resulted in hundreds of people being arrested in demonstrations in many places, and which was ultimately successful insofar as the government changed its legislation. Yet for the most part it was a localised and a fragmented dispute. More recently, the protests against the Criminal Justice Bill, which contained various new laws over what was and what was not acceptable behaviour, brought together a range of single-issue groups, who perhaps otherwise might not have seen themselves as having a common cause.

Indeed the mid to late 1990s witnessed a mushrooming of DIY political movements, where resistance is organised outside of the formal channels of government. High profile anti-globalisation movements have emerged in many parts of the world to oppose the actions of global capital. Uprisings against the policies of international financial and political institutions, such as the World Trade Organisation (WTO), marked a new departure in radical politics. At the same time, social criticism of the state continued to take different forms among different groups. While the new middle classes involved in contemporary social movements pursue participatory, small-scale, democratic association as an alternative to central state direction, poorer and weaker groups have other grievances and agendas.

One, indirect, source of change in the cities is the riot. Famously urban riots took place in the USA in the 1960s in the downtown areas of Detroit, Los Angeles and Newark. Riots in British cities in the early 1980s and again in the late 1990s and 2001 were likewise felt to require fresh schemes of social intervention. There is some disagreement as to whether riots are 'political'. Some would maintain that they are merely wanton disorder, deviance and lawlessness. It is, however, difficult sociologically to deny that they are an expression of protest and discontent. The fact that only some groups engage in riotous behaviour, and they are those without easy access to established political channels, is not incidental. Sites of riots in Britain have been ones where the poor live and where relations between local young people and police forces have been hostile and embittered. This hostility can often be along racial lines. For example, riots in Handsworth in Birmingham or Chapeltown in Leeds in the 1980s, and more recently in Bradford and Oldham, were at least partly triggered by the social and economic disadvantage felt by ethnic groups. This though is not always the case. In the early 1990s a serious of disturbances took place on the Meadow Well estate in North Shields on Tyneside, which has an almost entirely white population but where, it is estimated, 86 per cent of the residents were unemployed (*The Guardian,* 1 October 1991, p. 4). Young, unqualified white males, whose prospects for legitimate involvement in a consumer culture are severely restricted, have perhaps come to form yet another marginalised and excluded social category whose means of protest is limited to attacks on property and resistance to the police. Responses to these incidents are instructive: some authorities point to a need to relieve social deprivation, others to a need for more policing. During the 1980s, riot shields and CS gas, wielded by police, became a feature of life in parts of British cities, as well as in mining communities during the national strike of 1984–5. What these examples suggest is that informal political mobilisation and protest remains a major feature of urban life, and that this poses significant problems for the state. The state is therefore forced to intervene to retain authority and control of urban sites. Gottdiener has emphasised the importance of the state's role in enforcing social control (see also Cockburn, 1977). Gottdiener begins from the premise that 'the principal function of the local state is its role as the socially legitimated guardian of property expropriation. As such its fundamental purpose is social control' (Gottdiener, 1987, p. 195) This approach is especially relevant in the USA, where the state has intervened infrequently in comparison with the unitary states of Europe. According to Gottdiener, there has been relatively little direct state intervention in economic life (e.g. of corporatist types), or in reproduction of labour power.

Although Gottdiener's argument is insufficiently elaborate, it is suggestive of another important way of seeing local states. In his view one could see the conflict between the police and poor people in terms of state preservation of the fundamental security of property, both its own and that of private individuals. For one of the strong points of Gottdiener's analysis is his insistence that the state itself is a propertied body, that people frequently become resentful and that, as in tax revolts, contestation ensues. The state, it should be appreciated, often acts to expand its own powers.

This may sometimes result in state-led social reform for which there is no pressing social demand, on other occasions may mean the further expansion of bureaucratic agencies like the police force whose collective interest is its own expansion.

It is not, however, that the police alone are capable of securing safer streets. The introduction of new technology, most notably in the form of recorded surveillance cameras, has been one of the most important recent developments in efforts to promote safer cities. In almost every town and city up and down the British Isles, cameras monitored in back-street offices feed into police networks to extend the role of the state in regulating how individuals perform in public spaces. Despite this growth in surveillance techniques, one of the principal forms of gender inequality in the modern city remains: violence against women. Many feminist accounts describe how women are afraid to go out alone in the evening, especially after dark. This seems to be a greater fear in the USA and UK than in, for instance, Greece (Vaiou, 1991). Where there are well-used spaces, and where there is a vibrant public life, as in the Mediterranean countries, women's fear of violence on the streets is reduced.

7. 4.   Conclusion

We have argued that the terrain of urban politics shifts over time. Attempts to theorise the distinct function of urban politics, whether around consumption, boosterism, social control or even entrepreneurialism, fail to recognise the dynamic and reactive character of urban politics. We have argued that the contradictions of capitalism and modernity preclude political stasis. Nevertheless some general conclusions can be drawn about the changing nature of urban politics in advanced capitalist societies since the 1960s. The era of state welfare saw an urban politics of collective consumption. This state-welfare provision can be seen as the end product of major historical struggles by working-class movements, feminists and other social groups to achieve a basic level of security within capitalism. Yet during the 1970s and 1980s this political edifice was eroded in the course of massive economic restructuring and state policies to deal with financial deficits through welfare cuts and the promotion of popular capitalism. In the 1990s, in the face of ever increasing political pressure stemming from economic globalisation, the systematic erosion of welfare states quickened. The politics of urban boosterism is a concomitant of the globalisation of the economy, with the resulting need for political intervention to attract footloose investment. Yet we have also seen that such a politics in some ways marks a return to older political formations, with local élites playing important roles (Peck and Tickell, 1995; Tickell and Peck, 1996). Alongside state retrenchment and economic restructuring, political alignments have become more localised as the political forces created to organise social groups nationally attenuate. The result is to enhance a fragmented politics, in which local protest can take a variety of forms, some of them violent. Increasingly the state's role as law-enforcer and agent of social control is emphasised to deal with such problems.

It is wrong to see the recent period as the triumph of 'markets' over 'states'. The state continues to be at the heart of current forms of urban politics, as *organiser* of new forms of investment, market regulation, new forms of control and policing and as *disorganiser* of old forms of welfare provision and social collectivity. The state cannot resolve the problems of capitalism and modernity, with the result that one set of solutions becomes another set of problems. The move away from state welfare and towards market provision, for example in the form of what Peck (2001) terms 'emerging workfare states', is a response to the problems of fiscal crisis and the increasing demands made on the state for facilities and resources. But as we have seen, over the last decade the shift to market provision has created new problems of social justice and the maintenance of law and order, to which the state in turn has to attend, through means like increased use of CCTV.

8 Conclusion: Urban Sociology, Capitalism and Modernity

The late twentieth century witnessed growing doubts about the status of scientific knowledge. The problem, the philosophers observe, is one of finding some foundational grounding for affirming knowledge, truth and certainty. Enlightenment philosophers of the eighteenth century believed in the capacity of Reason to understand the world, whereupon planned interventions might secure human Progress. Western social thought developed largely under a wind of such a modern rationalist view, though there was always philosophical dissent. Today, the dissenters are in the majority. Post-modernists and post-structuralists deny that there can be any grounds for sustaining the narrative of Progress, of a singular, universal and developing core of knowledge to which science once pretended. We live in an age of radical doubt. While this condition might seem to undermine traditional histories of science as steadily improving towards perfect understanding, it makes little difference to an account of urban sociology, which has always been characterised by discontinuity, uncertainty and rediscovery.

Our review of debates has identified many significant issues and important findings, illustrating the diverse concerns that have been addressed under the auspices of urban sociology. That diversity poses again the question of what it is that constitutes urban sociology as a subdiscipline. We take the view that there can be no satisfactory delimitation of the concept of the 'urban'. The often confusing and obsessive debate in the field since the 1970s reached an appropriate conclusion that it is impossible to develop a scientifically useful concept of the 'urban'. In that sense, 'urban sociology' is mostly a convenient label. Nevertheless, it has a core set of concerns and practitioners of urban sociology have developed a distinctive and specialised corpus of knowledge. The historic core of urban sociology is best appreciated as a contextualised investigation of capitalist modernity.

For the past, urban sociology was more interested in the city as an emblem of modernity, and had less direct interest in its rule in social relationship. Much of the most valuable work arose from interpretive, and often impressionistic, attempts to dissect 'the experience of modernity'. The ethnographic fieldwork of the Chicago School on the nature of social order in an industrial city, Simmel's analysis of the culture accompanying the money economy and Benjamin's account of the relationship between tradition, experience and modernity exemplify the intellectual endeavour. They were concerned with the texture of collective experience, with personal identity and social relationships, in a tumultuous and disarticulate world. All sought to isolate the central, shared threads of everyday experience and the common meanings resulting from developments in Western societies between 1880 and 1940. The distinctive features of mundane experience came to be identified as the hallmarks of urban life. Metropolitan cities were seen as repositories of transitory, fleeting and contingent perceptions, and relationships as the locus of fashion, spectacle and novelty; as sites where new levels of personal anxiety, uncertainty, anonymity and dislocation emerged. These characteristics we now perceive as the traits of modernity.

Like many other people, we believe that urban sociology took a wrong turn in its championing of Wirth's essay 'Urbanism as a Way of Life', as a key formulation of the core issues of earlier sociology. The mistake, put simply, was to attribute the elements of the experience of modernity to urbanisation. So although Wirth accurately described some pertinent defining characteristics of cities and some of the behavioural traits of city-dwellers, he implied false casual connections between cities, as urban environments, and the social relationships and institutions of modernity. The aspects of human experience once attributed to the city *per se* are better conceptualised as elements of the experience of modernity.

In the early twentieth century the ambivalent experience of modernity was still in competition with older, traditional forms of social order. For this reason it made sense to study the large metropolitan city as the place where the culture of modernity was most evident – to use the city as a laboratory, in Park's phrase (1967). It therefore, perhaps, makes sense to distinguish a recent period of late or high modernity, for there are now few parts of the globe not thoroughly trammelled by a capitalist modernity. The experience of modernity has been diffused. It may still be that city-dwellers are the vanguard of social change, since many modalities of the experience of modernity are most strongly manifest in large cities. Their circumstances may thus repay the most intensive study. Cities may still fruitfully be used as laboratories for sociological observation, but they are no longer such privileged sites.

If Wirth confused the urban and the modern, his critics in the 1970s often made a parallel mistake in attributing the same experience of modernity almost entirely to forms of capitalist economic organisation. Marxist concerns with the role of the capitalist state in the maintenance of the social relations of economic production was a powerful corrective to those investigation of everyday life, such as the community studies tradition, which tended to ignore external economic and political determinations. The social power accruing to the owners of land and capital, and the impact of residential segregation on life chances were all identified as important material determinants of social inequalities. Uneven economic development on a global scale was dissected, showing that the process of industrial restructuring was beyond the control of the nation-state, increasing economic insecurity for many. The Marxist project uncovered submerged aspects of the capitalist structuring of everyday life.

However, although there is surely some elective affinity between capitalist economic arrangements and the experience of modernity, the one is not reducible to the other. Nor is it the case that class divisions, however important, are sufficient to account for the struggles and contradictions of the modern experience. Berman (1983) suggests that the modern experience cuts across other social divisions – of nationality, class, religion, etc. This is correct. However, currently there seems some danger that the universal aspects of the experience of modernity will again eclipse interest in the material bases of social divisions.

Sociological theory might be seen to oscillate between concerns with social inequalities and social disorganisation. The origins of social inequality lie primarily in differential access to material resources. Simplifying greatly, this is primarily attributable to the way in which private property, capital and labour markets operate to distribute rewards unequally between nations, regions, social classes, men and women, ethnic groups and age groups. Capitalist economic arrangements create material inequalities, though forms and levels of inequality are profoundly affected by political intervention and cultural representation. Welfare facilities, international trade agreements, class cultures, regional identities, etc. are effective components of the global structuring of resources. Urban sociologists have documented, explored and explained such inequalities at the localised level. Social segregation, the analysis of private and collective consumption and the politics of growth coalitions are important elements in a multifaceted understanding of inequalities and their effects on everyday life.

The specifically modern integument of capitalist relations creates a second set of political and cultural problems, which we term social disorganisation. As was pointed out in Chapter 7, political issues of social order cannot all be reduced to ones of material inequality. Indeed, some of the major 'urban problems' of the late twentieth century, concerning the environment, congestion, crime, etc., are more easily understood as the effects of the experience of modernity. In a cultural world where the search for excitement, power, joy and self-transformation (rather than acquiescence, security, reproducibility and self-maintenance) are central legitimate individual aspirations, harmonious social reproduction is inevitably rendered problematic. Material affluence secures neither restraint nor contentment; indeed it encourages competitiveness, fashion, mobility, restlessness, the search for novel experience – the very traits that classical urban sociologists saw as creating a difficult and fragmentary social world.

The social inequalities of capitalism and the social disorganisation of modernity are symbiotic. A precise and adequate formulation of the dialectic of capitalism and modernity has yet to be devised. One way of stating the paradox of modernity is that it constantly confronts people with a choice between opportunity and security. At one level we have, in the modern world, unparalleled freedom to change and develop, since, compared with other times, the force of legal, social and personal ties is much diminished. One cause of this is the fact that capitalist economic forms do not bind people together in permanent or personal ties. At the same time, however, such change and development threatens to remove the securities achieved through routine involvements and relationships. Insecurity and uncertainty may thus arise from our own actions. Moreover, we are liable to have our plans and hopes crushed, since the same forces that increase our opportunities tend to reduce levels of social control and allow other people similar freedoms, so that their behaviour becomes unpredictable and unreliable. Insecurity is the other side of opportunity.

In an unequal society, insecurity and freedom are felt in different ways depending upon a person's place in a material hierarchy. This means that by and large, the well resourced select the best means of minimising the risks and maximising the potential of modernity. In a sense, the middle-class retreat to the suburbs was a way of obtaining security and reducing the risks of life in central locations, where there are more dangers and unwelcome interactions with other social groups. Gentrifiers, by contrast, seek to maximise other potential gains of modernity – its excitement, its fashions, its amenities, etc. – by increasing their access to work, services and facilities, but this time protected from many of the negative aspects of inner-city living. By the same calculation, young working-class men looking for excitement, who become described as delinquent, are also maximising some of the possibilities of modernity, but under the constraint of more limited resources.

Many of the specialist contributions of urban sociology arise from the detailed examination of the localised intersection of capitalism and modernity. This intersection explains the strength of the principal form of urban politics – that concerned with collective security, providing a framework of welfare for expanding the opportunities of all citizens. Similarly, inequalities of condition both create and are reproduced through residential location: living in 'better neighbourhoods' gives opportunities to enjoy pleasant residential surroundings, ease of living in a concentration of people in similar material circumstances, acceptable journeys to work, better leisure facilities and less exposure to risks of theft and pollution. These inequalities affect not only mundane material existence but are also to do with cultural belonging, solidarity and identity.

Many so–called urban problems arise precisely because of the simultaneity of opportunity and insecurity. Although there is no useful theoretical application of the concept of the urban, there is a perfectly meaningful descriptive and practical dimension, which is the basis for the existence of interdisciplinary urban studies. Certain urban political and demographic features inevitably pose problems of management. Most simply, the city is a political jurisdiction in Western states with varied responsibilities for handling matters like congestion, hardship, homelessness, crime and social intolerance which arise more or less directly from the dense concentrations of heterogeneous groups of people. There is thus a need for information, planning, policy and regulation, which is supplied by urban managers and professionals. This provides the basis for a normal science of urban demography and policy, the domain of urban studies. Urban sociology contributes in varying degrees to this venture, but is not premised upon, nor provided with an intellectual rationale by, urban studies.

Urban sociology has exhibited a distinctive relationship to social theory. It tends to take a new turn when social theory throws up new theses that can be explored using the city as a research site. Waves of theoretical speculation about modernity, at different periods, have provided such occasions. Association and disorganisation are opposite sides of the experience of modernity. This central dilemma of forms of life in capitalist modernity has been developed by many social theorists. It is a process on which the specialised inquiries of urban sociology have gained some purchase. Some of the best studies in urban sociology implicitly bring abstract social theory to earth, or at least closer to the grounds of everyday experience.

Urban sociology is a fragmented and somewhat unstable subdiscipline precisely because many of the key practices of everyday life are contextual and configurational. It is context – the social interactions of individuals and groups – that is the backcloth to action. In previous urban sociologies context has often been reduced to, or conceived in terms of, its spatial dimensions. Gans (1984, p. 303) has argued, very plausibly, that urban sociology, has remained a field partly because it alone among sociological endeavours has emphasised spatial concepts, variables and factors'. But as we have seen, some of the ways in which it has conceived of space have been counter-productive. Context is more that spatial configuration. One aspect of the temporal experience of modernity is the normality of rapid changes of social context. As the social interactionist tradition in sociology has pointed out, deciding on an appropriate form of behaviour depends upon actors jointly recognising the social context in which their mutual responses are called forth. In a world of fleeting encounters this requires a considerable range of repertories of behaviour, strategic reflection and flexibility in mundane situations. Inventive and adaptive responses make for a huge variety of encounters, the context of which is not, or at least not easily, subject to generalisation. The specificity of an event, a situation or a location cannot be grasped abstractly, which is why ethnographic methods proved so essential to understanding modern experiences as they exist in everyday life in the metropolis. Many aspects of that experience cannot be appreciated using statistical methods. Rather the sympathetic reconstruction of everyday meanings accomplished by studies of small groups, subcultures, neighbourhoods, communities and localities provides the means to identify social organisation in modern situations. Such inquiries in part uncover unique configurations, which our analysis of place has recognised. At the same time, the unique dramatic episodes of everyday life constitute the fundamental and common characteristics of the experience of modernity.

Bibliography

Abrams, P. (1968) *The Origins of British Sociology 1834–1914* (Chicago: University Press of Chicago).

Abu-Lughod, J. (1980) *Urban Apartheid: A Study of Rabat* (Boston, Mass.: MIT Press).

Ackroyd, P. (2000) *London: The Biography* (London: Vintage).

Adams, R. and Allan, G. (1998) *Placing Friendship in Context* (Cambridge: Cambridge University Press).

Aglietta, M. (1979) *A Theory of Capitalist Regulation: The US Experience* (London: Verso).

Agnew, J. (1987) *Place and Politics: The Geographical Mediation of State and Society* (Boston: Allen & Unwin).

Alexander, J. (1982) *Theoretical Logic in Sociology* (Berkeley: University of California Press).

Alihan, M. (1938) *Social Ecology: A Critical Analysis* (New York: Wiley).

Allen, J. Massey, D. Pryke, M. (1999) *Unsettling Cities: Movement/Settlement* (London: Routledge).

Allan, G. and Crow, G. (1994) *Community Life: An Introduction to Local Social Relations* (London: Harvester Wheatsheaf).

Andersen, N. (1923) *The Hobo* (Chicago: University of Chicago Press).

Anderson, P. (1904) 'Modernity and Revolution', *New Left Review*, 144, pp. 96–113.

Arrighi, G. (1994) *The Long Twentieth Century* (London: Verso).

Augé, M. (1997) *Non-Places: Introduction to an Anthropology of Supermodernity* (London: Verso).

Badcock, B. (1984) *Unfairly Structured Cities* (Oxford: Blackwell).

Bagguley, P., Mark-Lawson, J., Shapiro, D., Urry, J., Walby, S. and Warde, A. (1990) *Restructuring: Place, Class and Gender* (London: Sage).

Bassett, K., Boddy, M., Harloe, M. and Lovering, J. (1989) 'Living in the Fast Lane: Economic and Social Change in Swindon', in P. Cooke (ed.), *Localities* (London: Unwin Hyman), pp. 45–85.

Bassett, K. and Harloe, M. (1990) 'Swindon: The Rise and Decline of a Growth Coalition', in M. Harloe, C. Pickvance and J. Urry (eds), *Place, Policy and Politics* (London: Unwin Hyman), pp. 42–61.

Bauman, Z. (1988) *Freedom* (Milton Keynes: Open University Press).

Bauman, Z. (1998) *Work, Consumerism and the New Poor* (Buckingham: Open University Press).

Bauman, Z. (2000) *Liquid Modernity* (Cambridge: Polity Press).

205

Baumgartner M. P.(1988) *The Moral Order of a Suburb* (Oxford: Oxford University Press).

Beauregard, R. A. (1986) 'The Chaos and Complexity of Gentrification', in N. Smith and P. Williams (eds), *Gentrification and the City* (London: Allen & Unwin), pp. 35–55.

Beck, U. (1992) *Risk Society: Towards a New Modernity* (London: Sage).

Bell, C. and Newby, H. (1976) 'Communion, Communalism, Class and Community Action: The Sources of the New Urban Politics', in D. Herbert and R. Johnston (eds), *Social Areas in Cities*, vol. 2 (Chichester: Wiley).

Bell, C. and Newby, H. (1974) *Community Studies: An Introduction to the Sociology of the Local Community* (London: Allen & Unwin).

Bell, D. (1973) *The Coming of Post-Industrial Society* (New York: Basic Books).

Bellah, R *et al.*(1985) *Habits of the Heart: Individualism and Commitment in American Life* (Berkeley : University of California Press).

Benjamin, W. (1969) *Charles Baudelaire or the Lyric Poet of High Capitalism* (London: New Left Books).

Benjamin, W. (1973) *Illuminations* (London: Fontana).

Benjamin, W. (1978) *One Way Street and Other Writings* (London: Verso).

Benstock, S. (1986) *Women of the Left Bank* (London: Virago).

Berman, M. (1983) *All That Is Solid Melts Into Air* (London: Verso).

Berman, M. (1984) 'The Signs in the Street: A Response to Perry Anderson', *New Left Review,* 144, 114–23.

Berthoud, R. and Gershuny, J. (eds) (2000) *Seven Years in the Lives of British Families: Evidence on the Dynamics of Social Change from the British Household Panel Survey* (Bristol: The Policy Press).

Bianchini, F. (1991) 'Cultural Policy and Urban Development: The Experience of West European Cities', paper delivered to Eighth Urban Change and Conflict Conference, Lancaster University.

Bondi, L. (1991) 'Gender Divisions and Gentrification', *Transactions of the Institute of British Geographers: New Series*, 16, 190–8.

Bondi, L. (1999) 'Gender, Class and Gentrification': Enriching the Debate', *Environment & Planning D: Society and Space*, 17, 261–82.

Borden, I., Rendell, J., Kerr, J. and Pivaro, A. (2001) 'Things, Flows, Filters, Tactics', in I. Borden, J. Kerr, J. Rendell and Pivaro, A. (eds), *The Unknown City: Contesting Architecture and Social Space* (London: MIT Press).

Bott, E. (1957) *Family and Social Network: Roles, Norms and External Relationships in Ordinary Families* (London: Tavistock).

Bowlby, S., Lewis, J., McDowell, L. and Foord, J. (1989) 'The Geography of Gender', in R. Peet and N. Thrift (eds), *New Models in Geography* (London: Unwin Hyman), pp. 157–76.

Bradbury, M. (1976) 'The Cities of Modernism', in M. Bradbury and J. McFarlane (eds), *Modernism* (Harmondsworth: Penguin), pp. 96–104.

Bradbury, M. and McFarlane, J. (eds) (1976) *Modernism* (Harmondsworth: Penguin).

Branford, V. (1926) 'A Survey of Recent and Contemporary Sociology', *Sociological Review,* XVIII, 315–22.

Branford, V. (1928) 'The Past, Present and Future', *Sociological Review*, XX, 322–39.

Bridge, G. and Watson, S. (2000a) 'Introduction', in G. Bridge and S. Watson (eds), *A Companion to the City* (Oxford: Blackwell).

Bridge, G. and Watson, S. (2000b) 'City Imaginaries', in G. Bridge and S. Watson (eds), *A Companion to the City* (Oxford: Blackwell).

Bridge, G. and Watson, S. (eds) (2000c) *A Companion to the City* (Oxford: Blackwell).

Buck-Morss, S. (1989) *The Dialectics of Seeing: Walter Benjamin and the Arcades Project* (Cambridge, Mass.: MIT Press).

Bulmer, M. (1984) *The Chicago School of Sociology: Institutionalisation, Diversity and the Rise of Sociological Research* (Chicago: University of Chicago Press).

Burawoy, M., Blum, J., George, S., Gille, Z., Gowan, T., Haney, L., Klawiter, M. and Lopez, S. (2000a) *Global Ethnography: Forces, Connections and Imaginations in a Post-modern World* (Berkeley: University of California Press).

Burawoy, M., Krotov, P. and Lytkina, T. (2000b) 'Involution and Destitution in Capitalist Russia', *Ethanography*, 1, 43–65

Burgess, E. W. (1967) 'The Growth of the City', in R. E. Park *et al.* (eds), *The City* (Chicago: University of Chicago Press).

Burrows, R. and Butler, T. (1989) 'Middle Mass and the Pit: A Critical Review of Peter Saunders' *Sociology of Consumption*', *Sociological Review*, 37, 338–64.

Butler, T. (1995) 'Gentrification and the Urban Middle Classes', in T. Butler and M. Savage (eds), *Social Change and the Middle Classes* (London: UCL Press)

Butler, T. (1997) *Gentrification and the Middle Classes* (Aldershot: Ashgate).

Butler, T. (2002) 'Thinking Global but Acting Local: The Middling Classes in the City', *Sociological Research Online*, forthcoming.

Byrne, D. (1989) *Beyond the Inner City* (Milton Keynes: Open University Press).

Castells, M. (1977) *The Urban Question* (London: Edward Arnold).

Castells, M. (1978) *City, Class and Power* (London: Macmillan).

Castells, M. (1983) *The City and The Grassroots* (London: Edward Arnold).

Castells, M. (1989) *The Informational City* (Oxford: Blackwell).

Castells, M. (1996) *The Rise of the Network Society* (Oxford: Blackwell).

Castells, M. (1997a) *The Power of Identity* (Oxford: Blackwell).

Castells, M. (1997b) *The End of the Millenium* (Oxford: Blackwell).

Caygill, H. (1998) *Walter Benjamin, the Colour of Experience* (London: Routledge).

de Certeau, M. (1984) *The Practice of Everyday Life* (Berkeley: University of California Press).

Christopherson, S. (1994) 'The Fortress City: Privatized Spaces, Consumer Citizenship', in A. Amin (ed.), *Post-Fordism: A Reader* (Oxford: Blackwell), pp. 409–27.

Christopherson, S. and Storper, M. (1986) 'The City as Studio: The World as Back Lot: The Impact of Vertical Disintegration on the Location of the Modern Picture Industry', *Environment and Planning D: Society and Space*, 4, 3, 305–20.

Clark, G. (1988) 'Review of Urban Fortunes: The Political Economy of Place', *Urban Geography*, 7, 374–5.

Clark, T. J. (1985) *The Painting of Modern Life* (London: Thames & Hudson).

Clarke, S. (1990) 'Precious Place: The Local Growth Machine in an Era of Global Restructuring', *Urban Geography*, 11, 185–93.

Clifford, J. and Marcus, G. E. (eds) (1986) *Writing Culture: The Poetics and Politics of Ethnography* (Berkeley: University of California Press).

Cochrane, A. (1988) 'In and Against the Market? The Development of Socialist Economic Strategies in Britain, 1981–1986', *Policy and Politics*, 16, 159–68.

Cochrane, A. (1991) 'The Changing State of Local Government: Restructuring for the 1990s', *Public Administration*, 69, 281–302.

Cochrane, A. (1993) *Whatever Happened to Local Government?* (Buckingham: Open University Press).

Cochrane, A. (1999) 'Redefining Urban Politics for the Twenty-First Century', in A. E. G. Jonas and D. Wilson (eds), *The Urban Growth Machines: Critical Perspectives Two Decades Later* (Albany, New York: State University of New York), pp. 109–24.

Cockburn, C. (1977) *The Local State: Management of Cities and People* (London: Pluto).

Cohen, A. P. (ed.) (1983) *Belonging: Identity and Social Organisation in British Rural Culture* (Manchester: University of Manchester Press).

Cohen, R. (1987) *The New Helots: Migrants in the International Division of Labour* (Aldershot: Gower).

Connor, S. (1989) *Postmodernist Culture* (Oxford: Blackwell).

Cooke, P. (1984) 'Regions, Class and Gender: A European Comparison', *Progress in Planning*, 22, 89–146.

Cooke, P. (ed.) (1986) *Global Restructuring, Local Response* (London: ESRC).

Cooke, P. (1989a) 'Locality, Economic Restructuring and World Development', in P. Cooke (ed.), *Localities* (London: Unwin Hyman), pp. 1–44.

Cooke, P. (ed.) (1989b) *Localities* (London: Unwin Hyman).

Cooley, C. (1909) *Social Organization* (New York: Scribner).

Cornwell, J. (1984) *Hard Earned Lives: Accounts of Health and Illness from East London* (London: Tavistock).

Cowan, R. S. (1983) *More Work for Mother: The Ironies of Household Technology from the Open Hearth to the Microwave* (New York: Basic Books).

Cox, K. (1991) 'Conceptualising the Local State', paper delivered to Eighth Urban Change and Conflict Conference, Lancaster University, September.

Cox, K. (1993) 'The Local and the Global in the New Urban Politics: A Critical Review', *Environment and Planning D: Society and Space*, 11, 4, 433–88.

Cox, K. R. and Mair, A. (1989) 'Urban Growth Machines and the Politics of Local Economic Development', *International Journal of Urban and Regional Research*, 13, 1, 137–46.

Crawford, M. (1992) 'The World in a Shopping Mall', in M. Sorkin (ed.), *Variations on a Theme Park: The New American City and the End of Public Space* (New York: Hill and Wang), pp. 3–30.

Crenson, M. A. (1971) *The Un-Politics of Air Pollution: A Study of Non-Decision Making in the Cities* (Baltimore: Johns Hopkins University Press).

Cressey, P. G. (1932) *The Taxi-Hall Dancers* (Chicago: University of Chicago Press).

Crewe, I. and Sarlvik, B. (1981) *Decade of De-alignment: The Conservative Victory in 1979 and Electoral Trends in the 1970s* (Cambridge: University of Cambridge Press).

Crow, G. (2002) 'Rethinking Community Studies', in P. Black *et al.* (eds), *Globalisation and Social Capital* (forthcoming).

Curtice, J. and Steed, M. (1982) 'Electoral Choice and the Production of Government', *British Journal of Political Science,* 12, 249–98.

Curtice, J. and Steed, M. (1986) 'Proportionality and Exaggeration in the British Electoral System', *Electoral Studies,* 5, 209–28.

Dahl, R. (1967) *Pluralist Democracy in the United States: Conflict and Consent* (Chicago: Rand McNally).

Davidoff, L. and Hall, C. (1983) 'The Architecture of Public and Private Life: English Middle-Class Society in a Provincial Town 1780–1850', in D. Fraser and A. Sutcliffe (eds), *The Pursuit of Urban History* (London: Edward Arnold), pp. 326–46.

Davidoff, L. and Hall, C. (1987) *Family Fortunes: Men and Women of the English Middle Class* (London: Hutchinson).

Davis, M. (1985) 'Urban Renaissance and the Spirit of Postmodernism', *New Left Review,* 151, 106–14.

Davis, M. (1990) *City of Quartz: Excavating the Future in Los Angeles* (London: Verso).

Davis, M. (1992) 'Fortress Los Angeles: the Militarization of Urban Space', in M. Sorkin (ed.), *Variations on a Theme Park: The New American City and the End of Public Space.*(New York: Hill and Wang), pp. 154–80.

Davis, M. (1999) *Ecology of Fear: Los Angeles and the Imagination of Disaster* (New York: Vintage Books).

Dear, M. and Wolch, J. (1987) *Landscapes of Despair: From De-institutionalisation to Homelessness* (Oxford: Blackwell)

Deas, I., Peck, J., Tickell, A., Ward, K and Bradford, M. (1999) 'Rescripting Urban Regeneration, the Mancunian Way', in R. Imrie and H. Thomas (eds), *British Urban Policy,* 2nd edn (London: Sage), pp. 206–32.

Dempsey, K. (1990) *Smalltown: A Study of Social Inequality, Cohesion and Belonging* (Melbourne: Oxford University Press).

Dennis, N., Henriques, F. M. and Slaughter, C. (1956) *Coal is Our Life* (London: Eyre & Spottiswoode).

Devine, F. (1997) *Social Class in America and Britain* (Edinburgh: Edinburgh University Press).

Dickens, P. (1990) *Urban Sociology: Society, Locality and Human Nature* (Hemel Hempstead: Harvester Wheatsheaf).

Dickens, P., Duncan, S. S., Goodwin, M. and Gray, F. (1985) *Housing, States and Localities* (London: Methuen).

DiGaetano, A. and Klemanski, J. (1993) 'Urban Regimes in Comparative Perspective: The Politics of Urban Development in Britain', *Urban Affairs Quarterly,* 29, 54–63.

DiGaetano, A. and Klemanski, J. (1997) *Power and City Governance: Comparative Perspectives on Urban Development* (London: University of Minnesota Press).

Dorling, D. and Woodward, R. (1996) 'Social Polarisation 1971–1991: A Micro-Geographical Analysis of Britain', *Progress in Planning*, 45, 1–66.

Duncan, S. S. and Savage, M. (1989) 'Space, Scale and Locality', *Antipode*, 21, 3, 179–206.

Duncan, S. S. *et al.* (1988) 'Policy Variations in Local States: Uneven Development and Local Social Relations', *International Journal of Urban and Regional Research*, 12, 107–28.

Duneier, M. (1994) *Slim's Table: Race, Respectability and Masculinity* (Chicago: University of Chicago Press).

Dunleavy, P. (1980) *Urban Political Analysis: The Politics of Collective Consumption* (London: Macmillan).

Dunleavy, P. (1990) 'The End of Class Politics?', in A. Cochrane and J. Anderson (eds), *Politics in Transition* (London: Sage), pp. 172–210.

Eade, J. (ed.) (1997) *Living the Global City* (London: Routledge).

Ellwood, C. A. (1927) 'The Development of Sociology in the US since 1910', *Sociological Review*, XIX, 25–34.

Fainstein, S. (1987) 'Local Mobilisation and Economic Discontent', in M. P. Smith and J. R. Feagin (eds), *The Capitalist City* (Oxford: Blackwell), pp. 323–42.

Fainstein, S. and Harloe, M. (2000) 'Ups and Downs in the Global City: London and New York at the Millennium', in M. Bridge and S. Watson (eds), *A Companion to the City* (Oxford: Blackwell).

Feagin, J. R. and Smith, M. P. (1987) 'Cities and the New International Division of Labour: An Overview', in M. P. Smith and J. R. Feagin (eds), *The Capitalist City* (Oxford: Blackwell), pp. 3–36.

Featherstone, M. (1987) 'Lifestyle and Consumer Culture', *Theory, Culture and Society*, 4, 1, 55–70.

Feigenbaum, J., Henig, J. and Hamnett, C. (1999) *Shrinking the State: The Political Underpinnings of Privatisation* (Cambridge: Cambridge University Press).

Fielding, A. J. (1982) *Counterurbanisation in Western Europe* (London: Pergamon).

Fincher, R. and Jacobs, J. (1998) *Cities of Difference* (New York: Guildford Press).

Finnegan, R. (1998) *Tales of the City: A Study of Narrative and Urban Life* (Cambridge: Cambridge University Press).

Finnegan, R. (1989) *The Hidden Musicians: Music Making in an English Town* (Cambridge: Cambridge University Press).

Firth, S. (1997) 'Popular Suburban Culture' in R. Silverstone (ed.), *Visions of Suburbia* (London: Routledge).

Fischer, C. (1975) 'The Study of Urban Community and Personality', *Annual Review of Sociology*, 75, 1, 67–89.

Fischer, C. S. (1982) *To Dwell Among Friends: Personal Networks in Town and City* (Chicago: University of Chicago Press).

Fischer, C. (1995) 'The Subcullinal Theory of Urbanism: a Twentieth-Year Assessment', *American Journal of Sociology* 101, 543–77.

Foster, J. (1997) *Docklands: Cultures in Conflict, Worlds in Collision* (London: UCL Press).

Fox, K. (1985) *Metropolitan America: Urban Life and Urban Policy in the United States 1940–1980* (London: Macmillan).

Frankenberg, R. (1957) *Village on the Border* (London: Cohen & West).

Frankenberg, R. (1966) *Communities in Britain* (Harmondsworth: Penguin).

Frisby, D. (1984) *Georg Simmel* (Chichester: Ellis Horwood).

Frisby, D. (1985) *Fragments of Modernity: Theories of Modernity in the Work of Simmel, Kracauer and Benjamin* (Cambridge: Polity).

Frisby, D. (2001) *Cityscapes of Modernity* (Cambridge: Polity).

Frobel, F., Heinrichs, J. and Kreye, K. (1980) *The New International Division of Labour: Structural Unemployment in Industrial Countries and Industrialisation in Developing Countries* (Cambridge: University of Cambridge Press).

Fyfe, M. R. (1991) 'Police, Space and Society: The Geography of Policing', *Progress in Human Geography*, 15, 249–67.

Gallie, D., Marsh, C. and Vogler, C. (1994) *Social Change and the Experience of Unemployment* (Oxford: Clarendon).

Gans, H. (1962) *The Urban Villagers* (New York: Free Press).

Gans, H. (1968a) *The Levtittowners: Ways of Life and Politics in a New Suburban Community* (London: Allen Lane).

Gans, H. (1968b) 'Urbanism and Suburbanism as Ways of Life', in R. Pahl (ed.), *Readings in Urban Sociology* (Oxford: Pergamon).

Gans, H. (1984) 'American Urban Theories and Urban Areas: Some Observations on Contemporary Ecological and Marxist Paradigms', in I. Szelenyi (ed.), *Cities in Recession: Critical Responses to Urban Politics of the New Right* (London: Sage), pp. 278–308.

Garfinkel, H. (1967) *Studies in Ethnomethodology* (Englewood Cliffs, NJ: Prentice-Hall).

Gasson, R., Crow, G., Errington, A., Hutson, J., Marsden, T. and Winter, D. (1988) 'The Farm as a Family Business', *Journal of Agricultural Economics*, 39, 1–41.

Gaventa, J. (1980) *Power and Powerlessness: Quiescence and Rebellion in an Appalachian Valley* (Oxford: Clarendon)

Gentle, C. (1993) *The Financial Services Industry* (Aldershot: Ashgate)

Gershuny, J. (1978) *After Industrial Society* (London: Palgrave Macmillan).

Giddens, A. (1971) *Capitalism and Modern Social Theory* (Cambridge: University of Cambridge Press).

Giddens, A. (1981) *A Contemporary Critique of Historical Materialism* (London: Macmillan).

Giddens, A. (1990) *The Consequences of Modernity* (Cambridge: Polity).

Giddens, A. (1991) *Modernity and Self Identity* (Cambridge: Polity).

Giddens, A. (1998) *The Third Way: The Renewal of Social Democracy* (Cambridge: Polity).

Gilloch, G. (1997) *Myth and Metropolis: Walter Benjamin and the City* (Cambridge: Polity).

Girouard, M. (1990) *The English Country Town* (New Haven, Conn.: University of Yale Press).

Glass, D. V. (1954) *Social Mobility in Britain* (London: Routledge & Kegan Paul).

Glass, R. (1989) *Cliches of Urban Doom and Other Essays* (Oxford: Blackwell).

Glucksmann, M. (1990) *Women Assemble* (London: Routledge).

Goffman, E. (1959) *The Presentation of Self in Everyday Life* (New York: Doubleday).

Goldthorpe, J. H. (1980) *Social Mobility and the Class Structure in Modern Britain* (Oxford: Clarendon).

Goldthorpe, J. H., Lockwood, D., Bechhofer, F. and Platt, J. (1968, 1969) *The Affluent Worker in the Class Structure* (Cambridge: University of Cambridge Press).

Goodwin, M., Duncan, S. S. and Halford, S. (1993) 'Regulation Theory, the Local State and the Transition of Urban Politics', *Environment and Planning D: Society and Space*, 11, 76–8.

Gordon, D. (1984) 'Capitalist Development and the History of American Cities', in W. Tabb and L. Sawyer (eds), *Marxism and the Metropolis* (New York: University of Oxford Press).

Gottdiener, M. (1985) *The Social Production of Urban Space* (Austin: University of Texas Press).

Gottdiener, M. (1987) *The Decline of Urban Politics: Political Theory and the Crisis of the Local State* (London: Sage).

Gottdiener, M. (1989) 'Crisis Theory and Socio-Spatial Restructuring: The US Case', in M. Gottdiener and N. Komninos (eds), *Capitalist Development and Crisis Theory: Accumulation, Regulation and Spatial Restructuring* (London: Macmillan), pp. 365–90.

Gottdiener, M. and Komninos, N. (eds) (1989) *Capitalist Development and Crisis Theory: Accumulation, Regulation, and Spatial Restructuring* (London: Macmillan).

Greer, S. (1962) *The Emerging City: Myth and Reality* (New York: Free Press).

Gregory, D. (1994) *Geographical Imaginations* (Oxford: Blackwell).

Gregory, D. and Urry, J. (eds) (1985) *Social Relations and Spatial Structures* (London: Macmillan).

Halford, S. (1989) 'Spatial Divisions and Women's Initiatives in Local Government', *Geoforum*, 20, 161–74.

Halford, S. (1992) 'Feminist Change in a Patriarchal Organisation: The Experience of Women's Initiatives in Local Government and Implications for Feminist Perspectives on State Institutions', in M. Savage and A. Witz (eds), *Gender and Bureaucracy* (Oxford: Blackwell).

Halkier, B. (1991) 'Greens in Movement: A Comparative Analysis of Friends of the Earth in Britain and NOAH in Denmark', MA thesis, Department of Sociology, University of Lancaster.

Hall, P. (1988) 'Urban Growth in Western Europe' in M. Dogan and J. D. Kasarda (eds), *The Metropolis Era*, vol. 1 (New York: Sage), pp. 111–27.

Hall, P. and Hay, P. (1980) *Growth Centers in European Urban Systems* (Berkeley: University of California Press).

Halsey, A. H., Heath, A. and Ridge, J. (1980) *Origins and Destinations* (Oxford: Clarendon).

Hamnett, C. (1989) 'Consumption and Class in Contemporary Britain', in C. Hamnett *et al.* (eds), *The Changing Social Structure* (London: Sage), pp. 199–243.

Hamnett, C. (1996) 'Social Polarization, Economic Restructuring and Welfare State Regimes', *Urban Studies*, 33, 1407–30.

Hannerz, U. (1980) *Exploring the City: Inquiries towards an Urban Anthropology* (New York: Columbia University Press).

Hannoosh, M. (1984) 'Painters of Modern Life: Baudelaire and the Impressionists', in W. Sharpe and L. Wallock (eds), *Visions of the Modern City* (New York: Columbia University Press), pp. 164–84.

Hanson, S. and Pratt, G. (1995) *Gender, Work and Space* (London: Routledge).

Harding, A. (1991) 'Growth Coalitions, UK-Style?', *Environment and Planning C: Government and Policy*, 9, 3, 295–317.

Harding, A. (1994) 'Urban Regimes and Growth Machines: Towards a Cross-National Research Agenda', *Urban Affairs Quarterly*, 29, 4, 356–82.

Harding, A. (1995) 'Elite Theory and Growth Machines', in D. Judge, G. Stoker and H. Wolman (eds), *Theories of Urban Politics* (London: Sage), pp. 35–53.

Harding, P. and Jenkins, R. (1989) *The Myth of the Hidden Economy: Towards a New Understanding of Informal Economic Activity* (Milton Keynes: Open University Press).

Hareven, T. (1982) *Family Time and Industrial Time: The Relationship between Family and Work in a New England Community* (Cambridge: University of Cambridge Press).

Harloe, M. (1984) 'Sector and Class: A Critical Comment', *International Journal of Urban and Regional Research*, 8, 228–37.

Harloe, M. (2001) 'Social Justice and the City: The New "Liberal Formulation"', *International Journal of Urban and Regional Research*, 25, 889–97.

Harraway, D. (1989) *Primate Visions* (London: Routledge).

Harris, C. and Ullman, E. (1945) 'The Nature of Cities', *Annals: American Academy of Political and Social Science*, 242, 7–17.

Harvey, D. (1973) *Social Justice and the City* (London: Edward Arnold).

Harvey, D. (1977) 'Labour, Capital and Class Struggle around the Built Environment in Advanced Capitalist Societies', *Politics and Society*, 6, 265–95.

Harvey, D. (1982) *The Limits to Capital* (Oxford: Blackwell).

Harvey, D. (1985a) *The Urbanisation of Capital* (Oxford: Blackwell).

Harvey, D. (1985b) *Consciousness and the Urban Experience* (Oxford: Blackwell).

Harvey, D. (1985c) 'Monument and Myth: The Building of the Basilica of the Sacred Heart', in D. Harvey, *Consciousness and the Urban Experience* (Oxford: Blackwell).

Harvey, D. (1988) *Social Justice and the City*, 2nd edn (Oxford: Blackwell).

Harvey, D. (1989) *The Condition of Postmodernity* (Oxford: Blackwell).

Harvey, L. (1987) 'The Nature of "Schools" in the Sociology of Knowledge: The Case of the "Chicago School"', *Sociological Review*, 35, 2, 245–78.

Hawley, A. (1950) *Human Ecology: A Theory of Community Structure* (New York: Ronald Press).

Heath, A., Jowell, R. and Curtice, J. (1985) *How Britain Votes* (Oxford: Pergamon).

Heath, A., Curtice, J., Evans, G., Jowell, R., Field, J. and Witherspoon, S. (1991) *Understanding Political Change* (Oxford: Pergamon).

Hechter, M. (1975) *Internal Colonialism: The Celtic Fringe in British National Development* (London: Routledge).

Hennock, E. (1973) *Fit and Proper Persons* (London: Edward Arnold).

Herbert, D. and Johnston, R. (1978) *Social Areas in Cities: Processes, Patterns and Problems* (Chichester: John Wiley).

Hetherington, K. (1997) *Badlands of Modernity* (London: Routledge).

Hill, R. C. (1987) 'Global Factory and Company Town: The Changing Division of Labour in the International Automobile Industry', in J. Henderson and M. Castells (eds), *Global Restructuring and Territorial Development* (London: Sage).

Hillery, C. A. (1955) 'Definitions of Community: Areas of Agreement', *Rural Sociology*, 20, 93–118.

Hobbs, D. (1987) *Doing the Business* (Oxford : Oxford University Press).

Hoyt, H. (1939) *The Structure and Growth of Residential Neighbourhoods in American Cities* (Chicago: University of Chicago Press).

Hudson, R. (1990) 'Trying to Revive an Infant Hercules: The Rise and Fall of Local Authority Modernization Politics on Teesside', in M. Harloe, C. Pickvance and J. Urry (eds), *Place, Policy and Politics* (London: Unwin Hyman), pp. 62–86.

Imrie, R. and Thomas, H. (1995) 'Urban Policy Processes and the Politics of Urban Regeneration', *International Journal of Urban and Regional Research*, 18, 4, 479–94.

Imrie, R. and Thomas, H. (eds) (1999) *British Urban Policy*, 2nd edn (London: Sage).

Jacobs, J. (1996) *Edge of Empire: Postcolonialism and the City* (London: Routledge).

Jacobs, J. and Fincher, R. (1998) 'Introduction', in R. Fincher and J. Jacobs (eds), *Cities of Difference* (New York: Guildford Press), pp. 1–25.

Jameson, F. (1984) 'Postmodernism, or the Cultural Logic of Late Capitalism', *New Left Review*, 146, 53–92.

Jameson, F. (1991) *Postmodernism or the Cultural Logic of Late Capitalism* (London: Verso).

Jay, M. (1993) *Downcast Eyes: The Denigration of Vision in 20th Century French Thought* (Berkeley: University of California Press).

Jay, M. (1996) *Visions in Context* (London: Routledge).

Jencks, C. (1984) *The Language of Postmodern Architecture* (London: Academy).

Jessop, B. (1990) 'Regulation Theories in Retrospect and Prospect', *Economy and Society*, 19, 2, 153–216.

Jessop, B. (1997) 'The Entrepreneurial City: Re-Imaging Localities, Redesigning Economic Governance, or Restructuring Capital?', in N. Jewson and S. MacGregor (eds), *Transforming Cities: Contested Governance and New Spatial Divisions* (London: Routledge), pp. 28–41.

Jessop, B. (1998) 'The Narrative of Enterprise and the Enterprise of Narrative: Place-Marketing and the Entrepreneurial City', in T. Hall and P. Hubbard (eds), *The Entrepreneurial City* (London: John Wiley & Sons), pp. 77–102.

Jessop, B., Peck, J. and Tickell, A. (1999) 'Re-tooling the Machine: Economic Crisis, State Restructuring and Urban Politics', in A. E. G. Jonas and D. Wilson (eds), *The Urban Growth Machines: Critical Perspectives Two Decades Later* (Albany, New York: State University of New York), pp. 141–62.

Jessop, B. and Sum, N.-L. (2000) 'The Entrepreneurial City in Action: Hong Kong's Emerging Strategies in and for (Inter-)Urban Competition', *Urban Studies*, 37, 2287–2313.

Johnston, R. (1986a) 'The Neighbourhood Effect Revisited: Spatial Science or Political Regionalism', *Environment and Planning D: Society and Space*, 4, 41–55.

Johnston, R. (1986b) 'Places and Votes: The Role of Location in the Creation of Political Attitudes', *Urban Geography*, 7, 103–16.

Johnston, R. and Pattie, C. (1989) 'Voting in Britain since 1979: A Growing North–South Divide?', in J. Lewis and A. Townsend (eds), *The North–South Divide* (London: Paul Chapman).

Johnston, R. and Pattie, C. (1998) 'Composition and Context: Region and Voting in Britain Revisited during Labour's 1990s Revival', *Geoforum*, 29, 309–29.

Johnston, R., Pattie, C. and Allsopp, J. (1988) *A Nation Dividing? The Electoral Map of Great Britain 1979–87* (London: Longman).

Jonas, A. E. G. and Wilson, D. (eds) (1999) *The Urban Growth Machines: Critical Perspectives Two Decades Later* (Albany, New York: State University of New York).

Jones, M. (1997) 'Spatial Selectivity of the State? The Regulationist Enigma and Local Struggles Over Economic Governance', *Environment Planning A*, 29, 831–64.

Joyce, P. (1980) *Work, Society and Politics* (Brighton: Harvester).

Jukes, P. (1990) *A Shout in the Street: The Modern City* (London: Faber).

Kahn, J. (2000) *Modernity and Exclusion* (London: Sage).

Kasarda, J. (1988) 'Economic Restructuring and the American Urban Dilemma', in M. Dogan and J. Kasarda (eds), *The Metropolis Era* (Newbury Hills, California: Sage), pp. 56–84.

Keil, R. (2000) *Los Angeles: Globalization, Urbanization and Social Struggles* (Chichester: John Wiley & Sons).

Kent, R. A. (1981) *A History of British Empirical Sociology* (Aldershot: Gower).

King, A. (1990) *World Cities* (London: Routledge).

Klein, N. (2000) *No Logo* (London: Flamingo).

Knopp, L. (1998) 'Sexuality and Urban Space: Gay Male Identity Politics in the United States, the United Kingdom, and Australia', in R. Fincher and J. Jacobs (eds), *Cities of Difference* (New York: Guilford Press), pp.149–76.

Kumar, K. (1978) *Prophecy and Progress* (Harmondsworth: Penguin).

Kumar, K. (1998) *From Post-Industrial to Post-Modern Society: New Theories of the Contemporary World* (Oxford: Blackwell).

Lal, B. B. (1990) *The Romance of Culture in an Urban Civilisation: Robert E. Park on Race and Ethnic Relations in Cities* (London: Routledge).

Lampard, E. (1965) 'Historical Aspects of Urbanisation', in P. M. Hauser and L. F. Schnore (eds), *The Study of Urbanization* (New York: Wiley), pp. 519–54.

Lash, S. and Urry, J. (1987) *The End of Organised Capitalism* (Cambridge: Polity).

Lauria, M. (ed.) (1997) *Reconstructing Urban Regime Theory: Regulating Urban Politics in a Global Political Economy* (London: Sage).

Lebas, E. (ed.) (1982) 'Trend Report: Urban and Regional Sociology in Advanced Industrial Societies: A Decade of Marxist and Critical Perspectives', *Current Sociology*, 30, 1–271.

Lee, D. and Newby, H. (1982) *The Problem of Sociology* (London: Unwin Hyman).

Lees, L. (2000) 'A Reappraisal of Gentrification: Towards a "Geography of Gentrification"', *Progress in Human Geography*, 24, 3, 389–408.

Lefebvre, H. (1991) *The Production of Space* (Oxford: Blackwell).

Leo, C. (1997) 'City Politics in an Era of Globalization', in M. Lauria (ed.), *Reconstructing Urban Regime Theory: Regulating Urban Politics in a Global Political Economy* (London: Sage), pp. 77–98.

Levitas, R. (1998) *The Inclusive Society? Social Exclusion and New Labour* (London: Palgrave Macmillan).

Lewis, O. (1951) *Life in a Mexican Village* (Urbana: University of Illinois Press).

Ley, D. (1983) *A Social Geography of the City* (New York: Harper & Row).

Ley, D. (1996) *The New Middle Class and the Remaking of the Central City* (Oxford: OUP).

Littlejohn, J. (1963) *Westrigg: The Sociology of a Cheviot Parish* (London: Routledge & Kegan Paul).

Lockwood, D. (1966) 'Sources of Variation in Working Class Images of Society', *Sociological Review*, 14, 249–67.

Logan, J. (1976) 'Industrialization and the Stratification of Cities in Suburban Regions', *American Journal of Sociology*, 82, 333–48.

Logan, J. and Molotch, H. (1987) *Urban Fortunes: The Political Economy of Place* (Berkeley: University of California Press).

Lojkine, J. (1976) 'Contribution to a Marxist Theory of Urbanisation', in C. Pickvance (ed.), *Urban Sociology: Critical Essays* (London: Tavistock), pp. 119–46.

Lovering, J. (1995) 'Creating Discourses Rather Than Jobs: The Crisis in Cities and the Transition Fantasies of Intellectuals and Policy Makers', in P. Healey, S. Cameron, S. Davoudi, S. Graham and A. Madani-Pour (eds), *Managing Cities: The New Urban Context* (Chicheste: John Wiley & Sons), pp. 109–26.

Low, S. (ed.) (2000) *Theorizing the City: The New Urban Anthropology Reader* (New Brunswick: Rutgers University Press).

Lowe, S. (1986) *Urban Social Movements: The City after Castells* (London: Macmillan).

Lowenthal, D. (1961) 'Geography, Experience and Imagination: Towards a Geographical Epistemology', *Annals of the American Association of Geographers*, 51, 241–60.

Lukes, S. (1974) *Power: A Radical View* (London: Macmillan).

MacAllister, I., Johnston, R., Pattie, C., Tunstall, H., Dorling D. and Rossiter, D. J. (2001) 'Class Dealignment and the Neighbourhood Effect: Miller Revisited', *British Journal of Political Science*, 31, 41–59.

MacIntyre, S. (1980) *Little Moscows* (London: Croom Helm).

MacKay, Loader I. and Sparks, R. (1997) *Crime and Social Change* (London: Routledge).

MacLeod, G. (1997) 'Globalizing Parisian Thought-Waves: Recent Developments in the Study of Social Regulation, Politics, Discourse and Space', *Progress in Human Geography*, 21, 530–53.

MacLeod, G. and Goodwin, M. (1999) 'Space, Scale and State Strategy: Re-thinking Urban and Regional Governance', *Progress in Human Geography*, 23, 503–27.

Marcuse, P. (1986) 'Abandonment, Gentrification and Displacement: The Linkages in New York City', in N. Smith and P. Williams (eds), *Gentrification of the City* (Boston, MA, Allen & Unwin), pp. 153–77.

Marshall, J. and Richardson, R. (1996) 'The Impact of "Tele-mediated" Services on Corporate Banking Structures: The Example of "Branchless" Retail Banking in Britain', *Environment and Planning A*, 28, 1843–58.

Marshall, G., Roberts, S. and Burgoyne, C. (1996) 'Social Class and Underclass in Britain and the USA', *British Journal of Sociology*, 47, 22–44.

Marshall, G., Rose, G., Newby, H. and Vogler, C. (1988) *Social Class in Britain* (London: Unwin Hyman).

Martin, R. and Sunley, P. (1997) 'The Post Keynesian State and the Space Economy', in R. Lee and J. Wills (eds), *Geographies of Economies* (London: Edward Arnold).

Massey, D. (1984) *Spatial Divisions of Labour* (London: Macmillan).

Massey, D. (1987) 'Heartlands of Defeat', *Marxism Today*, July, 18–23.

Massey, D. (1988) 'Uneven Redevelopment: Social Change and Spatial Divisions of Labour', in D. Massey and J. Allen (eds), *Uneven Redevelopment* (London: Hodder & Stoughton).

Massey, D. (1991) 'The Political Place of Locality Studies', *Environment and Planning A*, 23, 2, 267–82.

Massey, D. (1999) 'On Space and the City', in D. Massey, J. Allen and S. Pile (eds), *City Worlds* (London: Routledge).

Massey, D. and Meegan, R. (1979) 'The Geography of Industrial Reorganisation', *Progress in Planning*, 10, 159–237.

Massey, D. and Meegan, R. (1982) *The Anatomy of Job Loss: The How, Why and Where of Employment Decline* (London: Macmillan).

Massey, D. S. and Denton, N. (1993) *American Apartheid: Segregation and the Making of an Underclass* (Cambridge, MA: Harvard University Press).

Medhurst, A. (1997) 'Neogotiating the Gnome Zone: Visions of Suburbia in British Popular Culture', in R. Silverstone (ed.), *Visions of Suburbia* (London: Routledge).

Meegan, R. (1990) 'Paradise Postponed: The Growth and Decline of Merseyside's Outer Estates', in P. Cooke (ed.), *Localities* (London: Unwin Hyman), pp. 198–234.

Mellor, R. (1977) *Urban Sociology in an Urbanised Society* (London: Routledge).

Mellor, R. (1989) 'Urban Sociology: A Trend Report', *Sociology*, 23, 2, 241–60.

Merseyside Social Survey (1930) *The Social Survey of Merseyside*, ed. D. Caradog Jones (Liverpool: University Press of Liverpool).

Miller, W. L. (1977) *Electoral Dynamics in Britain since 1918* (London: Macmillan).

Mills, C. A. (1988) 'Life on the Upslope: The Postmodern Landscape of Gentrification', *Environment and Planning D: Society and Space*, 6, 2, 169–90.

Mingione, E. (1987) 'Urban Survival Strategies, Family Structure and Informal Practices', in M. P. Smith and J. Fagin (eds), *The Capitalist City* (Oxford: Blackwell), pp. 297–322.

Mingione, E. and Redclift, N. (1985) *Beyond Employment: Household, Gender and Subsistence* (Oxford: Blackwell).

Mohan, J. (2000) 'Geographies of Welfare and Social Exclusion', *Progress in Human Geography*, 24, 291–300.
Monbiot, G. (2000) *Captive State: The Corporate Takeover of Britain* (Basingstoke: Palgrave Macmillan).
Mollenkopf, J. H. (1983) *The Contested City* (Princeton, NJ: Princeton University Press).
Molotch, H. (1976) 'The City as a Growth Machine: Towards a Political Economy of Place', *American Journal of Sociology*, 82, 309–32.
Moorcock, M. (1997) *London Bone* (London: Scribner).
Morley, D. (2000) *Home Territories: Media, Mobility and Identity* (London: Routledge).
Mumford, L. (1938) *The Culture of the City* (Harmondsworth: Penguin).
Mumford, L. (1961) *The City in History* (Harmondsworth: Penguin).
Murray, C. (1990) *The Emerging British Underclass* (London: Institute for Economic Affairs).
Nelson, M. and Smith, J. (1999) *Working Hard and Making Do: Surviving in Small Town America* (Berkeley, CA: California University Press).
New Survey of London Life and Labour, 9 vols, London.
Newby, H. (1977) *The Deferential Worker: A Study of Farm Workers in East Anglia* (London: Allen Lane).
Newby, H. (1979) *Green and Pleasant Land? Social Change in Rural England* (Harmondsworth: Penguin).
O'Connor, J. (1973) *The Fiscal Crisis of the State* (New York: St Martin's Press).
Offe, C. (1982) *The Contradictions of the Welfare State* (London: Hutchinson).
Offe, C. (1985) 'New Social Movements: Challenging the Boundaries of Institutional Politics', *Social Research*, 52, 817–68.
Pahl, R. E. (1970) *Patterns of Urban Life* (London: Longman).
Pahl, R. E. (1978) 'Castells and Collective Consumption', *Sociology*, 12, 2, 309–15.
Pahl, R. E. (1984) *Divisions of Labour* (Oxford: Blackwell).
Papastergiadis, N. (2000) *The Turbulence of Migration* (Cambridge: Polity).
Park, R. E. (1921) 'Sociology and the Social Sciences: The Group Concept and Social Research', *American Journal of Sociology*, XXVII, 167–83.
Park, R. E. (1938) 'Reflections on Communication and Culture', *American Journal of Sociology*, XLIV, 187–205.
Park, R. E. (1967) 'The City: Suggestions for the Investigation of Human Behavior in an Urban Environment' (first published 1915), in R. E. Park, E. W. Burgess and R. D. McKenzie (1967) *The City* (Chicago: University of Chicago Press).
Parsons, T. (1937) *The Structure of Social Action* (New York: Free Press).
Parsons, T. (1951) *The Social System* (New York: Free Press).
Payne, G. (1987) *Mobility and Change in Modern Society* (London: Macmillan).
Peach, C. (1996) 'Does Britain Have Ghettos?', *Transactions*, IBG, 21, 216–35.
Peck, J. (1989) 'Reconceptualizing the Local Labour Market: Space, Segmentation and the State', *Progress in Human Geography*, 13, 1, 42–61.
Peck, J. (1995) 'Moving and Shaking: Business Elites, State Localism and Elite Privatism', *Progress in Human Geography*, 19, 16–46.
Peck, J. (1996) *Work-Place: The Social Regulation of Labor Markets* (New York: Guildford).

Peck, J. (2001) *Workfare States* (London: Guilford Press).

Peck, J. and Tickell, A. (1991) *Regulation Theory and the Geography of Flexible Accumulation*, SPA Working Paper No. 12 (University of Manchester).

Peck, J. and Tickell, A. (1992) 'Local Modes of Social Regulation? Regulation Theory, Thatcherism and Uneven Development', *Geoforum*, 23, 347–64.

Peck, J. and Tickell, A. (1995) 'Business Goes Local: Dissecting the "Business Agenda" in Manchester', *International Journal of Urban and Regional Research*, 19, 55–77.

Penn, R. Rose, M. and Rubery, J. (1994) *Skill and Occupational Change* (Oxford: Clarendon).

Perry, D. C. (1987) 'The Politics of Dependency in Deindustrialising America: The Case of Buffalo, New York', in M. P. Smith and J. R. Feagin (eds), *The Capitalist City* (Oxford: Blackwell), pp. 113–37.

Pfautz, J. (1967) *On the City: Physical Patterns and Social Structure* (Chicago: University of Chicago Press).

Philo, G. and Kearns, G. (1993) *Selling Places: The City as Cultural Capital, Past and Present* (Oxford: Pergamon).

Pickvance, C. (1990) 'Introduction: The Institutional Context of Local Economic Development: Central Controls, Spatial Policies and Local Economic Policies', in M. Harloe, C. Pickvance and J. Urry (eds), *Place, Policy and Politics: Do Localities Matter?* (London: Unwin Hyman), pp. 1–41.

Pile, S. (ed.) (2000) *City A–Z* (London: Routledge).

Pinch, S. (1985) *Cities and Services: The Geography of Collective Consumption* (London: Routledge).

Pinch, S. (1989) 'The Restructuring Thesis and the Study of Public Services', *Environment and Planning A*, 21, 905–26.

Piore, M. and Sabel, C. (1984) *The Second Industrial Divide. Possibilities for Prosperity* (New York: Basic Books).

Pollock, G. (1988) *Vision and Difference* (London: Routledge).

Pugh, S. (ed.) (1990) *Reading Landscape: Country City-Capital* (Manchester: Manchester University Press).

Quilley, S. and Ward, K. (1999) 'Global System and Local Personality in Urban and Regional Politics', *Space and Polity*, 3, 1, 5–33.

Redclift, N. and Mingione, E. (eds) (1985) *Beyond Employment: Household, Gender and Subsistence* (Oxford: Blackwell).

Redfield, R. (1947) 'The Folk Society', *American Journal of Sociology*, 52, 293–308.

Reff, T. (1984) 'Manet and the Paris of Hausmann and Baudelaire', in W. Sharpe and L. Wallock (eds), *Visions of the Modern City* (New York: Columbia University Press), pp. 131–63.

Reissman, L. (1964) *Urban Process: Cities in Industrial Societies* (New York: Free Press).

Rex, J. and Moore, R. (1967) *Race, Community and Conflict: A Study of Sparkbrook* (Harmondsworth: Penguin).

Riesman, D., with Glazer, N. and Denney, R. (1950) *The Lonely Crowd: A Study of the Changing American Character* (New Haven, Conn.: University of Yale Press).

Rose, D. (1988) 'A Feminist Perspective of Employment Restructuring and Gentrification...: The Case of Montreal', in J. Wolch and M. Dear (eds), *The Power of Geography* (Boston: Unwin Hyman), pp. 118–38.

Rowntree, B. S. (1941) *Poverty and Progress* (London: Longmans Green).

Sassen, S. (1991) *The Global City*, 1st edn (London: Routledge).

Sassen, S. (2000) *The Global City*, 2nd edn (London: Routledge).

Sassen-Koob, S. (1987) 'Growth and Informalisation at the Core: A Preliminary Report on New York City', in M. P. Smith and J. Fagin (eds), *The Capitalist World City* (Oxford: Blackwell), pp. 138–54.

Saunders, P. (1979) *Urban Politics: A Sociological Interpretation* (Harmondsworth: Penguin).

Saunders, P. (1981) *Social Theory and the Urban Question* (London: Hutchinson).

Saunders, P. (1984) 'Beyond Housing Classes: The Sociological Significance of Private Property Rights in the Means of Consumption', *International Journal of Urban and Regional Research*, 8, 202–27.

Saunders, P. (1985) 'Space, the City and Social Theory', in D. Gregory and J. Urry (eds), *Social Relations and Spatial Structures* (Basingstoke: Palgrave Macmillan).

Saunders, P. (1986) *Social Theory and the Urban Question*, 2nd edn (London: Hutchinson).

Saunders, P. (1990) *A Nation of Homeowners* (London: Unwin Hyman).

Saunders, P. and Harris, C. (1994) *Privatisation and Popular Capitalism* (Milton Keynes: Open University Press).

Savage, M. (1987a) *The Dynamics of Working Class Politics* (Cambridge: University of Cambridge Press).

Savage, M. (1987b) 'Understanding Political Alignments in Contemporary Britain: Do Localities Matter?', *Political Geography Quarterly*, 6, 53–76.

Savage, M. (1989) 'Spatial Divisions in Modern Britain', in C. Hamnett *et al.* (eds), *The Changing Social Structure* (London: Sage), pp. 244–68.

Savage, M. (1990) 'Whatever Happened to Red Clydeside', in J. Anderson and A. Cochrane (eds), *A State of Crisis* (London: Hodder & Stoughton), pp. 231–43.

Savage, M. (1992) 'Women's Expertise, Men's Authority: Gendered Organisations and the Contemporary Middle Classes', in M. Savage and A. Witz (eds), *Gender and Bureaucracy* (Oxford: Blackwell).

Savage, M., Watt, P. and Arber, S. (1992a) 'The Consumption Sector Debate and Housing Mobility', *Sociology*, 24, 97–117.

Savage, M., Barlow, J., Dickens, P. and Fielding, A. J. (1992b) *Property, Bureaucracy and Culture: Middle-Class Formation in Contemporary Britain* (London: Routledge).

Savage, M., Longhurst, B. and Bagnall, G. (2002) *Globalisation and Belonging* (London: Sage).

Sayer, A. and Walker, R. (1992) *The New Social Economy: Reworking the Division of Labour* (Oxford: Blackwell).

Scherzer, S. (1992) *The Unbounded Community: Neighbourhood Life and Social Structure in New York* (Durham, NC: Duke University Press).

Scott, A. J. (1988a) *Metropolis: From the Division of Labour to Urban Form* (Berkeley: University of California Press).

Scott, A. J. (1988b) *New Industrial Spaces: Flexible Production, Organization and Regional Development in North America and Western Europe* (London: Pion).

Scott A. J. (2000) *The Cultural Economy of Cities: Essays on the Geography of Image-Producing* (London: Sage).

Scott, A. J. and Soja, E. (1996) *The City: Los Angeles and Urban Theory at the End of the Twentieth Century* (London: University of California Press).

Sennett, R. (1977) *The Fall of Public Man* (Cambridge: University of Cambridge Press).

Sennett, R. (1990) *The Conscience of the Eye* (London: Faber).

Sennett, R. (1996) *Flesh and Stone* (New York: Norton).

Sharpe, W. and Wallock, L. (1984) *Visions of the Modern City* (New York: University of Columbia Press).

Shields, R. (1989) 'Social Spatialisation and the Built Environment: The Case of the West Edmonton Mall', *Environment and Planning D: Society and Space*, 7, 147–64.

Shields, R. (1991) *Places on the Margin* (London: Routledge).

Shields, R. (1992) 'A Truant Proximity: Presence and Absence in the Space of Modernity', *Environment and Planning D: Society and Space*, 10, 2, 181–98.

Silver, H. (1994) 'Social Exclusion and Social Solidarity: Three Paradigms', *International Labour Review*, 133, 531–78.

Silverstone, R. (1997) *Visions of Suburbia* (London: Routledge).

Simmel, G. (1950) *The Sociology of Georg Simmel* (edited by Kurt Wolff) (New York: Free Press).

Simmel, G. (1964) 'The Metropolis and Mental Life', in K. Wolff (ed.), *The Sociology of Georg Simmel* (New York: Fress Press), pp. 409–24.

Simmel, G. (1978) *The Philosophy of Money* (London: Routledge).

Sinclair, I. (1996) *Lights out for the Territory* (London: Ganta)

Smart, B. (1992) *Modern Conditions Postmodern Controversies* (London: Routledge).

Smith, D. (1988) *The Chicago School: A Liberal Critique of Capitalism* (London: Macmillan).

Smith, M. P. (1980) *The City and Social Theory* (Oxford: Blackwell).

Smith, M. P. (2001) *Transnational Urbanism: Locating Globalization* (Oxford: Blackwell).

Smith, M. P. and Tardanico, R. (1987) 'Urban Theory Reconsidered: Production, Reproduction and Collective Action', in M. P. Smith and J. R. Feagin (eds), *The Capitalist City* (Oxford: Blackwell), pp. 87–112.

Smith, N. (1979) 'Towards a Theory of Gentrification: A Back to the City Movement by Capital not People', *Journal of the American Planners Association*, 45, 538–48.

Smith, N. (1986) 'Dangers of the Empirical Turn: Some Comments on The CURS Initiative', *Antipode*, 19, 394–406.

Smith, N. (1987) 'Of Yuppies and Housing: Gentrification, Social Restructuring and the Urban Dream', *Environment and Planning D: Society and Space*, 5, 151–72.

Smith, N. (1996) *The New Urban Frontier* (London: Routledge).

Social Trends (2000) (London: HMSO).

Society and Space (1988) Special Edition on the New Geography and Sociology of Production, *Environment and Planning D: Society and Space*, 6, 3, 241–370.

Soja, E. (1989) *Postmodern Geographies* (London: Verso).

Soja, E. (2000) *Postmetropolis: Critical Studies of Cities and Regions* (Oxford: Blackwell).

Sontag, S. (1978) 'Introduction' to *One Way Street and Other Writings* (London: Verso).

Sorkin, M. (1992) 'Introduction: Variations on a Theme Park', in M. Sorkin (ed.), *Variations on a Theme Park: The New American City and the End of Public Space* (New York: Hill and Wang), pp. xi–xv.

Stacey, M. (1960) *Tradition and Change: A Study of Banbury* (Oxford: University of Oxford Press).

Stacey, M. (1969) 'The Myth of Community Studies', *British Journal of Sociology*, 20, 134–47.

Stein, M. (1964) *The Eclipse of Community: An Interpretation of American Studies* (New York: Harper & Row).

Stoker, G. (1995) 'Regime Theory and Urban Politics', in D. Judge, G. Stoker and H. Wolman (eds), *Theories of Urban Politics* (London: Sage), pp. 54–71.

Stoker, G. (ed.) (2000) *British Local Governance* (Basingstoke: Palgrave Macmillan).

Stoker, G. and Mossberger, K. (1994) 'Urban Regime Theory in Comparative Perspective', *Environment and Planning C: Government and Policy*, 12, 195–212.

Stone, C. (1989) *Regime Politics: Governing Atlanta 1946–1988* (Kansas: Kansas University Press).

Stone, C. and Saunders, H. (eds) (1987) *The Politics of Urban Development* (Kansas: Kansas University Press).

Storper, M. and Walker, R. (1989) *The Capitalist Imperative: Territory, Technology and Industrial Growth* (Oxford: Blackwell).

Strauss, A. (1961) *Images of the American City* (Chicago: University of Chicago Press).

Suttles, G. (1968) *The Social Order of the Slum* (Chicago: University of Chicago Press).

Swenarton, M. and Taylor, S. (1985) 'The Scale and Nature of the Growth of Owner Occupation in Britain between the Wars', *Economic History Review*, 38, 373–93.

Tanner, D., *Political Change and the Labour Party 1900–1918* (Cambridge: Cambridge University Press).

Taylor, B. (1980) *Eve and the New Jerusalem* (London: Virago).

Thompson, E. P. and Yeo, E. (eds) (1971) *The Unknown Mayhew* (Harmondsworth: Penguin).

Thrasher, F. (1927) *The Gang* (Chicago: University of Chicago Press).

Thrift, N. (1996) *Spatial Formations* (London: Sage).

Tickell, A. and Peck, J. (1996) 'The Return of Men's Words and Men's Deeds in the Remaking of the Local State', *Transactions of the Institute of British Geographers*, 21, 595–616.

Timberlake, M. (1987) 'World Systems Theory and Comparative Industrialisation' in M. P. Smith and J. Feagin (eds), *The Capitalist City* (Oxford: Blackwell), pp. 37–65.

Tomlinson, J. (1999) *Globalisation and Culture* (Cambridge: Polity).

Urry, J. (1990a) *The Tourist Gaze* (London: Sage).

Urry, J. (1990b) 'Conclusion: Places and Policies', in M. Harloe, C. Pickvance and J. Urry (eds), *Place, Policy and Politics* (London: Unwin Hyman), pp. 187–204.

Urry, J. (2000) *Sociology Beyond Societies* (London: Routledge).

Vaiou, D. (1991) 'Gender Divisions in Urban Space: Facets of Everyday Life in an Athenian Suburb', paper delivered to Eighth Urban Change and Conflict Conference, Lancaster University, September.

Wacquant, L. (1993) 'Urban Outcasts: Stigma and Division in the Black American Ghetto and the French Urban Periphery', *International Journal of Urban and Regional Research*, 17, 366–83.

Wacquant, L. (1997) 'Three Pernicious Premises in the Study of the American Ghetto', *International Journal of Urban and Regional Research*, 21, 341–53.

Wacquant, L. (1999a) 'America as Social Dystopia: The Politics of Urban Disintegration, or the French Uses of the American Model', in P. Bourdieu *et al.*, *The Weight of the World* (Cambridge: Polity), pp. 130–9.

Wacquant, L. (1999b) 'Inside "the Zone": The Social Art of the Hustler in the American Ghetto', in P. Bourdieu *et al.*, *The Weight of the World* (Cambridge: Polity), pp. 140–67.

Wainwright, H. (1987) *Labour: A Tale of Two Parties* (London: Hogarth).

Wakeford, N. (2002) *Networks of Desire* (London: Routledge).

Walker, R. A. (1981) 'A Theory of Suburbanisation: Capitalism and the Construction of Urban Spaces in the United States', in M. Dear and A. J. Scott (eds), *Urbanisation and Urban Planning in Capitalist Society* (London: Methuen), pp. 383–430.

Walks, R. (2001) 'The Social Ecology of the Post-Fordist/Global City? Economic Restructuring and Socio-Spatial Polarisation in the Toronto Urban Region', *Urban Studies*, 38, 407–47.

Wallerstein, I. (1974) *The Modern World System*, vol. 1 (New York: Academic Press).

Ward, K. (1996) 'Urban Regime Theory: A Sympathetic Critique', *Geoforum*, 27, 4, 427–38.

Ward, K. (2000a) 'From Renters to Rantiers: Active Entrepreneurs, Structural Speculators and the Politics of Marketing the City', *Urban Studies*, 37, 1093–107.

Ward, K. (2000b) 'A Critique In Search of a Corpus: Re-Visiting Governance and Re-Interpreting Urban Politics', *Transactions of the Institute of British Geographers*, 25, 169–85.

Warde, A. (1988) 'Industrial Restructuring, Local Politics and the Reproduction of Labour Power: Some Theoretical Considerations', *Environment and Planning D: Society and Space*, 6, 75–95.

Warde, A. (1990) 'Production, Consumption and Social Change: Reservations Regarding Peter Saunders's *Sociology of Consumption*', *International Journal of Urban and Regional Research*, 14, 228–48.

Warde, A. (1991) 'Gentrification as Consumption: Issues of Class and Gender', *Society and Space*, 9, 223–32.

Wellman, B. (2001) 'The Rise of Personalised Networking', *International Journal of Urban and Regional Research*, 25, 227–50.

Wellman, B. and Leighton, P. (1979) 'Networks, Neighbourhoods and Communities: Approaches to the Community Question', *Urban Affairs Quarterly*, 14, 363–90.

Wiener, M. (1981) *English Culture and the Decline of the Industrial Spirit* (Harmondsworth: Penguin).

Williams, C. and Windebank, J. (1998) *Informal Employment in the Advanced Economies: Implications for Work and Welfare* (London: Routledge).

Williams, P. (1986) 'Class Constitution through Spatial Reconstruction? A Re-evaluation of Gentrification in Australia, Britain and the United States', in N. Smith and P. Williams (eds), *Gentrification of the City* (Boston: Allen & Unwin), pp. 56–77.

Williams, R. (1973) *The Country and the City* (London: Chatto & Windus).

Williams, R. (1989) *The Politics of Modernism* (London: Verso).

Williams, W. M. (1963) *A West Country Village: Ashworthy* (London: Routledge & Kegan Paul).

Williamson, O. E. (1990) 'The Firm as a Nexus of Treaties: An Introduction', in M. Aoki, B. Gustafsson and O. Williamson (eds), *The Firm as a Nexus of Treaties* (London: Sage), pp. 1–25.

Wills, J. (1996) 'Geographies of Trade Unionism: Translating Traditions Across Space and Time', *Antipode*, 28, 4, 352–78.

Wilson, E. (1991) *The Sphinx in the City* (London: Virago).

Wirth, L. (1938) 'Urbanism as a Way of Life', *American Journal of Sociology*, XLIV, 1, 1–24.

Wolff, J. (1987) 'The Invisible Flaneuse: Women and the Literature of Modernity', in A. Benjamin (ed.), *The Problems of Modernity* (London: Routledge).

Wolin, R. (1983) 'Experience and Materialism in Benjamin's *Passagenwerk*', in G. Smith (ed.), *Benjamin: Philosophy, Aesthetics, History* (Chicago: University of Chicago Press), pp. 210–27.

Wright, P. (1991) *A Journey through the Ruins* (London: Paladin).

Young, M. and Willmott, P. (1962) *Family and Kinship in East London* (Harmondsworth: Penguin).

Young, M. and Willmott, P. (1975) *The Symmetrical Family* (Harmondsworth: Penguin).

Zorbaugh, H. W. (1929) *The Gold Coast and the Slum* (Chicago: University of Chicago Press).

Zukin, S. (1980) 'A Decade of the New Urban Sociology', *Theory and Society*, 9, 575–602.

Zukin, S. (1988) *Loft Living: Culture and Capital in Urban Change* (London: Radius).

Zukin, S. (1992) 'Postmodern Urban Landscapes: Mapping Culture and Power', in S. Lash and J. Friedman (eds), *Modernity and Identity* (Oxford: Blackwell), pp. 221–47.

Index

Note: f = figure, t = table.

232 Index

ST. PATRICKS
COLLEGE
LIBRARY